Polly Toynbee is the award-winning *Guardian* columnist and former social affairs editor for the BBC. Her previous books include *Hard Work: Life in Low-pay Britain*. Polly is chair of the Brighton Festival. David Walker was director of public reporting at the Audit Commission and founding editor of Guardian Public. Together they wrote *Unjust Rewards: Exposing Greed and Inequality in Britain* and *The Verdict: Did Labour Change Britain?*

Advance praise for *Cameron's Coup*:

'Polly Toynbee and David Walker at their forensic, polemic best – an account of Britain's dysfunctions that will leave you shaking your head at the impossibility of it all. But it happened all the same.'

Will Hutton

'Historians will read this book and damn Cameron's coalition. The rest of us must read it now to make them history.'

John O'Farrell

CAMERON'S COUP

How the Tories Took
Britain to the Brink

POLLY TOYNBEE
AND DAVID WALKER

First published in 2015
by Guardian Books, Kings Place, 90 York Way, London N1 9GU
and Faber & Faber Ltd, Bloomsbury House,
74–77 Great Russell Street, London WC1B 3DA

A CIP record for this book is available from the British Library

ISBN 978-1-78335-043-8

Typeset by seagulls.net

Printed and bound in Great Britain by
CPI Group (UK) Ltd, Croydon, CR0 4YY

2 4 6 8 10 9 7 5 3

Contents

Introduction

'I Thought I'd Be Good at It'

Asked why he wanted to be prime minister, David Cameron said, 'Because I thought I'd be good at it.' He wasn't. He bears direct and personal responsibility for (nearly) breaking up the UK, because of who he is and the policies he pursued as prime minister. With chillaxed nonchalance, what his government did on tax, spend and benefits, and housing, health and education, prised further apart region, class, generation, gender and race, driving deeper wedges between town and country, old and young, deserving and undeserving, lucky and unlucky, left and right. And, as it turned out, between the nations that make up the UK.

Cameron was in a coalition, but for most purposes the Liberal Democrats were a sideshow. Besides, this book is not about the Westminster charivari, the stuff that excites Nick Robinson on the *News at Ten*, the ins and outs or the mini-dramas that engross political journalists. Those aren't always insignificant but – as with our book *The Verdict*, on the Labour years – we want to audit what they did as a government, what effect their actions had on people's lives and paint a picture of the country under their rule.

We aren't naive. Many – increasing numbers – doubt the efficacy of politicians and policymakers, if they pay them any attention at all. People get on with their lives, talk about the weather, and fail to see connections between services, tax, job or wages and the decisions made by MPs and ministers. However, the Scottish referendum showed brilliantly how engagement might be electrically charged, albeit over a direct and straightforward question. By contrast, citizens' everyday experience of politics is rarely going to be as exciting, but it matters. One purpose of this book is to show how much.

We focus primarily on what the Conservatives did, yet it's hard not to query the personality at the top. One puzzle is that, unlike Margaret Thatcher, what you saw was not what you got: Cameron's strong ideological impulses were usually kept from view. He breathed an effortless trajectory from Eton to Oxford, to public relations and a safe seat in Witney. Harold Macmillan is supposed once to have been his role model; a picture of SuperMac hung in his office. For a while, Cameron tried to paint himself as a modern version of that other old Etonian, who had been a Keynesian, a builder of council houses and a prime minister deeply committed to the integrity of the country, from Scottish castles to Stockton-on-Tees to deepest Sussex.

There is no resemblance. Cameron sees the world through the narrowing prism of a social set and sectional interest. He trod the world stage as prime ministers do, but without any identifiable strategy, sense of history or grasp of long-run national interest; the idea of his turning to the classics or even Jane Austen for inspiration and proportion, as Macmillan did, is unlikely. At home, it was government by and from a coterie, half-barricaded in its southern English fastness, half-floating across the yacht-filled sea of globalised money.

The Tories came to power during what his partisans called a national crisis, claiming it demanded ruthless austerity. With admen's fluency, they produced sound-bite phrases, notably 'we're all in it together', but never tried to imagine the nation, let alone seek to strengthen unity in adversity. Deep and disturbing trends in capitalism left them indifferent. 'The fundamental promise of modern liberal economies – to make the broad majority of people gradually better off over time – is being called into question,' says Clive Cowdery, chair of the

Resolution Foundation, an independent thinktank that works to improve the lives of people on low incomes. Such adverse dynamics demand understanding – and political response.

Labour had taken a million children out of poverty. That progress has now gone into reverse. The great recession would have taken its toll across regions and classes but a good government would have looked to protect the weakest. Instead, they are the ones who have borne the brunt of deficit reduction, ministers bent on turning public opinion against the poor. The character of a government shows in the choices it makes about the distribution of pain. Whatever the balance of arguments about austerity, concerted assault on the bottom third of society is what must brand Cameron's reputation.

Writing about modern Britain, you have to rely on certain institutions, whose worth and reliability counterbalance the temptation to say everything is going to hell in a handcart, strong though that remains. We have used their work copiously, not always with full acknowledgement. Of course they include the *Guardian*, but also the *Financial Times* and its first-rate columnists such as John Kay, Martin Wolf and Janan Ganesh. Initials that crop up frequently include ONS (Office for National Statistics), PAC (House of Commons public accounts committee) and NAO (National Audit Office), and an organisation that has become de facto part of the constitution, so irreproachable its data and so incisive its analysis, the Institute for Fiscal Studies (IFS). Other indispensable sources are the pollsters, notably Ipsos MORI and one of the greatest of charities, the Joseph Rowntree Foundation (JRF).

Other initials include DWP (Department for Work and Pensions); FTSE (Financial Times Stock Exchange) 100, the list of companies on the London Stock Exchange with the highest capitalisation; NIESR (National Institute of Economic and Social Research); OECD (Organisation for Economic Co-operation and Development); OBR (Office for Budget Responsibility) and BIS (Department for Business, Innovation and Skills).

1

Unjust Britain

Take any route north and west of Oxford and, once across the ring road, you are soon in Cameron country. Despite his name, this is a long way from Scotland's craggy passions and collective self-assertion. This is also Clarkson country, with all the petrol-headed disdain for planet and public interest the TV personality stands for. He lives in Chipping Norton, which is also home to Elisabeth Murdoch and her father's favourite, Rebekah Brooks, the newspaper executive who had simply no idea how her brutish reporters were hacking and harassing.

Lush fields, luxuriant hedges and Jurassic yellow cottages announce the Cotswolds. Here and across England, farmers have done well – their real income after costs up by £1bn between 2010 and 2013. Prime arable land grew in value by 270 per cent, outstripping gold and even the Knightsbridge flats we visit later. The cause, reported Savills Estate Agents, has been 'rising global food demand, climate change and foreign investment attracted by liberal British laws'. Landowners in Scotland cashed in, too: prime fishing beats sold for £10,000 per salmon; business has never been better, say organisers of £15,000-a-day luxury hunting and shooting.

Here journeys are calibrated in hours by car from Notting Hill – about one and a quarter. Take a left beyond Woodstock and you reach Cornbury Park, which in early August hosts Wilderness. There's nothing wild about this annual music and arts festival, except its prices. To hire the Royal Safari Tent with its 'antique oak flooring, king-sized beds with memory foam mattresses, 200 thread-count Egyptian cotton bed linen, dimmable overhead lighting, botanical toiletries and complimentary bouquet of flowers' costs £2,000 for three nights plus £150 entry. Nicknamed Poshstock, it's a festival, joked one reviewer, where performers sing about Texas trailer parks to an audience more used to deer parks, where bands delight the offspring of bankers with folk laments for the decline of Clydeside.

Among Wilderness fans is the governor of the Bank of England and he does not need to rent a tent. Cornbury Park's sumptuous grounds belong to Mark Carney's sister-in-law, Lady Tania Rotherwick, and her husband, Robin Cayzer, 3rd baron Rotherwick, a hereditary Tory peer. Cayzer's first wife belonged to the McAlpine clan, now a long, long way from the glens and generous donors to the Tory party. Such is the interwoven nature of politics, high finance and class in Cameron's country, which yes voters in the Scottish referendum found so oppressive.

Carney is no outsider, despite his Irish name and birth in the far Northwest Territories of Canada. Thirteen years with Goldman Sachs buys inches of veneer and access all areas. His wife, Diana, was educated at Marlborough and comes from English country wealth, albeit generated by rearing pigs. She is an economist who wants global wealth rebalanced towards the poorest.

Carney himself has had a go. Capitalism's growing problem, he said in a speech in May 2014, is 'exclusivity'. His objection to accelerating inequality is not so much moral as economic: it fuels bubbles and banking instability. For the proceeds of growth to be sequestered by those at the top is dysfunctional. Social justice, the central banker says, is good for growth.

He joins a swelling chorus. 'Fiscal consolidation' – getting public revenues and spending into better balance – has to be perceived as fair, insists the OECD, thinktank to the wealthy nations, especially when spending cuts hit the poor harder than the well-off. Inequality of opportunity is detrimental to growth and wellbeing because it locks in privilege and chloroforms the 'animal spirits' that Keynes said are supposed to make capitalism tick.

Unequal Britain

Scotland's yes campaigners proved the OECD's point. The need for austerity was one thing; who bore its wounds was another. The poorest households had failed to keep pace with overall income growth, leaving them no better off than in the mid-1980s. As Carney put it, 'Distributional consequences of the response to the financial crisis have been significant.' That's about as close as a central banker would get to saying the coalition has been deliberately regressive, bearing down hardest on the poor, also on women, children and young people, who have started to call themselves 'generation rent'.

Don't get carried away by the banker's radicalism. In that speech and other pronouncements he has stayed well away from what his analysis tells us about modern Britain's inequalities. So, no allusion to the fact that Oxford and Cambridge together usually admit only 50 students who had qualified for free school meals, compared with 60 from a single public school, Eton, or the 65 from Westminster. *Floreat Etona* – Let Eton Flourish – it says on Cameron's escutcheon; his coalition deputy, Nick Clegg, is an Old Westminster, in his school's jargon.

Club government? Along Pall Mall the frontages are visible but what goes on behind them is secluded and inaudible. We know where the rich live – Kensington Palace Gardens is the country's most expensive street, with average property values at £43m (160 times the price of the average home). We know who lives there – super-elite residents including Chelsea Football Club owner Roman Abramovich and steel magnate Lakshmi Mittal; but we grasp little of their influence and networks. In the unexpected bestseller, *Capital in the Twenty-First Century,*

Thomas Piketty said, 'Wealth is so concentrated that a large segment of society is virtually unaware of its existence.' It's a profound point. Great wealth is greatly secret, especially its hold on power, and who knows what goes on over country suppers in the Cotswolds?

Registers and codes of conduct are supposed to govern contacts and gifts but MPs, ministers, civil servants and special advisers are susceptible. Economic power seizes political power. There's nothing new about that, but after 1945 its grip did loosen for a while. Then Thatcher broke the equilibrating power of the trades unions and her Big Bang deregulation of the City's unfettered greed. The OECD puts it coyly: 'The views of some socio-economic groups are better reflected in the design and implementation of policies, and policymaking itself is captured by the most privileged groups.' How easily the moneymen were ushered in; through outsourcing and the appointment of pals, the corporate chieftains *became* government. Citizens are semi-aware, knowing and unknowing about winners and losers. Blaming the political class rather than business for the recession and its unjust fallout, they seized chances, in Scotland and in voting for UKIP, to vent their rage and resentment.

Cameron's Conservativism

Neither austerity nor the way it was done was inevitable and unavoidable: there is always a choice. Policies were often visceral rather than deductive, but the Tories' instincts weren't random or accidental. They were not all of one mind, but they united broadly around the belief that theirs is the party of people with power, status and wealth and those who aspire to them, however wildly unachievable.

'Where there is discord, may we bring harmony,' intoned Margaret Thatcher on arriving at No 10 in 1979. She soon abandoned preaching for hectoring and hostility. Cameron, too, started soft, pulling a gauze of theory and thinktankery over the politics of division. Before the election one of the Tories' house intellectuals said Cameron was placing 'ideas of fraternity and social responsibility at the heart of British political debate'.[1] The catchphrase was 'compassionate conservatism', a shebeen brew of localism, autonomous schools and charity, with a deep underlying thread of anti-statism.

Because on screen the prime minister was reasonable and moderate, we need to emphasise just how *ideological* his party had become. That can still seem an odd word to use in a British context. But it's less grand theory than hard, driving belief – dogma.

There was no project, in the sense of a worked-out timetable – Cameron was too idle and disorganised for that. But he and the ministers he appointed had plans and a big picture: public bad, private good, with a wavy line around charities and the voluntary sector. A pattern forms around what they did. Differences were accentuated; the unity of the UK itself was set at naught. The Tories ya-booed the poor and idolised 'hard-working families' (who in fact were usually the same), demonised 'bureaucrats' and blessed enterprise. Communities secretary Eric Pickles was unleashed on council staff, their pay and pensions. Welfare recipients were divided into two groups, deserving and undeserving: the old (good); adults of working age, children and young people (bad). Social cohesion was subverted. Builders no longer had to include dwellings ordinary people could afford in new developments, thus filling new flats and estates with the same kind of people and undermining efforts to integrate different social, racial and religious groups in schools, work and localities. Capping housing benefit segregated poorer tenants in the cheapest parts of town. 'One nation conservatism' became an oxymoron; it was divide and rule.

Top of the Tree

Toryism 'aims on principle to keep wealth and power for those who have them, and keep them from those who don't'.[2] So did it? The wealthy remain entrenched. The top 10 per cent own half of the total estimated £9.5tn of all wealth. The 100 richest people, worth £257bn, own as much as the lowest third of the entire population. The UK is now one of the most unequal countries in the EU: our rich are richer. The top 1 per cent takes 13 per cent of all available income. That's more than double the share of total income taken by the richest 1 per cent in the Netherlands, King Willem-Alexander and Queen Maxima included.

Such concentration is not new; austerity has not loosened it. The UK is like a spacecraft with a tiny command module (5 per cent) sitting on top of a big body (70 per cent) with the legs and landing gear making up the remaining 25 per cent – the people who struggle, get by, sometimes sink into destitution. For Tory ministers the 5 per cent are your people, your wife's uncle, your host on your weekend in the Cotswolds, your school and university friends, and the few who have made it up to join the upper echelons from elsewhere. In an increasingly plutocratic country, top people have leverage on power, both directly and through agenda-makers in the media – which is why Rebekah Brooks is such an emblematic figure, married to a racehorse trainer who is an old Eton chum of the prime minister, bed partner of the man who becomes press secretary at No 10. It's no accident, as they say, that corporate lobbying has been a growth industry, despite a promise to corral it.

In just three days, the chief executive of a FTSE 100 company gets paid £27,000, a sum their average employee takes a whole year to earn. Executive median pay has risen to £4.4m a year. In the year to 2014 top remuneration climbed 5 per cent, four times faster than for the average earner. The speed at which the gap was widening picked up: the FTSE 100 executive who earned 'only' 47 times the average in 1998 now earns 143 times more than their staff. Later in the book we talk to Sir Martin Sorrell, chief of WPP, whose ratio is 780 times. 'The only reason why their pay has increased so rapidly compared to their employees is that they are able to get away with it,' says Deborah Hargreaves of the High Pay Centre.

This is the sort of income that feeds the lifestyle you can spy on in the *Financial Times* supplement, 'How to Spend It'. Try a 'stalking package' where, from £8,400 per couple, you are helicoptered to Petworth House in West Sussex to enjoy a weekend shooting deer – £12,000 if you occupy the Lady Hamilton suite. In 2013, a year when most people's real earnings were still falling, 62,000 more people joined the ranks of 'highish' net worth individuals, bringing the total to 527,000: this is a marketing category for those with investable assets of at least £600,000, not including their pensions, main home, art collection or vintage cars. Most joined the club not because of added productivity or enterprise but thanks to rising values of their second or other properties.

———————

Hard times never come to Knightsbridge. Lucy Morton, senior partner at upmarket estate agents WA Ellis, has never known a boom like it. Property values have risen by 20 per cent a year: there is a never-ending demand for Knightsbridge from buyers all over the world. 'Central London continues to be an investment sanctuary', says the Ellis brochure, and so it was for oligarchs, for Middle Eastern potentates and French bankers escaping François Hollande's taxes. Joining them in seeking a haven were our very own City financiers with more pay and bonuses than anyone could spend each year. Land in Knightsbridge, Belgravia, Kensington and Mayfair was better than gold ingots, a one-way bet in a soaring market. Lucy Morton found the boundaries of prime property were being pushed ever further. Surprisingly, she says, even Fulham is now attracting the same high-net-worth investors who might once not have ventured more than a few hundred metres from Harrods, banishing 'the ordinary English middle classes' to districts ever further afield. A lycée is now opening in Fulham, so that the children of wealthy French exiles can maintain their *bon ton, bon genre*.

Coincidentally on the day we visited, a Frenchwoman was worrying about the capital's property market. Christine Lagarde's IMF sounded the alarm over the gold rush, warning that as London prices rippled outwards, 'a steady increase in the size of new mortgages compared with borrower incomes suggests that households are gradually becoming more vulnerable to income and interest rate shocks', it said. Emergency measures should be considered. The government shrugged.

WA Ellis is no bubble company. Still on the same Brompton Road site where it was established in 1868, it looks out on the Armani Emporium, with Harrods and Harvey Nichols close by. In reception, a discreet display of properties includes a flat over-looking Hyde Park to rent for £25,000 a week – that's £1.3m a year. A house in Mayfair, with pool and indoor parking, can be had for £40,000 a week. Lettings for £5–6,000 a week seem standard. Sale prices run into the many millions for petite mews houses built for grooms and many millions more for mansions. Buyers are investment companies building prime property port-folios, often foreign, their real owners and landlords unknown. Residential streets around here are deserted, Lucy Morton says, as investors prefer to mothball their properties and not bother with tenants. Capital gain is the aim. WA Ellis disapproves and tries to encourage owners to let.

Lucy Morton has worked here for 25 years. Smart, warm, intelligent, she is at the helm of a business helping to make London property even more insane. She sees the same prop-erties bought and sold over and over, picking from the current files a pretty little bijou 'cottage' round the corner, 'in the heart of Knightsbridge village', with two bedrooms and a patio, that has sold five times over in recent years, its price multiplying by five to £2.7m – probably a snip in the present climate.

There is a curious wistfulness in Morton's view of the world. There she is, luring in foreigners – 75 per cent of her business comes from abroad – yet she muses whether there's a tipping point. 'Is there a time when the things they value about Englishness vanish, when everyone else is a foreigner, and everyone else in the private schools they value is foreign too, because the English have been pushed out?' Hot-housed children from the Far East are taking more prized top-school places. In Knightsbridge she hardly sees anyone these days who isn't foreign. 'Restaurants opening, the shops absolutely buzzing, but they're mostly foreign-owned, like so much in Britain. Harrods, Harvey Nichols, nothing is owned by us any more.'

She worries about how to bring up her children to understand life outside this bubble. An answer is taking her sons to a St Mungo's homeless hostel to see society's darker side, where the down-and-out and desperate are rescued by charities WA Ellis supports. 'We do what we call a spring clean once a year and clear all our old working clothes out of our cupboards and take them to a single mothers project north of Ladbroke Grove.' They raised £15,000 for charity last year. Rejoice, they might say, here is the 'big society' in action, from Knightsbridge to the badlands off the Harrow Road.

But Morton is not at ease. 'I see people in their 50s worrying more than they did, afraid that if they're not firing on all cylinders all the time they'll be out on their ear. They worry they won't get another job and they haven't got a good enough pension yet. There is a lot of worry, people are nervous.'

Those helping deposit global wealth in SW7 have enjoyed rich pickings, yet the mood music is discordant: even the Brompton Road doesn't feel like easy street.

––––––––

That sense of unease is pervasive. Yes, the pre-tax income share of the richest 1 per cent has increased in most OECD countries but the UK is far ahead. Ideas of fairness – however 'dysfunctional' in the eyes of business leaders and market theorists; however old-fashioned to visionaries and neoliberals – simply won't go away. Even four in five UKIP supporters tell pollsters the gap between rich and poor should be the government's highest priority.

The Elusive and Squeezed Middle

Despite this prevalent conviction that the UK is an unjust society, the Tories have enjoyed political success. That's because the 5 per cent can depend on support deep in society – English society. You can hear their voices in the chapters to come, such as those of Barbara Hatt of Sydenham and Chris Hill from Sheffield: they are not especially happy with Cameron, but unlikely ever to stray from voting Conservative. Their rallying cry is often tax.

It's also because of false sociology, propagated not just by the *Daily Mail* but by other editors and journalists who could usefully attend a course on basic statistics. We speak for the middle class, say Tories such as Dominic Raab. It turns out their 'middle' are people paying higher-rate income tax, which starts at just over £41,000, who are only 14 per cent of earners. The middle should be median earnings, £26,000. Here, incomes have stagnated in recent times. Or worse: disposable household income fell for four-fifths of the UK population in the year to 2013, but rose for the best off fifth.

The labour market looks to some as if it might be taking on a more 'Tory' shape. Self-employment, once a pointer to right-wards-leaning politics, has soared. But the new self-employed are poor, two-thirds earning less than £10,000; an army of mini-cab drivers, top occupation among the new self-employed.

More people are now classified as managers and directors; professional and technical employment has grown, too, as skilled trades have declined, along with sales, customer service and process, plant and machine operatives. In 2014, at the head of the list of the 20 fastest-growing jobs were supermarket checkout staff and shelf-stackers as well as therapists, solicitors, web design specialists, fitness instructors and estate agents. Not all chefs – another growth area – are Gordon Ramsay.

The 'squeezed middle' championed by Labour leader Ed Miliband has never had it so bad. Academics such as Danny Blanchflower and Steve Machin suggest the UK is taking the American road, its labour markets highly flexible, GDP growing but median earnings flatlining. This wasn't Cameron's doing directly, but his government did nothing to ease it; an aspect of his coup is to have succeeded politically despite what has happened to general living standards.

Median earnings in the UK had been rising till around 2005; by then, middling UK workers were 40 per cent better off in real terms than when Margaret Thatcher departed. But growth then evaporated and during the recession earnings dropped, losing about 2 per cent a year from 2008 onwards. By 2013, the IFS calculated, real median household income was 5.8 per cent below 2010. As recovery has taken hold, median earnings have barely budged upwards. Here's a household in June 2014: average weekly earnings were just 0.6 per cent higher than they had been a year before, but supermarket costs, energy and running the car were up 1.6 per cent. Real earnings kept falling.

Life at the Bottom

Pay disparity kept growing. Our poor are poorer than elsewhere; average income for the bottom fifth of UK households is well below France, the Netherlands or Germany. If the minimum wage had grown as much in the last 15 years as chief executive remuneration, the lowest paid would be on £15.30 an hour, not £6.30; the minimum is now worth £1,000 a year less in real terms than when it was introduced. Within sight of the general election, the government added pence to it; the campaign for a living wage won occasional polite words from ministers, but doing something would have been anti-market.

Incomes Data Services said wages were falling because low-paying sectors are creating far more jobs. High-paying finance and construction have shed jobs. More are working part-time, but want more hours; some 3.4 million are under-employed. Young people taking their first jobs in 2014 were earning 3.9 per cent less than new workers in first jobs the year before. Employees under the age of 30 have suffered a real-terms drop in weekly wages of around 10 per cent. The gap between women and men's pay had narrowed in the Labour years but has been widening again; women's low pay was an accelerator of inequality.

Poor Britain

In the recession, the UK suffered the biggest fall in working incomes among G7 countries. The share of GDP going into pay continued to fall, while the share going to profits rose. Yet income inequality had fallen during the recession despite wages falling; benefits for those made unemployed and welfare claimants were adjusted for inflation, with the result that the distribution of income got a little flatter. In 2013 income inequality was less than before the crash.

But pre-crash trends began reasserting themselves. The disposable income of the richest fifth of households grew by an average £940 between 2011and 2013, while the disposable income of all the other groups fell by around £250, with the poorest households experiencing the sharpest fall of £381. The recession had done little to change relativities. Before taxes and benefits, the richest fifth of households had an average income of £81,300 in 2013, almost 15 times greater than the poorest fifth, whose income was £5,500.

Before the election, the Tories had supported Labour legis-lation, promising to eradicate child poverty by 2020. But early on, the IFS predicted that coalition tax and benefit changes would increase the number of children in poverty by a fifth by

2020. Ironically, for the first few years the government could thumb their nose at the critics. The official figures said poverty had been reduced, despite benefit cuts, despite unemployment and low pay. Poverty is a measure of income against the median in any given year. Median incomes were falling so at first the proportion of those in poverty remained broadly level, a little down on 2010.

However, once the deepest cuts in benefits began in April 2013, this trend would surely reverse. To avoid the inevitable charge that this would be a poverty-generating government, ministers tried to move the goalposts. Poverty wasn't ultimately about money, they declared, but personal character – poor people failed to get married and are bad parents. Iain Duncan Smith, the work and pensions secretary, wanted a measure reflecting the 'moral' causes of poverty – the absent fathers and personal deficiencies. But these were as much the consequences of poverty as cause, and the statisticians cried foul. Later the DWP sheepishly announced that its search had ended.

It was never quite clear what Duncan Smith was after. The legislation already offered several definitions of poverty, and the Joseph Rowntree Foundation annually asked the public to define what they considered the minimum on which to get by. Unfortunately, paying for the resulting spartan list (including a spare pair of shoes, a one-week self-catering UK holiday and a modest birthday present for a child) cost a lot more than a job on the minimum wage would afford.

These years showed, again, the silence and 'apartness' of poverty. Low earnings and exiguous household income are hidden away. In Birmingham, over a quarter of children live in low-income households, higher than any other council area in England. The next highest numbers of poor children are not in big cities but in Tory Kent (50,000) and Tory Essex (43,000), spread in smaller towns and run-down seasides such as Margate and Jaywick. We visited Witney, in Cameron's constituency: the food bank is well used, but hidden away in a lockup garage.

The poor travel by bus; they shop differently. These were years when Poundland was being challenged by the 99p store and Poundworld, which is opening 150 new shops. 'There is strong demand for our value goods and everyday items,' said Chris Edwards, the chain's founder and owner.

His customers often relied on Wonga and payday loans, available (it said in the small print) at interest rates topping 1,600 per cent. This loan market increased in size from £900m in 2008 to £2.8bn in 2012. In poor districts such as Barking in east London and Hodge Hill in Birmingham, one in six families are covering their costs with payday loans or unauthorised overdrafts or by defaulting on household bills. The government, on the back foot, announced that from 2015 interest rates would be capped, but left unclear whether the total cost of credit or the annual percentage would be the target.

The facts of poverty have been fended off by Manichean rhetoric about benefits scroungers versus 'hard-working families', a phrase so overworked in the era it became a single word. However, the myth that poverty is caused by fecklessness and is the deserved fate of the workshy was exploded finally and for ever. The number of poor households where adults were in work rose: to be employed was not, as had been promised, the route out of poverty. Two-thirds of poor children have a working parent, many a single parent. But traditional two-parent families as approved by the moralists, with one 'breadwinner' and one parent at home caring for the kids, are also among the largest groups of households living in poverty – 31 per cent of the 1.3 million families with children living in poverty, the Joseph Rowntree Foundation found. Hard workers could toil all day and all night cleaning top people's offices, and yet still stay grindingly poor.

Towards the end of the 2010 election campaign, Citizens UK – an alliance of local community groups – summoned the party leaders to a campaign rally. The 2,500 people at Central Hall Westminster were drawn from faith groups and trade unionists, all campaigning for a living wage for cleaners, carers, caterers and security guards, the great army of the unseen, unheard and unrewarded.

Gordon Brown, the Labour prime minister, was on the platform when the event was electrified by a short speech from a 14-year-old, Tia Sanchez. She namechecked her family. 'This is my mum, Sandra, and my grandmother, Marta.' Then the bombshell. 'Both of them work as cleaners in the Treasury.' Sandra and Marta cleaned Brown's very own office, working for an outsourced company that made its money by paying its staff a poverty wage. Tia went on to describe the difference a living wage would make to her family. 'I might get the laptop I need for my school work. We wouldn't have weeks where we just eat lentils. My mum could afford to take the tube instead of three buses and I would have three more hours with her a day.' She broke down in tears, Gordon Brown hugged her and then he belted out the mantra, 'Wealth must serve more than the wealthy, prosperity must serve more than the prosperous and good fortune must help more than those who are fortunate.' Labour's own observance of that sentiment had been mixed: Blair and Brown left a million fewer children and a million fewer pensioners living in poverty – but they left the fortunes of the fortunate untouched and unquestioned.

Five years on, we caught up with Tia. Her speech had so moved a member of the audience that evening that he offered to sponsor her through university. But his business went bust, one of many who didn't make it through the slump, and he was forced to withdraw the offer. However, she did make it and she started a degree course at Royal Holloway, University of London in September 2014, a proud success for her family through all their struggles.

Her mother and grandmother still clean at the Treasury for the same outsourced company, still paid well below a living wage. Nothing has changed. We talked to Tia, but when we asked to speak to her family, they changed their mind and panicked: they had seen what happened to those who did speak out.

Valdemar Ventura cleaned the floors and toilets of the Cabinet Office. He was one of a number of Whitehall cleaners who signed letters to ministers. He handed his directly to Francis Maude, saying how hard they worked to keep government premises clean but were paid less than they needed to survive. He worked from 5 a.m. to 2 p.m., with an unpaid lunch hour, taking two buses to get home in time to collect his 11-year-old son from school. His wife Paula worked a later shift, as she studied for a quali-fication. On being interviewed by the *Evening Standard* he was suspended. His employer moved him to a heavier job, cleaning in a college, with eight floors, lifts, stairs and internal glass polishing to cover. At a disciplinary hearing his employer, ETDE ('Our values are embodied by respect, a commitment to practise what we preach'), accused him of gross misconduct, giving him a final warning for a 'security breach'. He lost his Saturday overtime, a crucial slab of his income. A living wage would deliver him £200 more a month, making the difference between scraping by, and sometimes not. Easy to forget how much every penny counts, until he described a special treat as being able to buy his boy a box of Cheerios for breakfast.

Ministers were embarrassed by the exposure of how little their cleaners earned. At the DWP, Duncan Smith said he would ensure the living wage was paid. But he didn't. In 2014 Frank Field MP found out the DWP still paid 5,000 staff less than the living wage. When pressed, Downing Street said a living wage might 'reduce business flexibility'.

Flexibility tends to be a quality those in power demand from employees or benefit receivers, not something they themselves exhibit – the flexibility, say, to accept more proportionate boardroom rewards or to break up concentrations of corpo-rate power. Similarly mobility: the government said it was all in favour of young people breaking out of deprived backgrounds to join the elite, but was reticent on the daughters and sons of rich people making room or old Etonians having to work in low-grade clerical jobs. Tia Sanchez deserves every success but there are a limited number of top-notch jobs in the law or in business. Markets have little evident interest in mobility: the 'Social Mobility Business Compact', which was cobbled together by Nick Clegg in February 2012 to give young people 'fair and open access to business opportunities', has had minimal impact on recruitment.

Going Up, Immobile Down

When a third of all wealth is inherited, mobility is circumscribed. Wealth stays where it is. Money increasingly partners with money as what sociologists call assortative mating (like partnering with like) becomes more common, not less. Later we discuss the coalition's pupil premium for poorer children – and the abolition of educational maintenance allowances and retreat from Sure Start children's centres. The Tories talked a lot about social mobility, even setting up a commission with Blair's former health secretary, Alan Milburn, as its chair. He duly reported that opportunity is closely related to household income and no scheme to fast-track poor children into higher education can combat that – anyway, the numbers on such schemes are marginal. Children's school performance remains tied to their background. JRF research showed that increasing the income of children eligible for free school meals to the UK average would halve the difference in test results at age 11 between them and the rest. That would cost £6,000 per child. This government was never likely to engage in redistribution on that scale.

Mobility is a matter of equality. All the evidence from Scandinavia says that where the ladder up is short, more children can climb. But it only works if there are snakes, too, and middle- and upper-class children drop down them to make room at the top. Inherited wealth and high incomes would always move heaven and earth to stop that. Places at Eton, Westminster, Oxford's Christ Church or Cambridge's Trinity are strictly limited. Besides, higher education was becoming more finely tuned to money and parental means. Austerity as practised by the coalition has been regressive, closing off opportunity. Social elites are not opening up.

Of course any picture of the UK in 2015 has to be dappled. Fortunes vary by class, of course, but also age, locality, luck and market. Managers at Morrisons, a company in difficulties, are facing the sack but Aldi has been expanding – it's cheaper and people have less to spend. Most people live in the middle, navigating straitened family incomes by shaving costs and crimped spending. People were getting by, but easily roused to tell pollsters of their resentment against anyone seen to be getting away with things – bankers, fat cat bosses, welfare claimants, foreigners or MPs.

We began at Cornbury Park. Poshstock it might be, but the festival leaves many a glamper happy, as do Latitude, Wickerman, Bestival and the rest, in a period of high artistic, musical and theatrical energy and creativity – some sparked by opposition to the regime. Despite hard times for many, the pursuit of fun and occasional discretionary spending on festivals still went some way down the income scale. The next chapter tries to catch the contrary tides.

2

Britain 2015 – A Snapshot

'We have not seen such a prolonged period of economic weakness since before even the 1930s,' said Paul Johnson of the IFS in January 2014. The verdict was, however, compatible with easy and prosperous living for many. Adam Smith, enjoying renewed fame as the emblem of Scotland's capacity, had said it: there's a great deal of ruin in a nation.

Even families with squeezed incomes could still afford (increased) season ticket prices to support their clubs. Theatre managers put out more 'house full' notices, not just in the West End: the Edinburgh festival reported record ticket sales. But companies and productions had been state-nurtured in a time of plenty, before the Arts Council budget was cut. Who stopped to thank Labour when the Imperial War Museum reopened in July 2014 with a new atrium and galleries after years of extensive redevelopment? Think ahead. This government will cast a long shadow. The 2014 Taking Part survey found a sharp fall in the number of children doing any arts: 35 per cent fewer took part in music activities, drama and dance than in 2010.

'They' Do Matter

Yet many don't make these connections between politics and 'life'. Barely four out of 10 ever discuss political affairs with friends or family, the Hansard Society found. People rarely measure out their existence by reference to governments. Their priorities are getting by, family, job, home, leisure and the fortunes of favourite teams. During the 2010 campaign, Cameron took a pot shot at Labour, complaining about '13 years of them going on television and never talking about what's actually happened or what real people have actually done. All they talk about is what they, the government, have done.' Yet the truth was the converse: Labour ministers had not done enough public tub-thumping or explaining; too often they pursued policies by stealth, frightened of what the *Sun* or the *Daily Mail* might say.

Our Picture

Labour had fattened public services, as we recorded in *The Verdict – Did Labour Change Britain?* Preparing it, we travelled the country, talking to people in varied walks of life – a Manchester head teacher, a reservist who has served in Iraq and Afghanistan. Some of them we have revisited. In 2010 we randomly chose Barbara Hatt from the list of staff on median earnings at the grocery chain for which she works. Neither her head office nor we knew anything of her life or views as, five years ago, she told us how she and her family had fared during Labour's 13 years. In 2014 we returned to her south London suburban home.

Barbara Hatt lives in Sydenham and works in Sainsbury's. Her husband, Brian, is a self-employed roofer and they have three grown-up children. They live in a modern house with a small garden in a cul-de-sac, over which have broken the waves of the property boom. 'I can't believe what's happened,' she says, with that mixture of shock and excitement that grabs homeowners in London and the south-east when they check the figures. They struggled to buy their own house on a mortgage in 1997. They paid £105,000 and now it's worth £375,000. 'It makes no sense.'

Yet individual and collective fortunes are bound together and Barbara is keenly aware of the knock-on effect of the boom on housing prospects for her children and their friends. 'No chance they can ever live near London. Something should be done by the government to stop this madness. They should be building more.' The Hatts have another problem, too: they had an all-too-close encounter with the UK financial sector. An endowment policy had been sold to them on the basis that it would pay off the mortgage. 'It went pear-shaped. It paid out in 2011 exactly the money we put in, but not a penny more.' They will have to find the money for mortgage repayments over more years.

When we first met her, we had no idea whether she had political views or even voted. It turned out she and her husband were what the 19th-century Tory prime minister Benjamin Disraeli called 'angels in marble'; they come from a long line of working-class Conservatives, without whom no rightwing government could ever have been elected. Her parents, grandparents and (she says) children always have and always will vote Tory. Always, that is, until the 2014 Euro elections. They all voted UKIP and gave the political establishment a nasty shock. Immigration was the main reason and remains a central issue; she is eager to leave the European Union, too. Yet, disaffected as they are, come the 2015 general election, the Hatts are all certain they will be voting Tory once again.

The Hatt family fortunes during the recession illustrate how individuals and households move up and down the income scales in tics and trajectories quite distinct from what is happening to the big picture. She herself did well, moving up a grade at Sainsbury's. At £29,000 her earnings are now a little above the median. Brian Hatt's roofing jobs took a knock, with no one buying or selling homes during the long slump.

She sees more shoplifting by people who are plainly hungry. She notices the struggles of the low-paid staff she supervises on the tills where she herself started 15 years ago. She's been keenly aware of rising prices and sees families cutting back and turning to cheaper stores. 'It is hard for so many. The benefits cutbacks, the tax credit rules changed, so they get a lot less. Staff working on the checkouts always want more hours, but I can't give them, when I only get a fixed pool of hours to share out every week.' She experiences welfare vicariously, through friends and staff. 'It's shocking how many can't get help or housing benefits because of the number of hours they work. I see people falling right behind with their rent. The bedroom tax, it's so wrong. I know quite a few in work who have to pay it but it's penalising the wrong people. I'd penalise the rich. Those bonuses are just so wrong.'

This isn't party-line Toryism. At the shop she helps collect groceries in the evening to go to food banks, 'Like out-of-date bread, dented tins.' She knows people who have to use the banks at the end of the week when their money doesn't stretch to payday. She was upset when, around Christmas time, she went to help a charity serve dinners to families without hot food. 'I'm really shocked by that – and I do know how genuine those people are.'

Working life has got harder. 'So much pressure, a lot are taking time off with stress. We have the mystery customer measure, when someone comes and looks at cleanliness, ease of exit at checkout, interactions with staff. They leave messages like "staff were robotic" or "open more tills". We only hit half the target, but if there are queues and I don't have more hours to hire people for longer, what can you do?' She has a personal development review twice a year, based on these targets. 'Jobs never used to be pressured like that. I think it's all these management consultants.'

When we talked in 2010, Mrs Hatt was grumbling about the NHS. This time she says: 'I think it's very poor, worse. I can't get a GP appointment.' Her case is dramatic. A few months ago she tried and failed to see her GP and then collapsed on the stairs with pneumonia, was unconscious for a day and in Lewisham hospital for two weeks. 'The GP said I should have seen him! I said: "What do I have to do to get an appointment? Drop down dead?" I nearly did.' She is one of public health's many head-aches as a long-time sufferer from emphysema who still smokes. 'Though a lot less than when you saw me last, I promise.'

For the Hatts, the clincher in their vote for UKIP and their biggest issue still is immigration. 'I just don't know why we let so many in. My brother's in Australia and we should be like them, shut the borders. I see a Bosnian selling the *Big Issue* on Sydenham High Street, well, what's he doing here?' Yet when she says, 'I've got nothing against foreigners,' she means it. 'I work with so many, have so many who are real friends – a really nice Polish friend, and she works really hard, a good person. There's Poles and Nigerians moved into this street since I saw you, nice people, work hard, buy their homes. But why are they here when we need the homes and the jobs? If we were out of Europe, we could put a stop to it.'

Barbara Hatt is hard to pigeonhole; her views clash with one another. She seems typical of the three-quarters of the public who tell pollsters they are happy with their lives but by a six-to-one margin also say the country is getting worse as a place to live. As for public services, she has always praised the local schools her children attended and she certainly wants a better NHS, in which she believes strongly. She wants more council and afford-able housing built and she wants more police on the streets, out there where she can see them. She doesn't particularly want lower taxes, because she thinks that means worse services and more benefit cuts.

All in all, here is no believer. She thinks things have got a lot worse in a number of ways. Yet she is definitely voting Tory in 2015. Party is a deep identity: it's who she is and where she belongs, a badge of belief in hard work and making your own way in life, as she feels she and her family always have. Labour is an alien tribe of which she is deeply suspicious. She echoes the anti-politics sentiments ricocheting around the land. Barbara Hatt yearns for clarity, simplicity and strength – yet is herself conflicted about what's right and fair. She is not a bad emblem for Cameron country – at least the English part of it.

––––––––––

As Ipsos MORI tracks public concerns it tends to find the economy causes the most worry, though as recovery began, anxiety lessened. Next, though often vying with fears for the NHS, comes disquiet over immigration, as talking to Barbara Hatt shows. In polling at the time of the 2012 Olympics, people applauded their own tolerance of diversity and yet four out of 10 said they would rather live where most people came from their own ethnic background. But people are now *less* likely to be living alongside their own kind; that's life in most inner London boroughs, in Slough, Luton and Leicester, all places where no single ethnic group now accounts for the majority of the population. Identity is rapidly changing: in Boston and the surrounding Fenland, as in Corby, Peterborough and parts of London (Walthamstow, Haringey, Ealing and Newham), shops feature a *polskie delikatesy*. In 2013, nearly half the mothers giving birth were foreign-born and the single largest group were Polish. The mix of races, demotic languages, types of schooling and religious observances has been permanently altered across tracts of England and to a lesser extent the rest of the UK, and change has accelerated during the past five years. In Birmingham, the fulcrum of tensions about Islamic practices in state schools, 38 per cent of children are white and the same proportion Asian, 7.2 per cent of mixed race and 11.9 per cent black. No one willed that demographic fact; it just happened.

Yet, however disturbing many find that, we saw with Barbara Hatt that their attitudes cannot be reduced to 'racism'. If anything, people are now more sensitive to racial, religious and cultural difference. Despite Tory journalists fulminating about 'political correctness', the public remain vigilant for signs of disrespect for heritage, ethnicity and religion, for all their uneasiness about Islamic radicalisation. In polls, two-thirds ask for more respect for the beliefs of different religions; the same proportion (maybe paradoxically the same people) think gay couples should be allowed to marry, up from a half in 2000.

Happiness

Concern over migration wasn't incompatible with high levels of 'wellbeing'. Cameron wanted better measures, less emphasis (he said) on mere money. It was a good ploy because pollsters have not in recent years found the country seething with discontent. On the ONS scale of 10, average satisfaction is 7.5, women higher than men, whites and Indians above black people, people in Northern Ireland and the south-west higher than people in Wales and the north-east. As recovery took hold, surveys found more people sort of smiling: eight out of 10 satisfied with their jobs, perhaps grateful to have one at all.

Measuring happiness is a mysterious art. The UK ranks above the EU average in recycling rubbish, but what does it mean when pollsters find that we are also above the EU average in life satisfaction? Ipsos MORI concluded: 'happiness in Britain has not fallen off a cliff during recessionary times but neither has it yet been lifted by the recent recovery.' Mona Lott, the wartime radio comedy tea lady, is alive and well. 'While the mood is stubbornly negative about the country, people are consistently more positive about their own prospects.'

That must be a result of Cameron's statecraft: the Tories could hardly complain at public contempt for politics and public affairs when their tone and style was to denigrate the NHS, councils and 'bureaucrats'. But consider the implications of a condition where you can't get government out of the picture because wellbeing depends on public help with caring for sick or disabled relatives. The incidence of dementia is growing. The Health and Social Care Information Centre says the number of people being diagnosed (in England) rose by a third – to 344,000 – in the seven years to 2014. Charities say that's an underestimate.

Demography

We don't live in some post-ideological age, when all governments are rendered impotent by global forces: that contention is itself ideological, and reflects vested interests. Governments are certainly not 'all the same'. And yet none are fully in charge. No government commands technological developments, demographic change, the transmutation of viruses or the rise of China, but governments do influence where costs and benefits fall.

People don't choose to age. They do choose to have children, often in defiance of conventional wisdom about their future income and comfort. The birthrate has risen steadily across all social classes. That half-explains the continuing strong growth in the population, now over 64 million; the other half is immigration (one in three of London's residents was born abroad). Even after the crash, mothers went on having more children, right through 2011 when the ONS recorded more babies born than at any time since 1972 (putting predictable strain on midwifery services the government had ignored). The UK population has been growing faster than elsewhere in Europe, adding five million since the turn of the century.

By 2020, the statisticians reckon on a further five million. But, in 2013, the ONS recorded the steepest fall in births for 40 years in a single year, down by 4.3 per cent. Reasons included 'uncertainty about employment (such as temporary, part-time, or zero-hours contracts), which can significantly reduce women's demand for children' and 'reforms to simplify the welfare system that may have influenced decisions around child-bearing'. (Note the official use of 'simplify' to mean 'cut'.)

'Broken Britain'

The Tory party, since Thatcher, has been riven between those who want economic dynamism ('creative destruction' is a key phrase) and proponents of order and stability, which historically were the bases of Conservatism. Cameron wanted both and got neither.

Metrosexuals and moralists battled for the Tory soul. Before the election Duncan Smith led a chorus booming out that Britain was 'broken'. Theirs was an odd cocktail of old-fashioned moralising, sexism (beware the fecund woman!) and a ploy to denigrate the welfare state, which of course was responsible for pregnancies and working-class fecklessness. Whatever was meant, Britain looks to have got more broken since they took office. If out-of-wedlock was (according to the cardinals) the cardinal sin, nearly half of all babies are now born to the unmarried. But then, as now, Duncan Smith had a problem with arithmetic. He claimed a staggering 54 per cent of 15- to 17-year-olds in the most deprived areas were getting pregnant; the correct figure was 5.4 per cent. On coming to power they tore down the ring-fence around funding for teenage pregnancy prevention and they excluded sex education from the revised curriculum, though both programmes had been phenomenally successful in reducing young pregnancies.

If a symptom of breakdown was young people having sex, the Wellcome Trust's regular survey of sexual attitudes and lifestyles reports that teenagers are neither having more sex nor having it younger than they were 20 years ago, when Tony Blair was boasting of his (self-reported) five times a night virility. Today's youth are, if anything, more docile: their consumption of drink and drugs has dropped to its lowest in a decade. Only 16 per cent admit to ever having taken drugs, down from 26 per cent in 2001. Polls report them working harder and going out less than their parents did when they were young. The explanation may be simple austerity, less money, tuition fees or worries about potential employers finding out. Another factor is culture: one in 12 of those aged under 16 is now Muslim and less likely to drink.

Successive governments have been tempted by the idea of an identifiable group of 'troubled families', mired in unemployment and misery, causing crime. Sir Keith Joseph, Thatcher's guru, believed in a core of poor families who, genetically and socially, transmit their bad habits down the generations (like the Savages in Aldous Huxley's *Brave New World*). So strong was his conviction that when the Social Science Research Council produced reams of research in disproof, he abolished it. Cameron and Duncan Smith harped on about a hardened group: one in 50 families exhibited multiple, transmissible problems. Unfortunately, the figure (120,000 such families in England) turned out to have been plucked from statistical nowhere. Worse, as the LSE's John Hills showed in his book *Good Times, Bad Times*, there is no such permanent core; families encounter problems from time to time, some move on, some fall back. A tough-talking civil servant, Louise Casey, was put in charge of a 'troubled families' programme, bombarding the selected households with attention from social workers, police and teachers. The case for intensive caseworking was not new and results were overhyped – by 2014 only a third of families were 'on track'. Advocates ignored the obvious. Troubled families' trouble starts with (lack of) money.

Old vs Young

Yet Britain was broken. The IFS's Robert Joyce says age became the key to disunity, more than class or place, and as a result of conscious policy. Once the old were most likely to be poor, but now it's the young. Since the crisis, young people have suffered the most severe income losses, while people over 65 have largely been shielded. The tax burden shifted from better-off pensioners to people of working age. Over retirement age, all income is exempt from national insurance.

Of course, low-earning workers do not suddenly become wealthy when they retire. However, the elderly have lately been clear winners in the policy stakes. When, early on, the DWP considered means testing pensioner privileges, the reaction from No 10 was sharp. Almost all pensioner benefits and perks – winter fuel allowances, free TV licences and free bus travel – have gone untouched, though changes were made to age-related allowances. Pensioners were exempted from the bedroom tax, although the majority of the nation's 25 million spare bedrooms are in old people's houses and flats. Pensioners were protected when even the poorest households were made to pay council tax. The state pension was 'triple locked', so its value will rise by whichever is the highest of the Retail Price Index (more generous than the index applied to welfare benefits), earnings in the economy at large or 2.5 per cent. By 2013, median income in pensioner households was 5 per cent higher than that in working-age households, having been 5 per cent lower as recently as 2008. 'The relative increase in pensioner incomes was in stark contrast to the fortunes of young adults, who saw by far the largest falls in income,' the IFS commented.

Just as the coalition took office, Tory minister David Willetts wrote *The Pinch*, deploring how the generation now retiring had sucked up money in generous pension pots and accumulated wealth from phenomenal house price rises, squeezing the living standards of their children and grandchildren, keeping the young off the housing ladder. The IFS says a majority of couples born in the 1940s are more than wealthy enough to sustain their standard of living through retirement, and more than two-fifths have more money in retirement than their average real earnings when they worked. Such plenty does not await tomorrow's retirees. Nearly half of people below retirement age have not paid into a private scheme; those in private schemes have seven times the wealth of the others. But neither Willetts nor his boss saw the consequent need for an open conversation about fairness, about services and the taxes needed to pay for them. That all sounded too collectivist, too critical of the imperfections of commercial society. It did not happen.

Instead the coalition gave every impression of indifference, either based on political calculation or a version of Tory hedonism-libertarianism, letting tomorrow take care of itself. Liberal Democrat pensions minister Steve Webb interpreted Osborne's 2014 budget as a licence for those approaching retirement to 'blow the whole lot on a Lamborghini' rather than an annuity to provide an income till they died. Never mind that abolishing the requirement to purchase an annuity would hit future state revenues, or that the Treasury had done scant modelling of the effects of the new policy, especially on paying for social care. If old people were profligate, wouldn't they end up unable to pay for care? Webb blandly said he did not believe many would put themselves at risk in this way, while admitting people were underestimating how long they were likely to live.

Voluntary arrangements were better, they believed. The government kept in place the National Employment Savings Trust invented by Labour, which will automatically enroll staff with no company or public sector pension. Employers are to pay 3 per cent, employees 4 per cent and the state will add 1 per cent tax relief. Roll-out to larger firms began auspiciously and, from July 2014, staff in firms with between 50 and 249 workers are being enrolled, unless they decide to opt out. But the scheme applies only to those on low incomes. The upshot is that from the next decade on many millions will retire, relying on highly variable pension pots that may simply be inadequate. Saving for a pension at 8 per cent of salary may well not be enough.

Being Young in Cameron's Britain

Tomorrow's poor pensioners are today's 18- to 30-year-olds, whose earnings have fallen 10 per cent, who face mounting rents and decreasing chances of buying their own home. In eight out of 10 local authority areas in 2014 house prices were more than five times the typical local salary, and that figure had increased eight-fold since 1997. Youth unemployment has become epidemic. The number of young people not in employ-ment, education or training (NEETs) had been on a rising trend and, at just under a million in August 2014 – 13 per cent of the age group – is now among the highest in Europe. A young person who ever became a NEET would lose up to £50,000 in earnings over their working life compared to someone who went on to train or get a job, or stayed in full-time education.

The recession hit twentysomethings especially hard. Their real living standards fell 13 per cent between 2007 and 2013. Participation in the labour market fell and a quarter still lived with their parents, many into their 30s. Ironically, this distorted the figures: adult children still living at home pushed up average household income. The rate of home ownership for 25-year-olds halved from 45 per cent in the 1990s.

The government appeared indifferent to those not destined for university: they killed off the Connexions youth service, which sought to bridge the gap between school and work. The UK, surveys showed, did relatively well for high-level skills. Where it was failing to keep pace was 'intermediate' skills. The UK Commission on Employment talked of 'occupational polar-isation', with a large gap to 'jump' between entry-level and higher-skilled roles. Where was the pressure on large employers to create genuine high-quality apprenticeships, as in Germany?

A survey of young people aged 11 to 16, conducted for the National Children's Bureau, found they were not keen on lowering the voting age; however, that might change after the Scottish referendum. The same survey uncovered the pessi-mism of young people: fewer than two in five expected their lives to be better than their parents', a profoundly depressing view that was shared by parents in other polls.

Children Take Their Punishment

In one of those pre-election sound bites that subsequently became such large hostages to fortune, this was going to be the most 'family friendly' government. Instead it has felt chillingly hostile. Cuts in benefits and services have hit mothers and children three times harder than pensioners. Since the recession, an LSE study found, 'the biggest losers in nearly all income groups are families with children – losing over 5 per cent of their income on average, and more than 4 per cent for those in the bottom three-tenths of the distribution'.

Perhaps children had now become an encumbrance, unwelcome in a market society. Janan Ganesh, pro-Tory columnist and author of *George Osborne – The Austerity Chancellor*, said out loud that the primacy of the individual had a logical conclusion – the 'childfree life'. Children were a cost centre, an unproductive nuisance.[1] Was this what the ultras now thought? Of a piece was the attempt by education minister Elizabeth Truss to improve productivity among childminders by specifying that each should care alone for six two-year-olds. Michael Gove ordered the sign on the Department for Children, Schools and Families to be taken down; he starkly renamed it Department for Education. Out went Labour's Every Child Matters wider vision of wrapping children into care, community schools and family support.

The Tories came to power with an often mindless determination to do away with Labour policies and institutions. The abolition of educational maintenance allowances flew in the face of evidence that they were encouraging young people from poor homes to stay on. Ministers had even wanted to drop free milk for the under-fives and, saving a trivial sum, kill Bookstart, which provided a package of books to parents when babies are born. Amid condemnation, neither proposal went ahead.

Schemes promoting sports and subsidies for free swimming for the under-16s were cut. The government even failed in their feeble gesture to force the Premier League to channel a little more money into maintaining local football pitches and coaches. Children were not just to be made productive, they were to be profit centres. By 2013, 34 per cent of special education and 46 per cent of foster care, along with 67 per cent of children's homes (measured by value of contracts), were run by for-profit firms, to a total UK value of £7bn. Child protection was to be handed to profit-making companies, outsourcing the most sensitive and perilous of the state's obligations, sifting who should join the 43,000 on child protection registers and the 68,000 in care. Forcing the government to U-turn on this proposal, a coalition of charities and unions complained that 'marketplace competition' in children's services had become an end in itself.

At first, the Liberal Democrats successfully insisted that the tax credits payable to low-income families would not be cut. But that protection lasted only until 2013. Families suffered a hailstorm of other reductions, in housing and welfare benefits and childcare, ministers refusing to assess the cumulative impact. Yet only one troubled the Tory backbenches. Osborne gestured towards the well-off sharing in austerity by taxing child benefit away from families where one parent earned over £44,000. A two-child family would lose £1,750 a year. But the proposal went pear-shaped when parents realised a couple on, say, £86,000 would keep it, if each earned £43,000. Because husbands and wives are taxed separately, there was no mechanism for taking it away from their joint income; a mess of tapers, bands and high withdrawal rates had to be devised and half a million indignant households had to fill out tax forms for the first time.

The government did not abolish the Children's Commissioner, who was supposed to advocate for children, but who was so quiet they might as well have done (holders of the office were more vocal in Wales and Scotland). Progress went into reverse: there are even signs infant mortality may have risen, after falling over many years. The Equalities and Human Rights Commission added that tax and welfare changes had been especially negative for families with a disabled child. Despite rising child obesity, the government resisted pressure to restrict the advertising of junk foods. Jamie Oliver protested vehemently when his work to improve school meals was immediately undone by Gove: for over half of secondary schools nutritional guidelines are now entirely voluntary. Public Health England reported on a steep rise in self-harm; more children have mental health problems but therapy and clinic places are in desperately short supply. Child neglect cases rose, perhaps linked to recession and austerity.

Child abuse was in the public mind amid revelations about predatory Jimmy Savile and cronies, grooming gangs in ill-run Labour Rotherham and dark suspicions about paedophiles and abusers in high (and Tory) places. An official review of child protection, commissioned from LSE Professor Eileen Munro in 2011, called for less red tape for social workers and the creation of a new post of chief social worker. Other recommendations fell under the chariot wheels, above all early intervention with families. Munro singled out the effectiveness of Sure Start, the early years community centres set up in disadvantaged areas by the preceding government.

Too late. Embarrassing pre-election promises to expand the Sure Start programme were wiped off the Tory archive website as, within four years, nearly 600 centres were closed. Although by late 2013 a million families were still able to use them, their services were often sparse; professional staff had gone and many now offered no childcare. The Tory thinktank Policy Exchange massaged the closure figures as 'mergers', but had to accept that Sure Start funding had been cut by 28 per cent, affecting the poorest areas most.

The coalition went ahead with Labour's plan to extend free nursery hours to two-year-olds but the £755m that local authorities were given in 2014 was not ring-fenced. Virtually all the places are in private and charity nurseries, forbidding comparison with what a decently funded public offer might be like. Academic evidence confirmed that a nursery place in itself made little difference to a child's later progress; what matters is the quality of care and early years' stimulus.

Childcare became the proverbial postcode lottery; the Family and Childcare Trust found that many areas are 'virtual child-care deserts'. Osborne adjusted tax reliefs so that, from 2015, higher earners can claim against nursery or nanny fees, a gift to better-off families. Meanwhile childcare tax credits, helping low-paid mothers take jobs, were cut by 10 per cent, a marked disincentive to mothers to enter the labour market, cutting the UK's employment ratio relative to elsewhere in Europe.

Typical of the coalition was to talk up a welfare initiative such as nurseries but fail to organise supply – partly because their favourite market solutions did not work; partly because they could not bring themselves to pay for energetic public provision. This was the story of the Liberal Democrat idea foisted on the Tories – free school meals for all 1.5 million infants up to the age of seven in English schools. It cost £1bn and was regressive: the poorest children already qualified for free meals. The Local Government Association reported two weeks before the new system was due to start in September 2014 that half its members had not received enough money from the government to cover kitchen improvements. The balance would have to be found from school budgets.

Calm Down, Dears

Even after the big reshuffle in July 2014, only five out of 22 cabinet members were women, and only 31 among 119 minis-ters. Cameron himself could be boorishly patronising, making bad jokes at women MPs. That matters when two-thirds of women think sexism is still a problem at work.

From 2002 to 2010, the pay gap between men and women had narrowed, but now it was growing again, to nearly 16 per cent. TUC research showed the majority of part-time female workers are paid less than the living wage in many areas. Women managers did no better, with those over the age of 40 earning 35 per cent less than their male equivalents. Women were clustered in minimum wage jobs yet 22 per cent of those female low earners have a degree. The Tories had signed the Equality Act, but refused to implement the section requiring large companies to break down pay by gender (as well as the gap between top and bottom earners).

Women were big losers from austerity: local public services have predominantly female workforces and, in caring for children and dependent relatives, women rely more on public services. Incidents of domestic violence rose 11 per cent between 2010 and 2013. After prevarication, the coalition instituted domestic violence protection orders, giving police stronger powers and providing better compensation for victims. But austerity and welfare cuts exacerbated domestic tensions; refuges have been closing, making it harder for women to escape abusive relationships.

Of the 2.5 million separated families in the UK, just under half used government-run schemes to assess, collect and make payments from parents, mainly men, to dependent children. The coalition tried, again, to repair the IT and other problems of the Child Support Agency. Its 2012 scheme introduced a new payments schedule and new IT system, but also new charges for using and enforcing the scheme, which are likely to be an active disincentive when they are introduced.

Geographical Gaps

The Scottish referendum became the most graphic exhibition of division in Cameron country, and we take that tale of disunity forward in the next chapter. Some places have done well, of course. Car production expanded in the north-east and West Midlands as motor manufacturing enjoyed a boom, albeit under non-UK ownership. Start-ups and small business have grown robustly in Cambridge, Edinburgh and Brighton, but in the small- and medium-sized enterprises (SME) league table Blackpool came last, behind Liverpool and Rochdale: these were among the towns and cities hardest hit by the recession, with fewest growth potential companies. The Fylde Coast, once a place of mirth, holidays and party conferences, won the black spot over and over again: highest for suicides is no accolade.

Once proudly industrial Coventry, a city that made things, lived with stagnant real disposable income – and this was a place that had not benefited from the boom in the 2000s. Gross value added per head, higher than the UK average in the 1990s, barely moved. In Coventry in 2010 the biggest employment sector was public administration, education and health, where a third of people worked. But here the axe fell. The blithe prescription was that by cutting the state you 'freed' enterprise. The state 'crowded out' business. The ideologues set their faces against the evidence showing how technological innovation depended, across the world and through the decades, on blending public policy and private enterprise. If you cut and denigrate public endeavour and investment then private entrepreneurs don't flourish either. From the internet to defence research, from the auto industry to pharmaceuticals and just about every major manufacturing tradition, in the US, Europe and developing nations, the state has played a central part in investment for progress.

There are major variations in the way recession and recovery are being played out, typically strengthening existing differences and raising the risk of further entrenching social inequalities, one study said.[2] The dominance of the south-east means that even if the other regions improved, they would need to travel that much faster over a longer period simply to catch up. And that's just England. On his watch the very unity of the United Kingdom came into play and remains there. Broken Britain indeed: Cameron narrowly escaped an epitaph as the man who broke the UK.

3

Our Disunited Kingdom

Disuniting the United Kingdom was not the result of deliberate policy. Like the creation of the British empire, it happened in a fit of absence of mind. Yet, with hindsight, jeopardising the unity of the UK had a lot to do with the Cameron style, and Tory ideology. It was not just Scotland. What are Conservatives 'conserving' when English Heritage is being privatised and the country's asset base hollowed out, let alone when they threaten such national unifiers as the NHS and the BBC? (A Murdoch news channel would never offer the BBC's careful and comforting selection of Scottish, Irish and English modulations.)

The elevation of Margaret Thatcher, in Scottish eyes for ever author of the notorious poll tax, was the beginning of the end of the Tories' ambition to be a national party, and her successor stumbled to its completion. Here was a prime minister of a country (the UK) who, until the last desperate days of the Scottish referendum campaign, avoided travelling to its northern third for fear of fomenting support for separation, which proved how under him 'national unity' had become so problematic both as an idea and practical politics. He looked baffled at the expression of identity by Scots yet this was a sundering foretold. Hadn't George Osborne's father-in-law, Lord Howell, spoken for them all when he called England's north-east 'desolate', adding that there's 'plenty of room for fracking well away from anyone's residence'? Anyone, that is, like them.

They arrived in Downing Street without any obvious commitment to territory or national (UK) integrity. Perhaps, for the Cameron set, it was the influence of adviser Steve Hilton (his wife a senior figure at Google) and the digital enthusiasts, who claimed the modern world had become weightless, stateless, instantaneous. In fact, they were utterly traditional in their lusting after money and material power. What they no longer cared about was *where*; Carmarthen, Cumbernauld or Coleraine were, at best, potential profit centres, at worst embarrassing reminders of yesterday.

The Tories had been visited with a kind of geographical aphasia. Over their horizon, parts of Britain had sunk below eastern Europe: GDP per person lower in west Wales than in Poland; GDP per person in Tees Valley and Durham lower than in the Czech Republic. Or perhaps it really was the triumph of market theory. Few Tories now followed Edmund Burke – after he was deemed surplus to ministerial requirements, the MP for Hereford Jesse Norman wrote an admired biography of the Irishman – whose 'age of sophisters and economists' had truly arrived. The set seemed to believe, in a complacent, Chipping Norton kind of way, that cultures and belonging and *identity* could take care of themselves. You could throttle public services, let markets rip, yet magically the people would bond together and things somehow just take care of themselves – the belief is an odd melange of middle Englandism, Von Hayek, Michael Oakeshott and Milton Friedman.

Strangely, not many believed it in the vast plains joining old Europe and Asia, or in the basin of the Tigris and Euphrates; and nor, closer to home, did the 1.6 million who voted yes to Scottish independence. Cameron simply could not comprehend the forceful assertion from the land of Adam Smith that community comes before market and demands self-realisation in creating a new state, split from the UK. Contracting, privatisation, the assault on the NHS and social cleansing through the bedroom tax had all been devised without any consideration for how they might play in *places*, on the periphery or in political cultures where Tories and their world-view are a minor or negligible presence, such as Scotland and most of Wales. The Burkeans had their moment in the sun, allowed to muse whimsically about the big society. No one really believed the sociological claptrap about residents running to man the fire-service hoses or check out books in libraries or enthuse disaffected teenagers in youth centres. No one had to look far to see that 'society' could embrace murderous religious faith, tribes and checkpoints or, UKIP's version, rejection of aspects of the modern world (conveniently summed up by the EU and mass migration) and nostalgia for lost togetherness.

Britishness Broken

In hindsight, Gordon Brown's stumbling, mumbling attempt to reinvigorate ideas of Britishness appears prescient. The Labour leader was derided, Cameron declaring that Britishness 'can never be defined by one motto or one politician'. SNP leader Alex Salmond agreed. Then Cameron too ended up mouthing platitudes. But he had either flunked O-level history or, as so many Scots believed, simply had no consciousness of the plural histories of the countries that make up the UK. The anniversary of Magna Carta, Cameron said, would be an occasion to mark 'British values'. Could he really be ignorant of the fact that in 1215 there was a dispute between French-speaking barons and a king of England who, though he might be Lord of Ireland, Duke of Anjou and *ci-devant* Duke of Normandy, at the time made no claim of feudal overlordship on the separate country of Scotland? When nationalism stalks the ground, historical detail matters.

And administration. Ministers made no apparent effort to think about how, with devolution, the parts of the UK had to be realigned. They clung to the old approach, equating England and the whole. A debate on British values was instigated in the House of Lords (the composition and constitutional standing of which would have to be thrown into the melting pot of a new UK). The government approved a motion promoting 'British values in all education institutions throughout the country', apparently oblivious of the fact that schooling in Northern Ireland and Scotland had never been London's to command, and in Wales was long fraught.

Cameron was a man caught, as the Americans say, between a rock and a hard place. Scottish voters wanted out of the UK; UKIP voters wanted out of the EU. Where was Britain? Attitude surveys showed the more British people feel, the more pro-European they also are. After the referendum Cameron might try but would not find it easy to fall back on 'England' either, both as a Tory toff whose acquaintance with the north and Midlands is slight and as the prophet of rootless, deracinated capitalism. What price England when the 'nation's' energy, utilities, healthcare and eventually schools and universities are available to the highest bidder?

Cameron's fate has been to preside during what feels like a transitional age – to what, nobody knows. About Britishness the public are not sure. It means, they tell pollsters, speaking English; for three-quarters it's bound up with being born in the country. Cameron said migrants to the UK should learn English and respect Britain's way of life. But what was 'our way of life' and which type of state was he talking about – one that embraces free markets, greed and social exclusion or the one represented by citizenship, the NHS and other national institutions?

Scotland and the UK

One version of the state certainly ends north of Carlisle and Berwick, where in the few years since devolution self-government has proved not just relatively efficient but exhilarating, albeit at the price of ignoring financial realities and pretending (a Nationalist habit) that depleting stocks of North Sea oil could pay for paradise in Paisley. Nonetheless, it wasn't obvious why Scotland had gone so swiftly from being a willing and enthusiastic partner in the union to coming within a whisker of finishing the UK off. Even if the answer lay within, to do with the eclipse of Labour (which itself had to do with the falling away of heavy industry), Cameron was required to try to understand a seething land, and practise statecraft. Late, very late, he told Scottish voters that the UK was innately pluralist and the 'effing Tories' would not be around for ever, but by then his pleading sounded like self-abasement, humiliating for both speaker and listeners.

The writing had been on the wall since the SNP took power as a minority government at Holyrood in 2007. Bumptious Alex Salmond's intentions were plain but neither Labour, with crash and recession on its mind, nor the Westminster Tories got his measure. Even after the SNP won an outright majority in 2011, they ignored him and, more importantly, any obligation to start rethinking the UK from the centre out. To diagnose myopia in the Whitehall hierarchy, among Labour's frontbench and in the media does not absolve the leader.

In hindsight, the government exhibited extraordinary naivety and complacency – or was it mere arrogance – not to factor in Tory unpopularity in Scotland, not to campaign for the unity of the UK, not to model constitutional futures, including England's. Not that the coalition did nothing. With the easy nonchalance that then, but no longer, characterised London's attitude, the coalition rolled with the recommendations of a commission on devolution set up under Labour, chaired by the academic Sir Kenneth Calman. The resulting bipartisan Scotland Act 2012 strode further down the devolution road, empowering Holyrood to issue investment bonds, to reduce income tax rates by up to 10 per cent or increase them by any amount, and keep the proceeds of stamp duty and landfill tax.

The Tories, relaxed in apparent indifference, were prepared to go further, devolving air passenger duty, housing benefit and full control of income tax. Cameron was apparently listening to the party's dynamic leader in Scotland, Ruth Davidson, taking the old Thatcher line on tax – the more visible and proximate, the more people would take agin it.

Against that background London treated independence as a sideshow, the referendum a ritual to be gone through. The Edinburgh agreement signed in October 2012 was soggy – signed, that is, by Cameron and the Scottish secretary, Michael Moore, from a Liberal Democrat party that had diminishing political presence in Scotland and which, when the campaigning started, simply went awol. Cameron traded control over timing for the nationalists' agreeing to drop a third option between independence and maintenance of the union, so-called devo max. A *politician* might have called Salmond's bluff and insisted on a speedy resolution, with a vote in 2013; instead the nationalists were allowed to organise and build momentum over 23 months. The litany of basic tactical errors goes on but centres, eventually, on the coalition's failure to make a case for union, until the last gasp. The feebleness of the Tory party in Scotland did not help. The mantra that the vote was for Scots alone seemed to concede the case: no one stood for the union. It was an extraordinary piece of historical amnesia from a party that had once backed military revolt (in Ulster) to support the union of the British Isles.

But a convincing Tory case would have demanded rigorous self-inspection. Take banking. Salmond was complicit in the fall of RBS; his model for Scotland relied on an overweight financial sector. To counter it, Cameron would have had to muster his own critique of imbalance and bankers' bonuses. Ironically, Scottish nationalism was offering its version of the globalisation the political right had been saying was fatefully unavoidable. Salmond glibly told yes voters it was compatible with social democracy. Cameron had nothing to say in reply, denial or agreement. The announcement of a 2017 European Union 'in/ out' referendum followed the Edinburgh agreement, throwing into the campaigning pot the prospect of Scotland voting no in 2014, then being ejected from the EU. The question continually put by the nationalists – whether the political cultures of north and south had diverged beyond reconciliation – was not even addressed until the last days. In the run-up to the September poll, the Scottish government's decision to abolish the right to buy for council tenants was telling. This emblem of Thatcher's English individualism was now being rejected as a dysfunctional measure reducing social provision.

Cameron symbolised both the limits of unionism and the absence of thought about an alternative. The coalition did commission a former Commons clerk, Sir William McKay, to look at MPs' territorial responsibilities and how to solve the fabled West Lothian question about excluding MPs from Scotland, Northern Ireland and Wales from voting on matters that affect only England. But it was a glance only at the Commons, ignoring the Lords and wider potential reforms. A pressing political problem was and remains that if Tory government at Westminster is the future of the UK, Scots do not want it. Of course, theirs, too, was a short-term view: it's extraordinary how in a polity that had been so stable for so long, such a major constitutional question could be debated as if it were just about the next Westminster government rather than institutions that would have to survive centuries. As the referendum approached, Cameron was pushed by Gordon Brown into going well beyond previous iterations of maximum devolution, with ad hoc offerings on finance and legislative autonomy – again without any strategic conception of what the results might be for the UK or attitudes in the rest of the country. London would have to resolve open questions about the principles on which UK public money was distributed to the constituent territories – a question made all the more urgent as the coalition approved new tax-raising powers for Cardiff as well as Edinburgh. Blathering, on both sides, about the Barnett formula (the mechanism that adjusts the amounts of public expenditure to the regions) usually missed the fundamental point – that people won't give up demanding social justice, however prevalent the markets or exacting the calculation.

rUK?

Wales was an afterthought. London had conceded further devolution to Cardiff before the shock of the Scottish referendum campaign, perhaps indifferently, probably complacently. The Tories' first Welsh secretary, Cheryl Gillan, was probably more worried about her constituency in the Chilterns, through which HS2 would barrel, but picked up Labour promises and launched a commission of inquiry, chaired by Paul Silk, former clerk to the National Assembly for Wales. In response the coalition agreed a suite of tax and borrowing powers for the government of Wales, including stamp duty from 2018 and the proceeds of landfill tax.

Offered a referendum on devolving a portion of income tax, Welsh ministers feared a trap. If yes, would that deprive them of the UK funds Wales could claim on the evidence of poverty and socio-economic disadvantage, let alone problems of rural sparsity and poor transport links? (The Treasury dashed hopes of support for a Welsh-promoted barrage across the Severn estuary.) If public spending were distributed on the basis of population, Wales could be £300m a year worse off than if based on social need. Wales pointed out how much less favourably it was treated than Scotland under the Barnett formula.

But Wales had its political uses. Cameron began kindly, talking on his first prime ministerial visit of a 'relationship based on respect'. The love-in did not last. Soon he was regularly making contemptuous remarks about the place at Prime Minister's Questions to score points against Labour. His disregard for unity and disdain for his own role as custodian of the cohesiveness of the United Kingdom dissolved as time and again he denigrated Welsh performance in health and education. Wales, said Tory MP Charlotte Leslie, was a 'nightmare vision of Miliband's Britain'.[1]

The truth is that the Welsh population is old (many move there to retire) and sick (with post-industrial diseases); compared with, say, the north-east of England, the Welsh NHS scores well enough. Welsh government employment programmes are impressive. We visited Jobs Growth Wales in Cardiff to find a successful transition to work scheme for 16- to 24-year-olds, utilising the European Social Fund, and low drop-out rate. The Welsh government did some things differently, such as charging for plastic bags in shops; it successfully fought off the coalition over abolition of the agricultural wages board. However, Welsh residents are not independence-minded, and immediately after the Scottish debate support for separation dropped to minuscule levels.

Northern Ireland was quiet and London was glad to neglect it after the long years of violence even if, internally, all was far from well. Underlying tensions erupted in riots over the decision by Belfast city council to fly the union flag on designated days only. The Northern Ireland Assembly governed, albeit through clientelism and tribal handouts. A 2012 survey found a majority believed self-government made no difference to the amount of say they had. Even the fiscal hard types in Tory ranks offended at the £1,600 per capita spending difference between England and Scotland did not quibble at Northern Ireland's public service spending per head at 20 per cent higher than the UK average (£1,200 above England's), or inspect too closely the effectiveness of capital investment in housing and roads in terms of patterns of residential segregation and inter-community rivalry, which were as intense as ever.

English Heritage

The preservation of England, it seemed, could safely be left to charity. English Heritage, the quango looking after monuments and castles, including Stonehenge – a site famous enough to attract the president of the United States into making a detour from the 2014 Nato summit – is being privatised. Sort of, anyway: it becomes an endowed charity, with the creation of a new mini-quango, to be called the National Heritage Protection Service. The stones of old England are formally to remain in public ownership, the charity given a long contract to extract revenue from charges, cafes, car parks and shops. The endowment, a one-off payment of £80m, is not going to be enough to keep the heritage in good nick, so there will be fraught annual battles with the Treasury over the subsidy required – which rather negates the point of the exercise, you might think.

Another piece of England's heritage, the canals and waterways, went to a new charity, the Canal & River Trust. So far it has been successful in mobilising volunteers, but if the charity is as entrepreneurial as the government envisaged, conflicts will arise as property developers sniff around urban canal basins and, for the sake of the bottom line, it lets the locks silt up.

The Tories are never likely to link such policies with the subtle question of 'England'. It does not follow that, because Scotland was invisible through a plutocratic prism, England had any more hold on their political imagination, even a deep, southern England triangulated by Cornwall (site of holiday photo ops), the Cotswolds and central London. Academic studies suggest the traditional passivity around English identity may now be changing, events in Scotland having jerked people out of diffidence. For some – not just defectors to UKIP – Englishness is how to express anxiety about migration, which also expressed itself in anti-European views.

It was time to pay urgent attention to the signs, symbols, institutions and funding flows that sustain unity. But the Tories no longer did togetherness: policies fragmented and marketisation broke bonds of belonging. Partly because of electoral geography, partly because they were intent on rescinding Labour creations (regardless of their success), the coalition's approach to England's regions was negative – the Liberal Democrats were impotent in preventing harm to areas such as the south-west, where they had seats.

Inner England

Ironically, Cameron had been offered an alternative vision of England, from within his own ranks. This was no Tolkienesque, Blakean waffling but a practical attempt to rethink England in terms of infrastructure and, critically, the mobilisation of 'place'. No 10 was polite to its author because he is a Tory grandee; they even gave him half an office in the Treasury. But Michael Heseltine was sidelined.

Heseltine, the saviour of Liverpool in the 1980s, creator of the London Docklands Development Corporation, was the man who dared tell Thatcher that her social policies were divisive and destructive. He was no egalitarian; he believed in profit, and the old snobbish dig (courtesy of Alan Clark) that Heseltine needed to buy his own furniture would not apply to his children, who will have the pick of a grand country house. But Heseltine also believed that private interest married public; state agencies created value by building infrastructure and charging or taxing the businesses that benefited.

He was despatched by the coalition to produce a report. The result, 'No Stone Unturned', was pithy and imaginative, urging new funds for regional economic development and collaboration between ministers and the great cities of England. This would not answer the 'English question' – how fair representation and decision-making for the inhabitants of England can be reconciled at UK level with more autonomy for the nations – but its practicality would be preferred by many to political vapouring. Here was a recipe for the clustering of growth, rebalancing of economic effort and – the reason it would never be adopted by the coalition – long-term *planning*.

A regional growth fund, with limited resources, was offered as a substitute for the coalition's vandalism in executing England's regional development agencies (RDAs). Cumbersome maybe, but they had pushed jobs and investment. An example: in 2014, the trust that looks after Hadrian's Wall, which had relied on One North East for support, closed for lack of funds. Tourists coming to England increased in 2013, by 7 per cent over the previous year. But of the 31 million who arrived, 16 million did not leave the capital. Without quangos, Visit England and the RDAs, who was going to mount the required campaign? Here was another instance of a holdover from Labour that, in 2010, could have been slimmed and improved; abolition left a gaping space.

Disparities in growth between the regions remained huge: in the north-east 67 per cent of working-age people are in employment compared with the UK average of 72 per cent, and 75 per cent in the south-east. The government's regional commitment was £6.2bn over the five years to 2015, it said, but that turned out to include £2.4bn spent by the despised RDAs. Total spending on local growth programmes (including funds from the equally despised EU) fell by nearly a fifth between 2010 and 2013. A welter of schemes were to plug the gap. The RDAs were replaced by Local Economic Partnerships (LEPs), but these glorified chambers of commerce covered smaller areas and had no money. Another scheme echoed Thatcher's enterprise zones. Whitehall said, a bit vaguely, that they would 'secure' between 6,000 and 18,000 jobs by 2015; the NAO found the arithmetic suspect.

The new regional fund was overtly ideological; it was aimed, the government said, at forcing 'areas and communities that are dependent on the public sector to make the transition to sustainable private sector-led growth and prosperity'. Another scheme was 'city deals', giving places such as Newcastle and Gateshead across the Tyne slivers of funding if they could show they were freeing up areas for development. This, ministers said smugly, proved their commitment to 'localism'.

Localism – A False Prospectus

When he came to power Cameron said 'devolve', but ministers were never likely to throw away the reins. The public did not particularly appreciate local authorities, even if they told pollsters they preferred councillors running local services; offloading cuts to councils was politically expedient. The Local Government Association (LGA), representing councils in England, was, till May 2014, Tory-dominated and supine.

Localism might have been a way of reviving politics, perhaps even assuaging the growing discontents of the inhabitants of England, but it was never likely to be much more than a gimmick once Eric Pickles was put in charge of local government. The former Tory party chairman had scuttled from his native Bradford to become MP for Brentwood in deepest Essex. He alternated between trying to please Tory councillors and contempt for the entire business of local democratic politics. Like Gove, he surrounded himself with particularly nasty special advisers, who collaborated closely with the *Daily Mail* in vilifying travellers, trade union officials and Labour councils that failed to fly the flag or hold prayers before they met – or failed to empty rubbish bins on the minister's schedule. He had a fetish for refuse, issuing a proclamation that bins be collected weekly.

The formula for allocating money to councils was doctored. All governments are tempted to favour friends. The coalition used weightings that benefited areas with more older people, with the result that Tory shires and suburbs did better. Studies found that councils in the most deprived areas did worst. The 10 most deprived areas of England lost £782 per household over the five years, compared with £48 per household in the best-off areas.

Where councils might have played a positive role, in stimulating jobs and growth, they were mostly excluded or enmeshed in elaborate bribes – if they permitted more housebuilding they would get extra grants or kickbacks from business rates (which were more tightly controlled by the centre). Pickles talked of community groups acquiring council property, but not where they would find the money to run a library or youth club.

Local authorities were in a vice. Pickles flourished his Localism Act, giving councils a 'general power of competence' – except the competence to raise money. Yet he threatened fire and brimstone if they dared increase council tax above his mark and forbade any thinking about tourist or sales taxes to augment stretched revenues. The government vetoed any revaluation of houses and flats, to update the basis on which council tax is levied. The LGA complained that the legislation actually handed scores of new powers to ministers and yet gaps had opened up in checking that money was being properly spent. Trust the people, said Pickles, in a pretence of democratic enthusiasm, but the people lacked intelligible data and he had killed off the quango that previously checked the accuracy of the figures, the Audit Commission.

Big Society

A few months after the coalition took power, we went to Aylesbury to visit Chris Williams, chief executive of Buckinghamshire county council. His solid Tory councillors took Cameron's big society to be cover for cutting spending and closing the youth service, libraries, day centres and clubs. There was even talk of issuing radar guns to village volunteers in the Chilterns, so they would publish the registration numbers of speeding motorists, parish by parish.

The big society was probably never much more than a phrase; polls found the public had no clue what it meant and a friend of the government, Peter Bingle, chair of Bell Pottinger Public Affairs, confessed, 'Perhaps it was a deliberate strategy for it to be nebulous and inchoate...or perhaps there was insufficient thinking before it was launched. Either way, nobody understands.'[2] Four years later, we returned to Bucks county hall, where the 'commercially minded' council has shed over 2,000 staff. The services they provided have been deleted or their work outsourced to contractors or big charities such as Barnardo's. A few of the council's smaller libraries are now run by volunteers, helped by some county cash and inter-library loans. Two community groups are involved in day centres in Princes Risborough and Bourne End. As for the radar guns, villages are involved in decisions when contractors install speed warning signs.

Big society was a gimmick. Voluntarism had and will always have strict limits; it cannot be relied on to provide basic services, especially where the poor and aged are concerned. That, after all, had been the reason government expanded in the late 19th and 20th centuries: the state alone could secure social justice.

The fate of TimeBank is illustrative. The charity, with support from the previous government, had built up a network of 300,000 people exchanging services with one another. At its 10th anniversary the new 'civil society' minister, Nick Hurd, offered congratulations for countering cynicism around big society. Within weeks, he axed TimeBank's grant and most of its projects died. Cameron made a highly spun speech promising a 'National Citizen Service', perhaps mindful of the party's old codgers and their lingering belief that youth needed discipline. There was a lot less here than the capital letters promised. The idea became summer and half-term courses for young volunteers from all backgrounds – admirable, except at the same time local youth services were suffering badly from cuts. But it turned out that the service would be run mostly by firms (including the ubiquitous Serco), with charities helping out. It was low-key and tiny – involving 37,000 people in 2013, at a cost per participant of £1,500.

For some, though, big society was big money. A group of Tory supporters seized the hour. One of their setups was the Big Society Network. A few months after the coalition took power, the Big Lottery Fund 'solicited' a bid for £830,000 from it for a loosely specified project to advance the 'objective of a big society'. Nesta, a Labour quango set up to kickstart innovations, later privatised, handed over £480,000. Later, the Charity Commission began investigating and the NAO examined the grants. Nothing illegal, it concluded, but the audit trail was murky and proper procedure had not always been followed. Shrinking the state was one thing; abstracting public money for jobs and emoluments was something else.

This was precisely what the Charity Commission should be on top of. But the government starved it of funds, then, to ensure it would not rock the boat, appointed as its chair a rightwing journalist, with biographies of the Queen Mother and Rupert Murdoch among his greatest hits. Under William Shawcross, the commission neither spoke up nor cracked down. The commission 'is not regulating charities effectively', the Comptroller and Auditor General concluded. 'It does not do enough to identify and tackle abuse of charitable status. Where it does identify concerns in charities, it makes little use of its powers and fails to take tough action in some of the most serious cases.'

Shawcross was predictably in favour of banning charity campaigning. The Tories took harsh legislative action to curb activity that could remotely be called political. As implemented by the Electoral Commission – a quango survival determined to lick the master's hand in gratitude – the Transparency of Lobbying, Non-party Campaigning and Trade Union Administration Act 2014 places strict limits on how much a charity can spend on anything defined as campaigning over the months leading up to a general election. Speakers during the bill's passage protested that the entirety of a charity's running costs, including websites and tweeting, could be counted in. And so it has turned out. Voluntarism was only welcome up to the point when volunteers started agitating on behalf of the people they cared for, the homeless, the indigent and needy. The big society needed a bag over its head.

'It was always a slogan without a policy.' Sir Stuart Etherington, the chief executive of the National Council for Voluntary Organisations, is jaundiced. No one from the Tories came to talk to him or colleagues about the coalition's cuts. 'They thought they could just roll back the state, and the community would take over, spontaneously, just like that! Of course, it didn't happen.' Nat Wei, a social entrepreneur, was brought in to encourage volunteering, and given a peerage. Etherington went to visit: 'They put him in a windowless basement in the Cabinet Office and they'd forgotten to tell him he wouldn't be paid.' Wei resigned within months. Volunteering has limits.

Etherington reserves special anger for the coalition's welfare programmes. Employment and training charities with a track record in helping prisoners and mentally and physically disabled people into work were encouraged to bid – only to be cast aside in favour of for-profits. Charities were left to pick up cases companies found too expensive, passing on little money. Employment programmes have been badly designed. 'Results are terrible. The companies cream and cherrypick. It needs a complete redesign.'

Social care charities have also been hard hit. 'Local authorities passed on disproportionate cuts.' Their day centres were axed first. 'Those that deal with hardship, with the poorest, struggling with the government's welfare reform – when their services are needed most, they've had their grants and contracts cut.'

What shocks him is the way the government deliberately chilled hearts and poisoned sympathy for those in most need. And now charity itself is in the firing line. Tory MPs such as Charlie Elphicke, Conor Burns and Priti Patel (who became a Treasury minister) are constantly harassing. Picking on Oxfam for daring to mention poverty in Britain, they forced a Commons debate on 'politicisation'. 'I just don't think the public was with them on this,' Etherington said. 'We resisted it and I think the government was wary of taking on the sector.'

Etherington worries that the curbs on lobbying mean that charities will self-censor and cease to speak. 'The trouble is, the guidelines are still unclear. But we'll say things! We'll say what we like but as we won't be intending to influence the outcome of an election, we shall refuse to register with the Electoral Commission.'

Charities have given the coalition an easy ride. They are far more trusted than politicians. If anyone can make bad governments quake, it ought to be their good people. 'Maybe we could have done more. I suppose we were focused on what was happening to us, to the disproportionate cuts we were suffering, and not on our clients.' He paused before adding that charities may have lost influence with the public once the government had done so much to persuade them that the poor were no longer deserving. Each charity had its own issues, he admitted. 'Scope would be talking about disability, Shelter about housing and so on. They did speak up but they didn't have a collective impact.'

There was, it seems, too much of that same individualism among the charities themselves. They, too, were not quite all in it together.

Profiting from Charity

Volunteering might make money. In April 2012 the government launched Big Society Capital, to lubricate private investment in charities doing public service work. For example with offenders. If voluntary bodies could cut reoffending, the government would pay them, and they would pass on a slice to the investors backing them. But a much-vaunted project involving prisoners released from Peterborough jail ran for barely two years; the sums did not add up and the 'social impact bond' returned no profit. The arithmetic the moneymen work with is too precise; real lives are messy and disordered. And, anyway, investment bonds crushed the life out of the charitable impulse, said Alex Whinnom, chief executive of the Greater Manchester Centre for Voluntary Organisations.

Recession brought a steep drop in the time people could give to volunteering. While rich areas saw only a blip, in the most depressed areas the drop was sharper. Of course, people would turn out for fun events such as the Olympics, where 240,000 applied to serve as unpaid helpers. But the government stubbornly refused to take the abiding lesson that volunteering is not a substitute for government action, but a complement: public services are enriched by unpaid participation. New charitable endeavour in response to the growing incidence of dementia proved the point. Dementia Friends, an initiative by the Alzheimer's Society, had to be supported from public funds.

Most people continue to give cash. In 2013, 88 per cent of adults had donated money in the previous 12 months, a similar rate to the year before. Donations from companies, however, fell. Gifts of over £1m totalled £1.35bn in 2012 – an indication of how concentrated wealth was – but fell short of the 2007 level. What did rise, the PAC found, were attempts to fiddle charity tax reliefs. The government had tried to cap relief on charitable donations in the 2012 budget – sparking an outcry from charity executives. Osborne U-turned.

Charity remains attractive as a means of creating a 'weightless state', offering a less controversial form of contracting. The Public Services (Social Value) Act 2012 started as a private member's bill from Tory MP Chris White and was then taken up by the government: it said that in outsourcing, the state could take into consideration wider social, economic and environmental benefits, as well as price. Little if anything changed. Charities won contracts, as they had before, only by cutting costs or acting as the backup to firms trying to offload the most difficult cases from their books. Later, to review it, the government appointed Lord Young, the Tory peer, 1980s minister and passionate privatiser. A rave from the grave, surely? But no, choosing David Young was yet another demonstration of Cameron's political roots, from which he drew sustenance in carrying out his great coup.

4

Cameron's Coup

Cameron was lucky. His coup would have been unthinkable without the great crash. The ill winds of recession blew him to success and in 2010 a sense of national emergency (inflamed by ideological allies such as Mervyn King at the Bank of England) gave his party cover to do what they would not otherwise have dared. A political tribe that once called themselves patriots ran down their country by wildly adding noughts to the UK's debt predicament: Osborne's comparisons with Greece were fatuous and disloyal. Exaggeration worked. Warnings of impending catastrophe proved more persuasive than the precise arithmetic of receipts and outgoings. The Tories, factious and ideologically incoherent, could unite around the prospect of a chainsaw massacre. Of the welfare state.

Here's the testimony of a man who has sat at the cabinet table with them for five years: the Conservatives, he says, undoubtedly 'see fiscal consolidation as cover for an ideologically driven "small state" agenda.' That's Vince Cable, the business secretary, and principal among the useful idiots supplied to the coalition by the Liberal Democrats.

Before opportunity knocked, the Tories had felt obliged to commit themselves to match Labour spending. 'Tories cutting services? That's a pack of lies', ran a headline in *The Times* in September 2007 as Osborne pledged 'year after year of real increases in public spending'. Crash and recession followed, but an ill wind was a political gift to the Tories, putting the axe of fiscal necessity into their hands. It's an unlikely image, true, but 2010 saw Cameron auditioning for the role of messiah.

He neither looked nor sounded the part. MPs such as David Davis thought Cameron's class origins a handicap: those vowels, his patrician descent from King William IV veneered with Eton and the Bullingdon into an effortless air of right to rule. He rode horses and would have gladly donned pink to chase foxes to death – except Labour had banned hunting with hounds and his PR training ensured he was never photographed doing anything else that would illustrate his privilege. Nor did he ever look a swivel-eyed doctrinaire. Breeding covered the ideological traces. Cameron could do emotional intelligence; he did reasonable; he did moderate. When required he was an old-style Anglican in whose hearing, he said, God came in and out like a distant radio station. Whatever else he was, this wasn't John Redwood or one of the ardent types on the backbenches.

The 'Stupid Party' Gets Ideas

Tories once thought ideas dangerous; its old moniker was the stupid party. Tories had avoided splits during most of the 20th century by not thinking much: 'they relied on intuition and common sense to awesome electoral effect', as *Financial Times* columnist Janan Ganesh put it.[1] But with Thatcher things changed. 'Now people believe there is Truth and it is knowable.'

But Cameron is no intellectual, no theorist: you could not imagine he, like Thatcher, would ever pull out of his bag dog-eared copies of ancient paperbacks by favoured gurus. Yet he, too, has strong, even protean beliefs, attested by the Thatcher poster on the wall of his college rooms, breathed through the walls of Conservative central office, where he had gone to work. Guy Black, head of the party's political section, recalled the early days. 'Four days after [Thatcher's 1988] Bruges speech, 21-year-old David Cameron walked through the doors to join the Conservative Research Department. We were pro-enterprise and hated state bureaucracy,' he says. They wouldn't let anyone in 'who wasn't committed to the revolution. We came to be known as the brat pack – there was nothing other than loyalty to Mrs T.'²

Let's ascribe to him not so much a set of propositions but rather reflexes, the working assumptions of his set, its journalist allies and the corporate chieftains he had served while in PR. The state is an impediment, an obstacle, oversized; the market solves all ills and returns a profit to our pals and our people, those who own the estates, the trust funds, the companies, the yachts and the Lear jets. Cameron's was always going to be a government of the rich, for the rich. 'I'm a tax-cutting Tory. Frankly I don't really like any taxes,' he told the Federation of Small Businesses. The manifesto promised to cut corporation tax, raise the threshold for inheritance tax and stamp duty.

To baseline Thatcherism was bolted a theory of the natural beneficence of 'society', which now was 'big'. Thatcher's aphorism about there being no such thing was junked. In came fey talk about charities and 'social enterprise', neighbourhoods and (a new one) 'free schools'. With one leap, the problem the more honest Tory thinkers had long recognised was solved: how to allow destructive free markets, low wages and macho hire-and-fire rules and yet still salve your conscience about the poverty and the social disruption these policies caused.

It was a hand-me-down from Thatcher's guru Friedrich von Hayek, who had preached self-generating order. Cut the state away and, hey presto, peace on earth and goodwill to all, who would immediately enrol in the 'little platoons' fantasised by Edmund Burke. The right wing thinktankers had plotted a formula: less state = more charity = solution to crime, unemployment and educational attainment. Making trendy reference to the theorising of Nobel Prize winner Elinor Ostrom about self-organising communities, they surfed an anti-government wave without sounding uncaring. State and civil society are in reality mutually dependent and locked in partnership, but now they became rivals in a zero sum game.

You could even blame social disorder on the state, which was the approach taken by Iain Duncan Smith. The welfare state *got in the way* of people's natural beneficence. When the prophet of 'broken Britain' became secretary of state, the line had to be adapted. Since he was now in charge, government could no longer be blamed. Instead, the Tories dusted off the oldest of mill-owner cliches: the poor themselves were responsible for their depravity; they were skivers and moral delinquents, redeemable only through a sharp dose of benefit reduction. It was a kindness to relieve them of their dependency by cutting their benefits.

If that sounds crude, listen to Lord Freud, the minister for welfare reform, a businessman who, like most previous transfers from the corporate sector to politics, proved to be both wooden and conceited (and offensive – because disabled people, he said, are incomplete, they don't deserve even the minimum wage). He was not a theorist; his views were functional. The point of Universal Credit – their grandiose and hubristic reform of welfare – was to push down 'quite sharply' the number of people who aren't working or looking for work. This wasn't so much neoliberalism as old-fashioned 19th-century doctrine of which Richard Cobden and other top-hatted Victorians would warmly approve.

Here's a caveat, which we will repeat at different points through the book. David Freud, evidently a Tory, had once been the apple of Tony Blair's eye and had served as an adviser when Gordon Brown was prime minister. Labour had been kinder and gentler, preferring to practise 'active labour market policy', offering carrots as well as brandishing sticks. The trouble was, under Labour as under the coalition, pushing people into low-income jobs did not solve much. They earned too little for decency or even to afford the rent, which is why (as ministers have started to admit) housing benefit took off in 2010 and is now reaching stratospheric heights. Besides, low-income jobs did not feel like the basis of sustainable prosperity in the hi-tech, high-skilled 21st century; the prevalence of low-income, low-productivity jobs helped explain why there are strict limits to UK growth: there's another chronic theme to return to.

Business is not a single interest; capitalism is not unidirectional. Some corporate executives were well aware of the self-defeating nature of the pile 'em high, get 'em cheap model for labour markets, but they tended to keep quiet. The point of Freud – not to be confused with Matthew Freud, Cameron intimate and PR chief – is that this was a government with crude ideas about what the private sector wanted. It rolled forward the post-1989, fall-of-the-wall, Thatcher idea that markets are 'natural', that alternatives were perverse, dangerous. Ministers did not think that marketising and shrinking the state were radical: they were merely tidying away the dust and detritus of misguided postwar statism. Thatcher privatised state-owned industries; they would complete the mission by privatising the functions of government itself – Royal Mail, the Land Registry, English Heritage – while liberating the people from the fetters of welfare dependency. Some Tories even modelled themselves on American Tea Party republicans.

Louche Leninists

Cameron was no Lenin. His Bolsheviks were not rabble-rousers; their PR advisers could never paint for them the striking picture of Thatcher's permed and handbagged supremacy in Downing Street. But there was no mistaking their purpose, or strength of instinct. They moved the markers of the politically possible, well beyond what she had thought achievable in her time.

During 2014, Monty Python reassembled to do live shows: Cameron's obstreperous party did sometimes resemble the Judean People's Front. How stupid were those badmouthing

him from the backbenches in failing to appreciate how successfully he used his apparent moderation. Rabid special advisers
feared they saw in Cameron a protagonist of 'one-nation'
Toryism. What they could not see was that this was as effective a defender of privilege and wealth as the Tory party was
ever likely to get and one, moreover, with an agenda that came
pretty close to the free-market right's all-time greatest hits.

We're using words such as reflexes, tics, assumptions,
accepting there was never such a thing as 'Cameronism'.
Rather, it was the same old, same old: diminish and under-
mine the state and the public sector. 'What takes me aback',
wrote Will Hutton, 'is their partisanship, the determined way
the national conversation is skewed towards the inadequacies
of the public sector, however concerning – avoidable deaths in
the NHS or extravagant pay-offs for BBC executives – without
any parallel focus on the inadequacies of the private.'[3] Beneath
his clowning, Boris Johnson said what they believed: restore
selective secondary schools, hail moneymakers, insist on the
'necessity' of inequality and exit the EU.

The house intellectual was Oliver Letwin, who took a backstairs role in 2010 in the Cabinet Office. He channelled the
pure doctrine of his (and Thatcher's) mentor Sir Keith Joseph.
During the 2005 election Letwin had let slip their long-term
intent to cut the state as a proportion of GDP to 35 per cent,
below even the US. The year before he had said out loud: 'The
NHS will not exist under the Tories.' Instead, government
would do vouchers, profit-making companies providing the
hospitals and surgeries. Which, pretty accurately, describes the
thrust of the NHS plan masterminded by Cameron's old boss
at central office, Andrew Lansley.

Nick Boles, an ex-thinktanker who became an MP then
minister, admitted on one occasion that the aim was to induce
chaos in public services. He meant promoting free markets and
competition, the opposite – as he put it – of planning, where
officials sit in a room and try to design the future: '"Chaotic",

therefore, in our vocabulary is a good thing,' as he put it in a debate in 2010. Chaos theory was probably never discussed around the cabinet table, but it wafted through the corridors. It borrows from the Austrian-American economist Joseph Schumpeter and the 'creative destruction' through which capitalism is supposed to renew itself.

It also links to the Tory philosopher Michael Oakeshott, who thought government – politicians and officials – would always get it wrong if they tried to organise social and economic reality. In the genealogy of ideas, Oakeshott was a potent influence on the London School of Economics political theorist Shirley Letwin and on her son, Oliver. His mother said the only important political question since the 18th century had been how big government should be, and the best way to cut it back might well be to make things fall apart, so the centre cannot hold.

Another metaphor: Leviathan (the 'big state') would be 'cowed'. Letwin said public sector staff needed 'fear and discipline'. An alternative tactic was dilution. Letwin helped write the 'Open Public Services' paper of 2012, which said: 'In the world we are now entering, all those who service the public will have a right to be recognised as public servants – regardless of whether the organisation for which they work are independent trusts, private enterprises, social enterprises.' So the very identity of the state dissolves into nothingness.

What Makeover?

The pitch began with a makeover. An heroic story was spun about the Tory party in the years since its catastrophic loss to Labour in 1997, both to sanctify Cameron's leadership and address the historical and ideological problem of how to sell markets. Like jackdaws on speed, they raided the policy cupboard and the thinktanks worked overtime. Cameron reconnected his party. The three leaders after Major were supposed to have been consigned to outer darkness as the sun rose to shine the way to a new compassionate future. Yet there, in 2010, were the discredited three, in prime positions: Duncan Smith as the scourge of welfare claimants; William Hague in a strong position at the cabinet table with time on his hands as foreign secretary. Even Michael Howard was still around as a grandee, channelling his hard line on crime through Chris Grayling.

The new leader of the opposition was too astute a tactician not to see that a full frontal assault on the welfare state was bad politics. At Cameron's side was fellow PR man, Steve Hilton, who had been Howard's policy coordinator before the 2005 election and saw close up the public's adverse judgment on the nasty party. Citadels fall to stealth and subterfuge and to commanders who wait in order to seize their opportunity. Step one in selling the Tories now looks comic: photo opportunities with huskies and hoodies. Step two was a storyline. However little attention the public pay to Westminster seminars, parties do need a 'narrative', if only to give party workers and candidates a sense of what they are up to. Cameron was proposing radical diminution if not outright destruction of the postwar welfare state, but he used the language of emancipation and empowerment.

So it made sense to pace the mean streets of city estates, cameras in attendance, proclaiming 'the political system is broken, the economy is broken and so is society. That is why people are so depressed about the state of our country.' It was clearly the fault of Blair, Brown and Labour since they were in power. But the trick was that deprivation and poverty (which the Tories acknowledged) would not be addressed with money and programmes, but by getting the bureaucratic welfare state out of the way. The problem was not insufficient benefits paid to poor households, but too much. Peel away welfare and charity would be reborn.

In retrospect, the confidence with which this non sequitur was advanced is breathtaking. It was founded on no sociological studies, no comparative analyses from countries that had advanced this formula (even the Tories hesitated to cite America here). The creed was 'localism' – but that didn't include councils. Instead, the people would take over their schools and get votes to veto council tax increases and choose crime commissioners.

Schools, transport, health, welfare, probation, economic development – any public service you cared to name – was 'overly centralised and complex'. In practice, localism was contradictory and confused. Did the Tories even want more participation? School governors were removed; NHS commissioning was handed to new unelected bureaucracies. But that came later as gradually we got the point: messiness was part of the purpose. Confused accountability and competing mandates helped the project, making government seem less legitimate, more of a burden.

That may sound too pat, too schematic. Ministers did not all read their crib sheets. Downing Street turned out to be ramshackle and Osborne, always more likely to assume the role of master manipulator, was never interested enough in administrative detail. Throughout this book, we have to keep balancing their broad ideological aims against sloppiness in execution.

Thatcher had arrived in power with at least one playbook – the plan for taking on and beating the trade unions devised by John Hoskyns and Norman Strauss. This time there was nothing so specific, even though the thinktank schemes and Letwin's plans had direction and method. The aim was to destroy the welfare state in ways that a successor Labour government could not repair within its likely time span. Tory planners knew that with weak electoral support, theirs might be only a one-term government and, if so, the coup required making permanent changes fast.

Into Power

After the crash, as the economy plunged, Labour had a dud prime minister and no excuses. 'We did not have an explanation for what was happening,' David Blunkett admitted later.

A part-excuse was the condition of politics, especially the sharp public reaction to disclosures about MPs' expenses. Guilt was shared between the parties – Tory MPs were disproportionate claimants because of their disproportionate personal wealth – but the Tories salvaged some credibility (though not, as it turned out, a House of Commons majority) by providing a simple reason for crash and decline: Labour's overspending.

Of course Labour had spent. The state had mobilised huge sums of public money to save individual banks and the financial sector. But the Tories could not admit it without accepting that the state had an inalienable role to play in stability and security, and – through taxation and spending and public service provision – in fending off the chaos of the markets. We began the chapter calling Cameron lucky; his fortune held. Crisis in the eurozone was also opportune. It was also the fault of government. 'The state bailing out banks is terrible for neoliberalism, while a story based on the evils of excessive government spending fits perfectly,' wrote Simon Wren-Lewis, professor of economics at Oxford.[4]

This was more than just a coup in the banal sense that you voted for Dr Jekyll and find you've elected Mr Hyde. The tide of opinion was running rightwards. In 1997 people had willed the broad thrust of Labour policies, especially higher public spending on health and other public services. Then came the crash and recession and, looking at Brown and at least some of his frontbench, that phrase coined by Disraeli to describe Gladstone's cabinet came to mind – a row of exhausted volcanoes.

But that does not imply anything like a 'settled will' in favour of drastic spending cuts, or the assault on welfare – which might have justified the post-election volte-face. Spending had to be cut to pay off the national debt (31 per cent strongly agreeing in May 2010, 27 per cent tending to assent), and spending had to take the rap rather than increased income tax. But attitudes are often inconsistent and 75 per cent also thought the government's priority should be protecting those most in need.

Whatever the state of opinion, the electoral fact was that the Tories missed a majority even against the most unpopular of prime ministers after the crash of a lifetime in a country in a slough of despond. Shouldn't that failure have pointed towards caution, incrementalism, the slog of winning assent for policies where we were indeed all in it together? The electoral evidence pointed to unassuaged suspicions of the atavistic Toryism the 2010 MPs represented. Little noticed, the candidates selected to stand shifted the centre of gravity of the party to the right.

An acolyte, the assistant editor of the *Daily Telegraph*, put it like this: 'In the end, you are either a big-state person, or a small-state person, and what big-state people hate about austerity is that its primary purpose is to shrink the size of government spending.' With the callousness towards ordinary people struggling to live decent lives on low incomes that so typifies the 'high journalism' of the right, the writer pronounced himself 'bored' by discussions about spending cuts. 'The bottom line is that you can only really make serious inroads into the size of the state during an economic crisis. This may be pro-cyclical, but there is never any appetite for it in the good times; it can only be done in the bad.'[5]

An expert on the Tories, Professor Tim Bale, noted 'the extremity and outspokenness of the 2010 intake': was there any longer a Tory mainstream, he wondered. 'The right – free market, small state, low tax, tight borders, tougher sentences, eco- and Euro-sceptical – is where the solid centre of the party now resides.'[6] And so it proved in office and, broadly, in the selections made for the cabinet, which remained unusually stable, at least until the summer of 2014. Then, attention focused on Cameron's dropping his friend Michael Gove. But, more importantly, the reshuffle was the night of the long knives for old-style centrist Toryism. The shift to the right among MPs finally caught up with the remaining few, Kenneth Clarke, the last pro-European, and Dominic Grieve, the attorney general, who had stoutly resisted the groundswell for withdrawing from the European Convention on Human Rights, which would have propelled the UK out of the community of civilised nations.

Coalition Collaborators

Yet around the cabinet still sat Vince Cable, Ed Davey and the other Liberal Democrats, and their contribution to the coup needs unpacking. By electoral luck, Cameron acquired a two-party vehicle for pressing on down a one-way street. The glaring psephological fact is the absence of public will in favour of the hardline programme the coalition delivered. Cameron's detractors missed the extent to which coalition meant Tory hands tight on the steering wheel with their partners strapped into the child seats in the back.

It's *Cameron's* coup; the Liberal Democrats drift in and out of the story, making an occasional impression but as bit-part players, rhubarbing away, occasionally making a dash to centre stage. In 2010 they did less well than the pre-election hype presaged, but suddenly in May they were enough of a parliamentary presence to be the inevitable adjuncts of the government.

In hindsight, two things stand out. One is that power sharing had hardly been anticipated, despite the pollsters' predictions. The second is how little that mattered to the Tories was ever seriously challenged, not the depth of the cuts or their cosy relations with business, not their sycophantic dealings with Murdoch or their demolition of the postwar welfare consensus.

Part of the reason for that was the Liberal Democrats' own ideological battle during the preceding decade and the rise of a substantial group with clear affinities with Cameron's crew: these were the MPs who had produced a volume of essays (*The Orange Book – Reclaiming Liberalism*), most of which set a version of the case for free markets and less state.

Clegg is called 'socially progressive', a badge you get if you are in favour of gay marriage, but you don't lose if you are against redistributive taxation. Some Liberal Democrats shared the anarchistic streak noticeable on the right. What else to make of the pensions minister's response to Osborne's abolition of compulsory annuities? Jeremy Browne – for a while a junior minister at the Home Office – wrote a book in 2014 calling for his party to move towards 'unbridled, authentic liberalism': *Race Plan* proposed a 40p top income tax rate and a state smaller than 38 per cent of GDP – then drew the obvious conclusion and urged merger with the Tories.

Coition in the Cabinet Room

The homoerotic encounter in the Downing Street rose garden marked the climax of frantic grappling. What those 'days in May' proved was lust for office. Marriage or, some might say, backstairs coupling was pimped by officials from the 'deep state'. These included the governor of the Bank of England, preaching a doctrine on spending, tax and policy that masqueraded as objective analysis but was freighted with partisan assumptions and biases. Sir Gus O'Donnell, cabinet secretary and head of the civil service, was also an orthodox economist who lent his weight to the theory of fiscal emergency.

Cameron boxed clever. He dipped the Liberal Democrats' hands in the blood of Tory spending cuts while conceding trifles, including a referendum on the mildest measure of electoral reform. Clegg then failed to get a guarantee of support for constitutional reform, and the Tories went on to scupper both. The Tories took complete control of public finances and economic policy; Danny Alexander, the junior Liberal Democrat planted at the Treasury as chief secretary, rapidly went native and, as a born-again prophet of austerity, became a doughty shield for a party his own north of Scotland constituents would never dream of supporting. But they relished pork barrel. While preaching austerity to others, Alexander's own hand reached deep inside the feeding trough to bribe his constituents. Specific interventions from the Treasury had secured special funding for a tourist railway in his Inverness seat, a bailout for the Inverness sleeper train, one-off tax breaks just for the ski lifts in his constituency and a generous alloca- tion (from the UK government) to the Highland council to fund exemptions from the coalition's bedroom tax. 'This is the payoff. Danny is loyal to George, and this is what he gets in return,' said a senior Liberal Democrat.

Perhaps, if he had not driven so recklessly on the motorway then treated his wife and family so badly, Chris Huhne might have been more effective in standing up to the Tories – though his record in office puts that in doubt, having gulped down previous Liberal Democrat anti-nuclear commitments. Like Cable a clever economist with real-world experience, he cannot be excused by the defence of not understanding the effects of austerity or the way the Tories were using fiscal consolidation as a cover for realising their political ambitions. Other Liberal Democrats were like rabbits caught in headlights, blinking nervously and running to get out of the line of fire. Ed Davey, taking over as energy secretary, disappeared from political sight, as his policies became confused and his resistance to Tory market models and their friends in the energy companies crumbled. A small Liberal Democrat-inspired green investment bank eventu- ally arrived in their last year, lacking freedom to borrow to invest.

The Coalition

The 'Coalition Agreement for Stability and Reform' committed the parties to maintain the government in office for a fixed five years. Meaningless clauses were inserted, saying, for example, that special advisers 'must at all times act in the interests of the government as a whole': the subsequent ruthlessness of the Tory special advisers showed how naive the Liberal Democrat negotiators had been in failing to secure any concrete commit- ments or sanctions in case of breach. The most doctrinaire Tory could not have wished for more suggestive language: it promised to disperse power, break 'open the state monopoly in schooling' and stop 'the relentless incursion of the state into the lives of individuals'. The ragbag even included a 'compassionate' promise to employ precisely 4,200 extra health visitors.

In retrospect, it's hard not to laugh. The coalition agreement pledged directly elected people on primary care trusts (PCTs); within a year the coalition was legislating to abolish them altogether and rigorously exclude democracy from clinical commissioning. A promised Post Office Bank disappeared, along with 'honesty in food labelling' and a ban on the sale of alcohol below cost price. A peculiar promise 'to encourage live music' was never heard again. The coalition would start a national tree-planting campaign – but was that to be before or after the selling-off of the national forests and woodlands that the Tory environment secretary began preparing within weeks of taking office, but which was not mentioned in the document?

Other commitments were airily aspirational; for example, 'concerted government action to tear down barriers and build a fairer society'. Even conceding there might have been some sincerity behind that promise on the Liberal Democrat side, we must ask whether Clegg and his colleagues had the remotest idea of the impact of austerity on fairness – or even think of insisting on evaluations and evidence. Did they stop for a moment to consider how committed the Tory party was historically to fortifying those social 'barriers'?

Elastoplast was liberally applied to contentious areas. Trident missiles were to be renewed; the Liberal Democrats did not like that, so would be 'exploring alternatives'. Once in office they were allowed nowhere near the Ministry of Defence. Liberal Democrats crowed about securing a top-up grant to schools based on the number of children poor enough to qualify for free meals, but asked for and got nothing on the bigger question of school funding allocations, a grave omission given the financial favouritism that would be shown to the Tories' free schools and academies. We will discuss Clegg's misunderstanding of the tax system: he failed to grasp how raising the income tax threshold to £10,000 was regressive and benefited higher-rate taxpayers much more than the low earners he was claiming to help.

Later, Clegg took to the airwaves on LBC. He claimed that he had stopped Tory ideologues imposing their experiments on English schools. 'I said to them, "No, you can't turn the clock back to a 1950s-style exam system which divides kids up; you can't introduce profit-making into state schools."' But why had he signed a coalition agreement so loose that the ideologues had such ample space? The falsity of Clegg's position is demonstrated by his own nominee for the education department – David Laws. During his short stint at the Treasury before resigning over suspect expenses claims, Laws had proved holier than Pope Osborne as a priest in the cult of austerity. Was he really cut from cloth different to the Tory education secretary's? Laws was the man who, after all, had written in 2004 in favour of abolishing the NHS and moving to American-style insurance, allowing patients to pay top-ups (if they could afford it) for private care. When the tide later turned, he upended the boat, talking of the Tories' desire 'to shrink the state long after the deficit has been cleared'.

The coalition agreement had a hole in it the size of Durdle Door. Nowhere was there any hint of what was to happen in health. The words were incontrovertible: 'We will stop top-down reorganisations of the NHS [and] stop centrally dictated closure of A&E and maternity wards so that people have better access to local services.' The NHS must be chalked up as one of the Liberal Democrats' greatest derelictions of duty, given what they had said and continued to say they stood for. It was also a puzzle. Did their MPs and peers – Shirley Williams the biggest culprit – understand the implications of what the Tories proposed: how could they not see what was being rendered in Lansley's NHS bill? The coalition agreement had hardly been encrypted. 'The only feasible way of making gains in quality of service … is to introduce competition, choice …'

The agreement contained not a word about higher education finance. Yet in 2010 some 400 parliamentary candidates had signed a declaration vowing to abolish university tuition fees. In a famous photo, Clegg was pictured writing: 'I pledge to vote against any increase in fees'; use your vote to block fees, he had told students in marginal seats. This betrayal has become a touchstone for electoral cynics to parrot the cliche that they're all the same. When Clegg demanded that the Tories take similar strain and agree to means test pensioner benefits such as the winter fuel allowance, he was brushed off. Electoral damage was not to be equally shared.

The paradox was that time and again they saved the Tories from dangerously extreme policies that might have sunk a single-party government. Above all, they made it impossible for Europhobes to demand an in/out referendum in this parliament. Governing alone, Cameron would have had no excuse for resisting his hot-headed Euromonomaniacs. The Liberal Democrat mantra was that they 'stopped the Tories from being far worse'. But stopped what? Tory ministers learnt they could win political kudos with their own party by floating extreme ideas secure in the knowledge that the Liberal Democrats would torpedo them – the restoration of charges at the national galleries and museums, for example.

Liberal Democrats donned the motley to camouflage true Tory purposes. If Simon Hughes, Davey and Cable had voted for it, surely coalition policy must be justified and reasonable? Their acquiescence certified that cuts must be necessary, not an emanation of doctrine. So the Liberal Democrat role was to normalise or 'de-ideologise'; they draped a veil of legitimacy over policies too scary for the Tories to get away with by themselves. Austerity introduced by the Tories alone would have been seen as merely vindictive but, commentators noted, when signed off by the Liberal Democrats it became unavoidable. MPs on the right never understood the accidental good luck of taking in the Liberal Democrats as sleeping partners.

The 2015 election will confirm the evidence from local authority and European Parliament elections over recent years that Clegg made a catastrophic misjudgment. Even if he sincerely believed that in the circumstances of May 2010 the 'national interest' compelled his party's adherence to the Tories under the terms of the coalition agreement, Clegg or his aides should surely have drawn on history. Apart from wartime, 'national' governments have always been constituted to favour the Tory side. National interest turns out to be sectional interest. In 1931, the Liberals were destroyed as a political force for a generation by swallowing Tory austerity. In many parts of England and Wales – their future in Scotland is also in jeopardy – the Liberal Democrats may have been fatally contaminated and removed as a potential electoral threat to the Tories. The human shields took the heat and melted.

Cleverer than Clegg, the business secretary qualified himself as standard-bearer for what remained of the party's conscience. But taking Cable's ministerial performance at face value – what he did rather than what he said – we would have to conclude that his failure was stark. Where was the state-inspired economic activism promised by the Liberal Democrats before the election, their infrastructure bank or their young persons' workplace scheme, let alone their constraints on corporate greed? When we interviewed Cable a few years ago, he had clearly said, 'The way to deal with fat cat salaries is to have a tax system that is more progressive, and I have argued for a higher rate of tax on people earning over £100,000 a year.' The words were often strong and his judgment sharp – as when Cable attacked the Tories' 'ideological' plans to cut welfare and acidly observed how fragile were the foundations of UK economic recovery. But words were not matched by deeds. In this pact, Mephistopheles gave little away and, beyond enjoying the perks of office, Faust got little in return for his soul. Whatever intellectual credibility Cable could claim diminished every time he parroted the Tory cliche about 'the mess Labour left us'.

He knew full well that whatever disagreements there might be about the scale and extent of fiscal consolidation, the cause had been the banks, and sorting them out was the task he was struggling to complete.

The final page of the coalition agreement document contained a clause easily missed after the welter of odds and ends. It overrode everything else: 'Deficit reduction takes precedence over any of the other measures in this agreement.' No sums are attached. A short note added: 'The main burden of deficit reduction will be borne by reduced spending rather than increased taxes.' That became the basis and point of austerity, as practised by George Osborne at the Treasury.

5

The Cuts

Running through the Derbyshire village of Kilburn near Belper is Church Street. It's an A road and busy. For years the children at the junior school have been shepherded across by a lollipop lady. But no longer. The county council is now demanding a further 2,000 cut in headcount on top of the 1,600 posts culled since 2010. It is getting rid of the crossing patrol, which school head Nigel Pratley says he can't raid school funds to keep.

There, in microcosm, are the cuts, so far. By 2018, Derbyshire county council has to lop a further £157m off its annual budget. The disappearance of Kilburn's crossing patrol is not the end of the world: the school goes on educating children. But teachers' pensions and salaries have suffered. Students, soldiers and benefits claimants are worse off; investment, school buildings and infrastructure projects have been cancelled.

That's not much when set against restoring the public finances and rescuing the economy, say defenders. But austerity was not necessary on the timetable or to the depth they chose. Their cuts weren't pragmatic but dogmatic. They acted with malice aforethought, their decisions on tax and spending springing from a distinct anti-welfare, anti-government rather than technical judgment on how to respond to the emergency circumstances of the crash.

And now: there is no renaissance in enterprise. It's British business as usual: low wages, low productivity and low investment.

After five years, Osborne raised the annual growth rate from Labour's 2 per cent in early 2010 to 3 per cent in 2014, with a big dip in between, and at considerable social cost. Kilburn's lollipop lady is one tiny instance. Social policy effects will scar the life chances of many of the children who are growing up dependent on food banks.

Labour's Legacy

Between 2000 and 2007, spending on public services grew more quickly than over any other seven-year period since 1945, from 36.6 to 41.1 per cent of GDP. Public servants, lollipop ladies included, enjoyed Labour largesse. Austerity is about rolling back those years. By 2016–17 spending will be the same proportion of national income as in 2000, despite the changing size and age of the UK population.

Labour had been profligate – in this sense. It had not undergirded necessary increases in spending by raising tax. In technical terms, the structural deficit had grown. In opposition, the Tories had promised independent scrutiny of their fiscal judgments and once in power Osborne swiftly established the Office of Budget Responsibility (OBR). The boss was the Olympian Robert Chote, former head of the Institute for Fiscal Studies. Reports exuded gloom, which suited advocates of austerity. But the OBR says plainly that crisis and recession *were not caused* by Labour tax and spend (though public finances could have been in a more resilient state when the train hit the buffers). The jump in public spending to 48.1 per cent of GDP was caused by the impact of crash and bailout. The budget deficit – the annual gap between government income and outlays – ballooned to £159bn, or 11.2 per cent of GDP, in 2009–10, which was big, but still less than in the US and Japan. This wasn't 'socialism' or 'Labour excess' but the price of rescuing capitalism from itself.

In the closed setting of the World Economic Forum in Davos in 2013 Osborne admitted it.[1] The reason why the UK economy fell off the cliff was its outsize banking sector, the same size as America's, in an economy one-fifth the size. When the mics were on, Osborne stuck with his script. We have to pay tribute to his political flair. He saw a chance to accomplish the goal of pushing back the state and opening it to the market.

Days in May

Labour failed to explain the inevitability of financial imbalance in the depths of recession; it failed to extol the beginnings of recovery; it failed to nail the Tories' primitive analogy between the macro-economy and a household budget, let alone Osborne's 'the country maxed out its credit card'. The UK – with its own central bank and currency – was able to borrow at historically low rates throughout the recession under both Labour and coalition governments.

The accumulation of past borrowings (the national debt) was manageable; much was long term and would not need refinancing for years. The debt was high but not out of kilter with the US or Germany, and the cost of borrowing remained preternaturally low. But the Tories, echoed by the Liberal Democrats, preferred a Greek drama: riots on the streets of Athens filled the nightly news. The implication was that the UK would also collapse. It wasn't true and they knew it. Imagine the chief executive of a big corporate had declared they were close to bankruptcy. 'The detached observer', said one such, the economist John Kay, 'would conclude that the UK government failing to repay its sterling obligations is a risk commensurable with the prospect of a meteorite falling on one's head. The observable reality is that the British government can borrow for 50 years at an interest rate of about zero in real terms, the lowest in centuries.'[2]

But economics is a bun fight, as much about sentiment and political sympathy as hard analysis. 'The markets' are actually pinstripe suits with political views. A Tory chancellor can rely on a chorus of bankers and journalists and tycoons; they backed immediate and drastic fiscal 'consolidation'. That anodyne phrase meant cuts to planned spending and some increases in tax.

Net public debt as a proportion of GDP had to be lowered and it had to be lowered to 30 per cent, the lowest ratio for 300 years. Whence such precision? Debt and growth were not inseparable twins; history offered no predictable point where national debt has a detrimental impact on economic growth. Nations with higher average debt-to-GDP ratios had not lost out on long-term growth performance. Economists who assert that beyond a certain level of debt (90 per cent was plucked out of the air) a country is heading for perdition are like yokels scratching up folk wisdom.

The Growth Record

GDP was expanding until the middle of 2010: during Alistair Darling's final three months, the economy grew by 1 per cent, a quarterly rate faster than before the crash in 2007. Of course, a hypothetical post-2010 Labour or alternative government would have been hit by recession in the eurozone and weakness in export markets. But its 'consolidation' would surely have been more pragmatic, uninflected by a partisan bid to tilt the balance. 'The coalition has seized the opportunity at the moment of the UK's greatest economic crisis since the 1930s, and the widespread uncertainty about its causes, to impose a protracted fiscal contraction with the aim of reducing the tax burden,' said the veteran economist Brian Henry.[3]

To fanfare, Osborne announced in summer 2014 that the UK economy was as big as it had been in early 2008, with GDP worth £1,600bn. Leave aside for the moment that most incomes were still no higher than in 2003 in real terms, or that with a growing population, GDP per head was still 4 per cent lower than at the 2008 peak. His story is not compelling. He came in, he cut, the economy contracted and not until the autumn of 2013 did it recover in aggregate, with growth in 2014 set to be 3 per cent (off a reduced base). Those are the bare facts of Osborne's tenure as master manipulator of the macro-economy. They leave a lot of room for argument about cause.

And contention continues: when you hear certainty on either side, be suspicious. The years since the crash have been 'a period of missed forecasts, the collapse of cherished models and the emergence of new puzzles', said Chris Giles of the *Financial Times*.[4] Yet modesty and humility aren't characteristic of economics as a discipline, let alone practitioners in high places such as the International Monetary Fund. In October 2008 the IMF had predicted the UK economy would grow by 12 per cent by 2013; in fact, it contracted by 1 per cent. In June 2010 Osborne predicted net borrowing would be £37bn in 2014–15; it was closer to £100bn. The coalition's initial target was missed by so many miles that it inadvertently disproved Osborne's dire warnings of the consequences of failing to abolish the deficit fast. The UK even lost the triple A credit rating Osborne had said was vital for survival – and nothing happened.

The IMF changed its mind. Towering over Osborne at their occasional joint press conferences, its stately chief executive Christine Lagarde – unlike her disgraced predecessor never likely to be impersonated by Gerard Depardieu in a *film à clef* – brought conventional wisdom to bear in appraising the UK. But conventional wisdom had been sore wounded by the crash. Suddenly, no one (including Nobel laureates) was quite sure what money was or whether limits existed to banks' capacity to create it. Pompous and staid as a breed, after quantitative easing the central bankers resembled Tommy Cooper shambling through a trick: hundreds of billions magicked out of thin air, just like that. Magicians' money added 3 per cent to GDP overall from 2009 to 2013, according to Martin Weale, of the Bank of England's monetary committee.

In 2012 Lagarde had unveiled the IMF annual assessment of the UK economy, saying she shivered in trying to think about the public finances without the benefit of Osborne's austerity. But a year later, another IMF voice, its chief economist Olivier Blanchard, said the opposite, warning that the coalition was 'playing with fire' over austerity, which had cut demand and delayed recovery. In summer 2014 Lagarde reversed the judgment. But then she admitted: 'We have learnt there is no single way to reduce fiscal deficits', adding a postscript to the effect that improvements in the public finances 'should strike a balance between revenue and expenditure measures'. In other words, a better balance with more taxing and less cutting.

Public Finances

Osborne's initial catechism said it was absolutely essential to eliminate the structural deficit in the public finances during the life of the parliament, by 2015. This meant 'fiscal tightening', taking £40bn out of the economy – nearly 7 per cent of GDP. Things did not go to plan: the green shoots proved stubbornly subterranean; the Treasury did not get the money and had to keep paying for social supports in a recession-bound economy. Instead of eliminating the annual deficit by 2014–15, he had to shift his target date to the middle of the next parliament, in 2017–18. Ah, he said, but the target remained sacrosanct; he even tightened it – to take 10.3 per cent of GDP out, albeit over a longer period of pain. All is now to be well by 2018. The political plan was to get unavoidable tax rises over with, but to leave the worst of the spending cuts till later, hoping in between there would be wiggle room enough to pay for pre-election giveaways.

OBR estimates of growth and revenues went awry. In June 2010, it predicted national debt at 69 per cent of GDP by 2014–15, with Osborne on course to get rid of the deficit.

But by 2013, the OBR's forecast for what Osborne needed to borrow during the five years had risen from £322bn to £564bn. Despite Osborne's dire 'Greek' warnings about losing international creditworthiness, this £242bn slippage in the UK state's need to borrow had precisely zero impact on long-term interest rates.

Osborne had failed. By 2014, UK borrowing was at record levels despite recovery. The deficit came down, yes, but the plan was in tatters. Cutting the deficit was to 'work' by reducing spending; business activity would catch light in a sort of spontaneous combustion. But cutting spending harmed the overall economy, as well as individuals and households. The OBR queried the extent, saying household spending had kept going, but inflation was also higher than expected, so households were still feeling the pinch and household spending didn't contribute as much to economic growth as forecast. But threats to cut and the wild talk of 2010 undoubtedly damaged confidence. The pace of activity did not pick up; more money had to be spent on welfare for those out of work and tax credits and housing benefits for those finding jobs that barely covered their living costs – with the paradoxical effect of reducing Osborne's proposed cuts in total spending.

No one, including the OBR, disputes that Plan Osborne kept GDP depressed. It's a question of by how much: nearly 2 per cent in 2012, 3 per cent in 2013, according to some estimates. Austerity can't account for all the losses in GDP – which also have to do with problems of growth that lay abroad, depression in the eurozone and the failure of business to kickstart investment, preferring to amass piles of cash – yet from Osborne's first budget in June 2010 the case for slower austerity had been repeatedly made. Economists, far from infallible and all grappling with uncertain data, are divided. Those who had not accepted that austerity killed growth in 2011 and 2012 had, for consistency's sake, to refuse to give Osborne credit for the return of growth in 2013.

Osbornomics

In 2015 the budget deficit is set to fall to just under 5 per cent of GDP, with the national debt still rising at about 77 per cent of GDP. But the return of growth and a falling deficit has allowed Osborne to say he is back on track: three years late, maybe, but in time to give a fillip to the campaign for the 2015 election. Right up to August 2013 renewed recession – 'triple dip' – threatened, but eventually the figures showed the economy spluttering back to life. Abatement of the euro crisis helped, along with a boom in equity prices and – once again – that precious British inflation in house prices, aided and abetted by the Treasury itself. The problem remains the flow of revenue, lumpy and subject to gaming. Of course, a housing market boom swelled Treasury funds in late 2014, thanks to stamp duty and corporation tax.

Osbornomics did not just belong to the chancellor: it was the belief system of a secure coterie of friends, relatives and the like-minded, who could be called upon to protect the flanks. Bank of England governor Carney was a good example. Recruited for the ostensibly technocratic job of running the central bank, he could be relied on to practise the mystic art of quantitative easing. Mystic, because you did not have to be Penn and Teller to wonder why it was possible for the Bank of England to print money to give (yes, not lend) to banks for them to lend to businesses, but it was impossible for the Bank to lend (not give) the money to local authorities for them to build real houses for which tenants would pay real rents. When the banks didn't spend but kept the money for themselves, they were given more.

Money In

Osbornomics can be summed up from the coalition's 2010 programme: the main burden of deficit reduction falls on cuts in spending rather than increased taxes. This is the fault line.

'Cuts in the welfare state', says the LSE's John Hills, 'bear much more heavily on those with low incomes than those with high ones, while tax increases tend to hit people in rough proportion to their incomes.'[5] Having decided that four-fifths of deficit reduction would come from cuts and one-fifth from tax increases predetermined where the pain of austerity would be felt.

In his first act as chancellor, Osborne's most symbolic decision was to cut the top rate of income tax from 50p to 45p. This tolled the knell for all-in-it-togetherness. This was the centrepiece of what became his omnishambles 2012 budget, when the wheels came off one measure after another, forcing his retreat on a new charity tax, a caravan tax and even a pasty tax, where Cameron was caught out pretending he'd once eaten one of Cornwall's finest on Leeds station.

Dropping the top rate showed the government's essence. Dispute raged over how much the 50p rate had brought in. Thinktanks dusted off their ancient 'Laffer curves', renamed dynamic scoring, to show that, thanks to their tax cut, executives worked harder, earned more and so brought in compensatory revenue. Curiously, the same behavioural dynamic did not apply to the poor: they would only work harder if their benefits were cut.

Public indignation boiled over as firms, including Goldman Sachs, proposed to delay payments to staff in order to get the 45p rate from April 2013 – this a firm that was a major bene-ficiary of public spending. They backed down after pressure from the Bank of England and the Treasury.

The Free Enterprise Group of Tory MPs and ministers complained of the unfairness that top earners 'shoulder' a large fraction of total tax paid; Boris Johnson, ever the class clown, said they should be bestowed with knighthoods to mark their 'heroic contribution'. The government asserted that the richest 20 per cent of households 'continue to make the greatest contribution towards reducing the deficit'.

But the tax system is *designed* to be progressive. Taking taxes and benefits including education into account, 52 per cent of households receive more than they pay in taxes. That is the only way of running a society where market rewards are skewed. So, it's true that 300,000 individuals at the very top of the scale account for 7.5 per cent of all the UK government's tax revenues. House price inflation has been raising the proportion of stamp duty revenue accruing from mansions. Sales of housing in only two London boroughs, Westminster and Kensington and Chelsea, accounted for more than 14 per cent of the tax take from all residential transactions in 2013. But that's all evidence of growing inequality, mitigated only slightly by the tax system, and few if any deliberate decisions by the government.

A Fiscal Drag Act

Looking at the pressures on spending in an ageing society, let alone the overhang of debt from the recession, no prudent chancellor should be cutting revenue streams. Fiscally, things could only get worse. Tax revenue from the North Sea and from motorists is falling. The OBR sees fuel duties falling from 1.8 per cent of GDP today to 1 per cent by 2030, an annual revenue loss of more than £10bn. How to replace the money while encouraging greener travel? 'If we are to meet our carbon reduction targets we will need to replace all of the more than £30bn a year we raise from tax on road fuel,' said the IFS's Paul Johnson. Osborne did the opposite and cut the take from fuel tax. Osborne was lucky, putting VAT on fuel up to 20 per cent, so raising pump prices, but at a time when international oil prices were falling. The juggernauts were carbon and costs. Duties are producing less as cars and lorries become more fuel-efficient. Charging for road use might have been a better source of revenue and would have helped to lever people out of cars into trains and buses. Difficult, but the UK is not alone.

Angela Merkel's coalition is debating whether to force lorries to pay an annual charge for using the Autobahn.

Like chancellors before him, Osborne could rely on the extra revenue that comes from holding tax thresholds while prices and, hopefully, earnings rise. The starting point for 40 per cent tax was actually cut, by £2,000, to £41,865, to adjust for the rise in personal allowance, with the result that between 2010 and 2014 the number of higher-rate taxpayers increased from just over 3 to 4.4 million, causing much harrumphing on the Tory backbenches.

That resulted from having to accommodate the Liberal Democrats' push to raise the threshold over which people pay income tax. Nick Clegg had negotiated a deal: cut top tax in exchange for cutting the personal allowance – no one earning under £10,000 would pay income tax. The cost was high, £10.7bn in lost revenue, and most of the benefit would go to those higher up the earnings scale whose tax liabilities would also fall. Besides, low earners still paid national insurance starting at 12 per cent of their earnings on anything over £153 a week. Worse, for low earners, most of the gain from paying less income tax was clawed back in a deduction from their tax credits under Duncan Smith's new Universal Credit scheme. All taxpayers benefit when the threshold is raised but, it turned out, low-paid families gain least. On average, taxpayers gain £200 for every £1,000 the threshold is raised, but low earners who need tax credits only get £70. Raising the tax threshold is a gift to higher-income households: three-quarters of the value went to households in the top half of the earnings distribution.

To get money in, the government raised the main rate of VAT to 20 per cent – a sharp reversal after Labour had cut VAT to stimulate consumption. In the UK, a lower proportion of consumer spending is subject to VAT than elsewhere in Europe, with fuel and food exempt. It would have been fairer to extend the scope of the tax, compensating the poorest through tax credits and benefits, but that was never going to happen. Taking all taxes into account as a proportion of incomes, the ONS reported the top fifth pay 35.5 per cent of their income in tax, while the bottom fifth pay 36.6 per cent, because a higher proportion of their income is taxed through VAT and sales taxes.

Osborne proclaimed he would clarify tax, and even set up the Office of Tax Simplification, which identified 1,042 separate reliefs. He then succeeded in abolishing 48 while creating others; under him the total actually grew. For all the talk about the cleansing force of markets, Osborne prevaricated in the face of lobbies. Labour had promised the video games industry relief similar to that enjoyed by films; Osborne stopped it, only two years later to change his mind following a campaign by games developers, who threatened to decamp to Canada, which offers concessions.

No wonder the IFS said the coalition has made tax more opaque and even held back recovery with a string of tax changes that make the system 'more complicated, less efficient and less transparent'. An example is the Tory belief that tax arrangements for men and women living together cement marriages and inhibit divorce. In 2014 Osborne enacted a new marriage tax allowance costing £600m. It affects only a third of married couples and the great majority of them are likely to be pensioners. The divorce rate is unlikely to alter as a result.

The Tax Gap

Billions are owed to the government, even now after all the pain of austerity. In addition to the £22bn owing (at March 2013) in uncollected fines and debts, there is the 'tax gap' between what companies and individuals pay and what the assessment slip says. Estimates vary but £35bn is a conservative starter from the Treasury. Add in, says the NAO, transactions that are criminal and fraudulent and off the books, probably worth £50bn a year, and the total loss to the exchequer is £100bn.

The government brought in a General Anti-Avoidance Rule, but wily corporate lawyers needed tougher restraint. The 2014 budget proposed that HMRC should be allowed to tap directly into bank accounts of those who owe more than £1,000 in tax. The plan provoked the bankers and an odd bunch of allies in the civil liberties and poverty charities. Progressives had to rub their eyes. Here was Osborne going much further than Labour had dared. Once on the statute books, these powers would surely be as effective as a deterrent as they were practical tools.

Yet Osborne continued to say that his ambition is to cut taxes. Hearing the mood music, officials were reluctant to push too hard, even for what was owing. But the government's hand was forced by acclamation for the redoubtable Margaret Hodge, chair of the PAC, in exposing and haranguing tax avoiders. Under political instruction, however, HMRC hesitated. An HSBC employee in Switzerland disclosed the names of 130,000 potential tax cheats, but the ensuing inquiries were slow; Spanish and French tax authorities have recouped more. A UK-Swiss Tax Agreement, which came into force in January 2013, brought in £1bn by 2014, significantly less than HMRC expected.

Glacial, too, were the government's efforts to curb tax avoidance and evasion offshore. In austerity, the OECD, once a happy hunting ground for free marketeers, has become a cheer-leader for international collaboration to staunch losses from the tax system and for tighter regulation of tax havens. UK government representatives have not been conspicuous. The Channel Islands claim to be more forthcoming, but the UK still provides cover and protection for a string of islands where rich people sequester their gains, legal and illegal. The government, like its predecessor, looked away and a massive potential source of revenue continues to go untapped.

At home, HMRC published a hit list of avoidance schemes and sent out 'accelerated payment notices' with some 33,000 individuals and 10,000 businesses in sight; potentially £7.1bn of revenue was in play. For once, the media had a field day not with benefit cheats but with denouncing well-heeled entertainers and corporates sheltering their income from tax. A Tory minister – David Gauke – stood tall and defended the scheme as simply putting rich taxpayers on the same footing as self-assessment taxpayers who pay upfront. Gary Barlow OBE was one caught in the furore and Cameron had to call Jimmy Carr's Jersey-based avoidance 'quite frankly morally wrong'.

The evidence swings both ways on the government's tax-collecting efficacy. HMRC was ordered to cut staff by 5,000 a year, which was daft when for years it could show that each extra tax official brought in substantial sums. The Association of Revenue and Customs (ARC), the senior tax managers' union, said every £312m spent on tax officers brought in another £8bn to the exchequer. Scrutiny of 'high net worth individuals' with assets worth more than £20m brought in £1bn 'extra' between 2009 and 2014, the financial secretary to the Treasury claimed. Were there really only 6,200 of them in the UK's tax net? Despite staff cuts, HMRC planned to recruit dozens of lawyers to tax tribunals to hear appeals resulting from its crackdown. Although more cases were going to court, the PAC complained of an enormous backlog, with 43,000 cases pending.

But by no means all accountants were in the business of denying the Treasury its fair due in tax. We talked tax in South Yorkshire, where recession had bitten hard, and found that among business people – natural supporters of the Tories – the behaviour of the banks and the big accountancy firms was profoundly resented. They didn't like income tax, no question, but nor did they like the idea that the tax system could be scammed or manipulated by cheats and the very rich. Ideas of fairness are never far away, on all sides of the political divide.

———

The senior partner of Hawsons Chartered Accountants sits in the boardroom of Pegasus House, with fine views across Sheffield, a city with many more hills than Rome's seven. Chris Hill, large and emphatic, leading light of the chamber of commerce, gets a good overview of the city's business life. Recovery is in the air. His offices are on the road to Glossop and Manchester across the peaks, and he hears the heady talk about new trans-Pennine links and northern revival. But this dignified old firm has looked after the accounts of Sheffield businesses for 160 years, ridden many economic cycles and managed to escape the jaws of the giant combines that have eaten up so many medium-sized prac- tices, so its partners have learnt a certain circumspection.

Hill recollects when the crash hit. 'We were getting calls for help every day of the week. People asked us what was going to happen next.' The building industry took the hardest fall. When the music stopped at the height of the property mania, developers were left with brand-new flats in the city centre and tracts of land they couldn't sell. One large investor had just flattened an entire block – and the gap-tooth space sits empty still. 'Banks pulled their loans. They found excuses, covenants stating the loan to value must be 90 per cent, so when property values dropped they could back out. We had six or seven that went to insolvency.' He fears another bust when interest rates rise: paradoxically, as property values rise, so banks will foreclose when they see the price is right.

'We tried hard not to let staff go, though other firms did. We know our people and their families, and we just didn't want to make them redundant. Normally, there would be 5 per cent turnover, but no one left, which made it harder.' He echoes other employers we've talked to: how they held tight to as many staff as they could, more than they needed. It's reflected in the surprisingly low unemployment rates during the recession. But Hawsons did stop giving jobs to their graduate trainees on completion, letting them go after their three years of training – again reflecting national figures for shrinking graduate jobs. 'Normally, we'd take them all, a scarce resource, always being poached by the Big Four once we'd trained them up,' Chris Hill says.

The Big Four loom large in his demonology, the monster accountancy firms that act like a cartel. 'They can play both sides, all things to all men, auditors and advisers to the same companies. We can't do that. I don't know how they get away with it.' How cleverly the Big Four act, helping draw up contracts for outsourcing public services then bidding themselves or acting for the private bidders.

He spreads out his wide hands in mock shock at what he sees: 'How can it be that people from the Big Four go into HMRC for a while on secondment to help them out on tax matters – and then they go back to their own companies as tax advisers again?' The poachers turn gamekeepers all the better to poach again.

There is an old-world probity about his disdain for clever modern tax dodges. 'If people want that sort of thing, it's not us. It's for specialist boutique firms or the Big Four.' He refers to EBTs as if they were some form of accounting pornography. 'Employee Benefit Trusts, we don't do those. A company loans money to an EBT and gets tax deducted from their corporation tax. Then the trust loans it to the beneficiaries, who are the company directors, so they pay less tax.' Why doesn't the government close such loopholes?

Hill talks about HMRC, which has been shutting its local offices. He reckons that not only quality of service but tax revenues have suffered: HMRC must have lost considerable sums by losing local knowledge and expertise. 'Before they shut down, you could call a local inspector who knew us and knew the client. You could talk to someone who knew what you were talking about. Now you get a call centre somewhere and someone who just takes notes but has no idea what you mean. They say someone will call you back but they don't. They tell you to write, they don't reply.' Inspections are rarer and inspectors no longer quite know what to look for. Clients struggle with self-assessments, unable to get any advice, investigations left hanging for years.

The coalition's new tax allowances have encouraged more research investment, he says, pointing to a high-end acoustics manufacturer that has recently upped its R&D spending by 125 per cent, taking on three new graduates to develop new products. But what counts as R&D? You can claim a proportion of salary and heat and light. 'A whole industry of R&D specialist tax advisers has sprung up,' he says, adding: 'It's very cutting edge', with a faint whiff of disapproval.

Chris Hill blames increasingly elaborate avoidance schemes on the 50p tax rate. 'Clients just thought it was wrong to pay half their income. Why should they bother working any extra, if they'd lose half of it? It was psychological. They talked of not taking so much income but leaving their money in a company, knowing that if they sold it they qualified for entrepreneurs' relief, so they ended up paying only 10 per cent in the end – that sort of thing. Our clients were a lot happier when it came down to 45 per cent.'

Here is a businessman, in a northern city that even before the recession was struggling to recover an economic identity after the collapse of manufacturing and mining in the 1980s. Yet he is convinced Osborne called the economy right – despite the three flatlining years after 2010, when the forecasts had to be downgraded over and over. Hill buys TINA, the Tory argument that There Is No Alternative: 'Osborne couldn't have done any different.' He sees the effects of the cuts in the libraries and in road maintenance. Sheffield council cut its grant to the museum of industrial heritage, where he's on the board. He worries about social care for the old. But the cuts were necessary, he believes.

Like many in secure, well-paid skilled work, Hill and Hawsons have been largely untouched by crash and recession, personally insulated from austerity and the cuts. During the past five years, they sailed comfortably by. And now, he says, things are on the up. 'At a chamber of commerce wine tasting last week, you could feel how confidence was returning. Bankers, solicitors, accountants, some of our clients, you feel a new buzz in the air.'

That's news all chancellors want to hear. 'Buzz' means extra revenue from VAT, national insurance and other taxes. Like chancellors before him, Osborne was delighted to see house prices rise, pushing up the related tax streams from stamp duty, inheritance and capital gains tax to their highest share of GDP for half a century. Rising prices pushed more transactions into the higher-rate bands; as a result, stamp duty raised £9.5bn in 2014 and was on course, the OBR said, to double in value by 2018. Similarly, the number of estates liable to inheritance tax was rising, with the tax itself producing an extra 11 per cent a year. Inheritance tax proceeds were heading towards 0.3 per cent of GDP, higher than Labour had ever got, even during the Denis Healey era when he merrily talked about squeezing till the pips squeaked. This wasn't a sign of Osborne's latent social democratic character, but the coarse arithmetic of fiscal drag. The threshold was frozen in 2009, with the result that more estates fell liable – from about one in 14 to nearer one in 10.

Nonetheless, the UK has a far from rigorous or fair system for taxing wealth. The total yield from capital taxes will still reach only 1.8 per cent of GDP in 2018, not much above its 1.6 per cent peak in 2008. Tax thinkers said the burden should be borne more by inert wealth, property and unearned income, but the earnings of hard work still bore more of the brunt. Latter-day Tories could never bring themselves to utter the words of their revered if maverick predecessor, Winston Churchill, who extolled estate or 'death' duty as 'a certain corrective against the development of the idle rich'.

(Less) Money Out

Public spending had increased by 3.2 per cent a year on average between 1956 and 2010 and by even more, 4.7 per cent, in the Labour years between 2000 and 2010. Osborne jammed on the brakes and made them squeal. Public spending is now falling by 0.3 per cent a year on average in real terms. Considering the cost of servicing debt and supporting more pensions and the cost of unemployment, the squeeze on every-thing else represents 'the most prolonged period of spending restraint since the second world war', according to the House of Commons library.

Osborne targeted welfare for families and people of working age, pensioners as ever protected, except those in the public sector. Also defence, where spending fell 8 per cent from 2011 to 2014. Cuts hit capital spending, civil service jobs, councils, police, prisons, probation, defence, universities, the immigration service, the arts – and regional and industrial support. The schools and NHS budgets were ringfenced, but that did not mean protecting spending per head. Or pay. The freeze on pay for clinical staff applying in 2015 means a real pay cut for the sixth year in a row. For equivalent jobs, public sector pay is now behind the private.

One exception to austerity was the 28 per cent real terms increase for the Department for International Development, which reached the UN target of 0.7 per cent of GDP for aid in April 2014. A small proportion of total spending, aid was a fig leaf for Liberal Democrats who voted through the other cuts. In September 2014 MPs approved a private member's bill making that 0.7 per cent a statutory commitment: only a handful of backbenchers voted against, including Philip Davies MP. The bill, he said, would push disapproving Tories into UKIP and only serve to keep 'Guardian-reading, sandal-wearing do-gooders' happy.

Elsewhere, the cuts were not scientific or strategic: the government deployed no evidence about what programmes and services were yielding good results for their costs. Ministers cut within their departments often without knowing what functions they were losing, mocking quangos and programmes whose names they didn't understand, later having to restore them fast.

Shrinking Public Sector

The coalition set upon the public sector. Over the four years from May 2010, public sector employment fell from 21.6 per cent of the UK workforce to 17.6 per cent, about 900,000 people, leaving 5.4 million in public sector jobs as of summer 2014, which is pretty much the figure when Labour took office in 1997. The IFS observed that the nature of the UK labour market was changing dramatically, especially where – in the north-east, Northern Ireland and Wales – people traditionally relied most on public employment. By 2013, the public workforce made up about one job in every five, a lower figure than at any point during the past four decades. Some public sector employees found their jobs were reclassified into the private sector – such as teachers in further education and sixth form colleges, and employees of nationalised banks. Employment totals in the NHS stayed the same; civil service full-time equivalents fell by 80,000.

The pay and conditions of local authority staff and civil servants had been under rightwing press attack for some time, amplified after the 2010 election. But simplistic pay comparison was usually misleading. It neglected the way outsourcing had reduced the proportion of blue-collar jobs in the public service and the fact that, because staff tended to be teachers, social workers, lawyers and engineers, they would inevitably be paid for their qualifications. But they made easy targets, still.

Osborne's inaugural budget in June 2010 froze pay for two years. Some staff, especially in health and local government, could rely on reasonably automatic increments, but for many the five years from the election saw their pay decline in real terms, provoking strikes but not the all-out confrontation some Tory hawks had hoped for. Osborne and Francis Maude, minister for the Cabinet Office, announced that public sector pensions would be cut by £2.8bn and employees would contribute 50 per cent more, without waiting for the review they themselves had commissioned from ex-Labour minister John Hutton. In addition, the price index for both existing and future public pensioners was to be switched, slicing at least a fifth off the value of their pension every succeeding decade. Public opinion warmed to the government's argument that public pensions were on average twice as generous as the private sector's (and two-thirds of private employees have no pension at all from their employers). Yet while 78,000 out of 4 million retired public pensioners do have pensions above the average wage, the average male public sector employee pension was just £4,000 a year and a woman's £2,800. Both the NAO and the OBR said firmly that future public pension commitments, already adjusted down by Labour, were affordable.

Cuts, But Who Bled?

Awareness of the cuts depended on who you were. The poorest and disabled people could hardly fail to notice if they had to pay council tax for the first time, or were struck by the bedroom tax. General perceptions are skewed by those with megaphones in well-heeled newsrooms. The under-reporting of the cuts, especially in welfare, was a kind of conspiracy to deceive.

Pollsters and trend-spotters regarded attitudes to tax and spend as thermostatic: when Labour governments spend, the public gradually turns against state generosity. Spending cuts by Tory governments sooner or later cause dissatisfaction and demands for more spending, as each round of cuts gets closer to the bone. But there are lags in perception. By October 2013, 40 per cent were telling pollsters they found public services worse. But 42 per cent found them the same and 15 per cent even reported them better.

At any one time, not many people have children in schools, and people only use maternity services for a very short time. Nurseries are of interest for perhaps five years in a family's life. University likewise, for a shortish time in the life cycle. Young adults use few services and see less point in them, until they have children. The crisis conditions in social care take most families by shocked surprise only when they suddenly need them for an aged parent. Concern for the NHS is universal because everyone fears they might fall ill or under a bus. But only one person in 50 is a heavy council service user at any given time. As long as there are no scandalous deaths among the frail, most voters might never notice the cuts.

But by late 2013, the mood was turning, seven out of 10 worried about social support. The cuts most noticed affected hospitals and care for the elderly. Difficulty getting a GP appointment registered with many, but potholes topped the list, as road mending was axed: 67 per cent said highway maintenance was worse. Libraries quickly became an early target for local authority cuts because their statutory obligations were less specific than for, say, child protection. Closure of branch libraries provoked demonstrations in many places and, in some, attempts to keep book borrowing going through volunteer schemes. A survey in 2014 asked about adult use and only 35 per cent said they had been in a library during the preceding 12 months, a big drop from the Labour era when, in 2006, 48 per cent had.

That fits the pattern of the age. Children don't vote and their parents are much less politically visible than elderly citizens, who do vote. Only poorer people and tenants need housing advice or a social fund for emergencies. Services for them are always the easiest to cut.

The Heaviest Cuts

Council spending was disproportionately hit, cut by 29.1 per cent between 2010 and 2015, taking inflation into account. Despite an ageing, increasing population, and more people in hardship, by 2015 councils will be spending in cash terms the same as they did nine years ago, in 2006. The cuts have been getting heavier each year, with big reductions of up to 6 per cent being made in the single year 2014–15.

Devolve the axe, ministers said: let councillors be blamed for shutting swimming pools. Time and again, confronted with complaints, ministers said it was up to councils how to spend their funds. They could increase council tax by up to 2 per cent, but if they went above that, they had to hold a local referendum – expensive and unlikely to be won. Councils by and large took it on the chin, protesting in private but not vigorously in public. Even Labour councils, additionally hit by changes in the way the government grant was distributed, were reluctant to say they weren't coping. They tended to boast to their voters about how well they were managing, which gave the government an easier ride.

Visits to frail old people in their homes by underpaid care workers lasting only 15 minutes became notorious. Social workers with caseloads of children at risk were burning out, constantly threatened with public shaming if they failed to rescue a child. Numbers in care rose as a result, costing councils more. Councils lost 2,000 youth worker jobs and closed 350 youth centres. There were too few childcare places in deprived areas that needed them most, children's centres closed or cut back on services within them.

Cuts have fallen heaviest on housing, highways and transport investment. Culture and the arts are in the firing line, which is why municipal museums are auctioning off paintings and statues. Parks are a precious resource, with most people living an urban life. But half of councils are considering selling them, the Heritage Lottery Fund found. Four out of five council park departments had lost skilled management staff since 2010. Yet – here perhaps lies the reason the public were so oblivious – the condition of public spaces had improved and more people were using municipal green spaces.

In town and county halls, however, the pain was real. Doncaster council is cutting 1,200 jobs to 2017, closing old people's homes, increasing fees and charges. By 2018 Birmingham is to cut its workforce from 13,000 to 7,000 – job losses double those the city suffered when the Longbridge car plant was shut a decade ago. That's compared with 2010's workforce of 20,000. Coventry city council lost 1,000 staff from 2010–14, and is now planning to make a further 1,000 staff redundant in order to save £60m by 2018. 'There's no doubt we will be a smaller organisation and delivering fewer services with fewer employees,' Cllr Damian Gannon, the finance chief declared.[6] It wasn't just poor inner cities. In another part of England, West Somerset district council, faced with an unbridgeable budget gap, warned that it would have to give up altogether and become 'virtual'.

Derbyshire's lollipop ladies, where we began this chapter, are going in a second round of job cuts. 'The government has left us with no choice,' complained council leader Anne Western.[7]

6

Waging War on Welfare

If an abiding impression from the Thatcher era was Covent Garden opera-goers stumbling over rough sleepers in the Strand, Cameron's is food banks. A million people are being fed from them, though the Trussell Trust says its 400 banks are still meeting only a fraction of the need. They are spread across the UK, often hidden from public view in well-off areas, inside churches to avoid embarrassment for the recipients of food parcels and shame for the rest of us. Outside supermarkets, volunteers collect tins, baby food and toilet paper. Shoppers give generously: the polls show they supported benefit cuts in general, but were shocked to find so many fellow citizens in one of the most affluent countries in the world reduced to queuing for handouts.

During the 1980s, the Church of England published a report called 'Faith in the City', which was sharply critical of growing deprivation. At Easter 2014, 45 bishops wrote that policies had created a 'national crisis' and leaders' moral duty was to act on the growing numbers going hungry. Cameron ignored them and even tried to claim that food banks were a manifestation of the big society. His ministers were less charitable. Lord Freud sniffed at 'an almost infinite demand for a free good', apparently unaware that use of the banks is carefully rationed by means of vouchers from councils and his own Department for Work and Pensions jobcentres. Duncan Smith, in remarkably unchristian spirit, sneered that the Trussell Trust was politically motivated, as if it were deliberately giving people food in order to shame the government.

When we visited, St George's Crypt in Armley in Leeds was taking delivery of crates of free fresh bread from a generous local bakery: food banks touched the national conscience. Among those we met in Leeds were many bedroom tax victims. One was a chronically depressed man who most days couldn't leave his flat, made desperate by a demand to pay £14 a week from his £72 benefits for his spare room. Spare? His grown son comes to care for him when he sinks into crisis. Here, too, was a woman in her 50s with learning difficulties, dumbfounded at losing all her benefits for an infraction of rules she can't comprehend: letters and appointments were often made deliberately confusing.

Another Leeds woman, in tears, had worked all her life until recently overcome by osteoarthritis. The bedroom tax tipped her over the edge, but she was unusually lucky and had found somewhere smaller to move into, swapping with another council tenant in need of more room for her children. But she can't move until she pays £300 in bedroom tax arrears, which just go on building.

Now his sons have moved out, a 59-year-old widower with a recent heart bypass must pay the £18 a week room tax, which has left him destitute. 'I've always lived here, my friends are here, I've redone my home over the years, put in the fireplace, crazy-paved the garden, I can't go.' But he can't pay either – and there's nowhere smaller to move to.

In a council office we visited in Stoke-on-Trent, now shut, queues of people and staff were struggling to answer the phones. Some callers were in tears, others shouting in frustration after a series of rebuffs; some have mental health problems. Jobcentres used to pay out small sums to the utterly destitute from the Social Fund; it was abolished, with responsibility for emergency aid transferred to councils. But they lack cash; in Stoke, council staff were handing out vouchers for charity food, and for those who could walk no further, they kept an emergency cupboard with beans, pasta and tinned tomatoes, but only for those they could check on their database. For some they could top up electricity and gas keys.

Entrenching Family Poverty

Staff sighed that the DWP office in the city sent them people it had disqualified or whose benefits were delayed in a chaotic system. DWP harshness was not random. It followed inexorably from the announcement a month after the coalition came to power that the social security budget would be cut by £18bn, a total later extended to £25bn. This was the 'main burden' of Osborne's deficit reduction plan we described in the previous chapter. The DWP took by far the heaviest hit. Benefits cuts were to fall hardest on people of working age and their children, on disabled people, but not on pensioners.

In other countries, too, people of working age were in the firing line – in 2012 more than two-thirds of OECD states were cutting spending on benefits. But, the OECD noted, the UK welfare system is entrenching poverty for families, in or out of work. 'As benefit reductions cumulate over time, it could also partly reverse progress made over the past decade in reducing child poverty, and create a need for costly social interventions in the future.'[1]

Another UK characteristic was growing public intolerance of welfare, fanned by the government. In 1999 four in 10 thought the state should spend more on welfare, even at the expense of higher taxes. Ten years later this was down to two in 10. Public hostility had, it seemed, increased in years when social benefits rose in real terms. The reasons for that growth were more complicated than socialist generosity: the bill had risen due to disability, low pay and ageing. But here was a ripe political opportunity: the coalition could make cuts and score points with the public.

Cameron's U-turn on the Poor

In his cautious years, Cameron broke with old Tory dicta by declaring that no, wealth doesn't trickle down to the poor, nor does the rising tide lift all boats. We went to Easterhouse, the sprawling estate on the outskirts of Glasgow, where Duncan Smith once claimed to have had an epiphany that transformed him into a champion of the poor. Bob Holman, the renowned community organiser, was sitting in the cafe run by unemployed volunteers he founded years ago. Duncan Smith, penitential, had been photographed in front of an evocatively boarded-up tenement – an opportunity set up by Tim Montgomerie, his adviser, later a Murdoch editor. The purpose of the visit, Montgomerie had said, was to display 'compassionate Conservatism'. Holman shakes his head in disbelief at what Duncan Smith has done since to those who formed his backdrop.

In the campaign specific promises were made. Child benefit would not be means-tested. (It was.) Labour's education maintenance allowance to help teenagers stay in school would stay. (It was abolished.) No disabled child would ever suffer. (Many did.) Looking at what happened to social security, the 'coup' metaphor is given added emphasis. A sincere, fair-minded government, even one of the centre right, might have come to power and said: the fiscal situation is terrible, Labour did not let on how bad it is and it needs dramatic action, but with the pain fairly shared. But this government piled the deficit burden on the backs of the poorest, not by accident but with intent. Then – this was Duncan Smith's specialty – it used the DWP press office to conduct a campaign of vilification and stigmatisation of those claiming social benefits. The DWP's relationship with the truth was fleeting. 'A life on benefits will no longer be an option,' he said in 2011, implying a dense, swarming population of lifelong idlers when, in fact, of the 1.5 million claiming the jobseeker's allowance, barely 0.3 per cent had been claiming for five years or more – a grand total of 4,220 people.

There was no grand blueprint: the welfare state was cut with a rusty axe wielded with malice. Free-market radicals believed that widening inequality was functional, as lowering benefits must surely drive more people into work and keep wages usefully low; they forgot that workers are also consumers and taxpayers and low wages suppress demand and revenues. But who cared if the economics was erroneous when there was a culture war to be fought? Osborne exploited the case of a benefits-dependent household where the father was imprisoned for causing the death by fire of six of his 17 children. However atypical, it was too good to ignore: 'I think there is a question for the taxpayers who pay for the welfare state – subsidising lifestyles like that.' The chancellor might have mentioned his gratitude that £16bn in benefits goes unclaimed by those who are entitled. Or compare minor social security fraud with massive tax evasion, proportionately a much greater offence against the public purse. They were playing to the gallery, and the public, it seemed, wanted to believe the ministers' and media one-sided evidence.

Polluting Hearts and Minds

The DWP budget was a soft target. Few claimants are Tory voters, and claimants had no voice beyond the bleating of charities and clergy. Each family affected would struggle alone and unseen behind their front doors, making no political noise. Contrary to the stories, people did not like claiming because they knew, and evidence confirmed, that work increased life satisfaction while dependency had a measurably negative effect on wellbeing. Channel 4's *Benefits Street* was a notorious exploitation of people living on James Turner Street in Birmingham, who proved the old adage about cameras creating their own reality.

But the focus groups and polls said 'cut'. YouGov found 76 per cent in favour, along with 71 per cent of Labour voters. Duncan Smith's charge that 'the incubation of the benefits culture was Labour's greatest sin' struck home: when asked to associate something with Labour, the public no longer selected the old cloth cap symbol of the working man, but instead picked a fat man lolling on a settee with a can of lager watching daytime television.

That social security was 'spiralling out of control' was a persuasive argument as long as no one examined any details. The DWP's budget was 23 per cent of public spending, but half of it went to pensioners and there was nothing any government could do to prevent baby boomers claiming their due, even if the retirement age was raised. As for working-age benefits, they had become miserly, with an adult expected to live on just £72.40 a week. Only 3 per cent of total benefit spending went to the unemployed, whatever the public believed.

Ministers had to accept there is a minimum a 'hard-working family' needs to survive: that was the basis of tax credits. But more were qualifying for these in-work benefits as better full-time jobs were lost and replaced by low-paid and part-time employment. In response, tax credits were cut, for example the allowance previously given for reductions in income during the year. Labour had brought in an official minimum wage but its value had been allowed to fall by £1,000.

It was the same story with housing benefit. Private rents were skyrocketing, pulling up the cost of the housing benefit bill. Addressing these basic market dysfunctions was never on the coalition's agenda, so the social security budget took the strain and the government blamed the poor.

War on Welfare

The most devastating cut was invisible to the naked eye. From 2010 all benefits (other than pensions) have been uprated annually using a lower measure of inflation, the Consumer Prices Index (CPI), which does not include housing. (The higher measure, the Retail Prices Index (RPI), was kept for tax thresholds and grants to business – and pensions.) As a result claimants are losing at least 10 per cent of the value of their benefits over the next decade and onwards. This not only cut the DWP bill, it guaranteed the poor would go on getting poorer in relation to everyone else. Here, the Tory legacy is formidable. In addition, the government decreed an even more direct cut in the value of benefits: from 2013 to 2016 no payments are to increase by more than 1 per cent – except pensions.

Twin caps were set, one affecting individual households, the other the overall budget. Stopping any household getting more in benefits than the national average income of £26,000 sounded absurdly generous to many, but it caught some 67,000 families, mainly in London and the south-east, mainly larger households paying sky-high rents for expensive temporary private housing where councils had billeted them. By the end of 2013, over 27,000 households had been capped, their average benefit cut £83 a week, leaving many with little to live on after rents were paid.

In addition, the coalition announced a limit on the total benefits bill from 2015, excluding pensions and jobseeker's allowance. (The cost of the latter for the unemployed rises or falls according to the economy and unemployment levels.)

Slash and Burn

At high speed, ministers slashed in all directions. Local authorities were conscripted as agents in hounding the poor: council officers were made to administer the bedroom tax. The benefit helping poor households pay council tax was cut. From April 2013 councils had to devise their own systems, but must exempt pensioners. Support grants were cut by 10 per cent, so councils either passed the cut on to the poorest or subsidised payments out of their depleting resources. The majority pushed the reduction on, but within a year arrears were mounting among the 2.3 million households required to pay council tax for the first time.

In 2013–14 Liverpool collected about two-thirds of the council tax due from poor households, leaving the city short by £3.5m, with similar non-payment rates in Birmingham. In London, 15,000 claimants' debts had been referred by councils to bailiffs.

With the Social Fund, some of its previous value was allocated to councils and the devolved administrations, but from 2015 you are on your own, chums, as Duncan Smith was wont to say. 'Local authorities will still be able to provide to the appropriate level,' the government said speciously. We saw in Stoke how they struggle. Different cuts rained down on the same households time and again, but the government refused to do the research to show the cumulative impact. Jonathan Portes of NIESR pointed out 'an almost complete lack of attention to cross-cutting issues' as to how the cuts 'combine to produce disproportionate impacts on vulnerable groups'.[2] An exceptional meanness: 25,000 families where under-16s struggle to look after a sick parent have been hit, as adult dependents lost between £55 and £70 a week in severe disability premium.

Punishing Claimants

To ratchet up the pressure, the DWP set thresholds for the number of people to be thrown off benefits by Jobcentre Plus, its network of offices where claimants were processed. Duncan Smith kept denying these were 'targets' but, failing to hit them, staff were still fired. Many claimants are semi-literate, mentally ill or have bad English and can't use the internet; try finding a payphone to take coins to call the DWP office. A study found letters going astray, going unread, yet still sanctions – reductions in payments – were applied.

If the screw was tightened on claimants, life for the screw-tighteners got tough, too. A DWP official in a Midlands Jobcentre Plus office agreed to meet if she could remain anonymous. We met – we'll call her Janet – in a railway hotel. She is a junior manager who has worked for the DWP for over 10 years. She used to like the work when it was about trying to help people into jobs and sort out their problems.

She'd had her own difficulties, having been out of work, leaving a retail job in order to care for her sick mother. But she is allowed no sympathy for claimants. The new rule is to excise as many claimants as possible from the benefits register in any way possible, however unscrupulous and sometimes downright cruel. It meant poor people getting even less, many 'sanctioned' off benefits to live on thin air.

'You park your conscience at the door. Sanctions are applied for anything at all, just to hit the targets.' Officially the government always denied having targets to reduce claimant numbers. The word 'target' is not used. Janet gives us a printed sheet displaying 37 'spinning plates', inside each is a number; numbers actually reached are written in green for a hit, red for a miss.

'Many claimants don't know what's happened until their benefit suddenly stops. Many can hardly read. It's very easy to hand someone two sheets of A4 and get them to agree to 50 "steps" towards work, but they don't know what a step is, so they're sanctioned; their claim is shut down and they disappear from the figures.' People are often sanctioned for failing to appear at appointments they never knew about. If they call to rearrange, 'we don't answer the phones'. A flowchart on the wall shows how to raise a successful sanction. Someone with a disability who is knocked off employment and support allowance (ESA) can lodge a further claim while awaiting an appeal. 'But we are explicitly forbidden from telling them that – it says so in black and white in the briefing pack. These often very ill, confused and low-capability people are easy meat.'

ESA is the main benefit for people who are ill or incapacitated – there are about 2.5 million claimants. She showed us the spinning plates that specified 'off flows' at 50.5 per cent. It was a target the office had narrowly missed. Managers verbally instructed DWP staff to 'disrupt and upset' claimants – in other words, bully them. The official manual says 'offer further support'.

She showed us a letter sent to vulnerable claimants who, because of their condition, are not legally required to present themselves in the office; its wording is so deliberately ambiguous that most recipients could only read it as an instruction to attend, so the very ill stagger in. Tricks are played. People who have paid national insurance contributions qualify for a year on a type of ESA available regardless of claimants' income. If they are still ill at the end of a year, they have to fill in a form to qualify for a means-tested version of ESA. But offices are forbidden to stock these forms.

She says the DWP is striving in whatever way it can to make it as difficult as possible to pursue a claim. Then, catch-22, 'when people drop out the DWP will say that's a sign they must have been cheating in the first place'. Which is exactly what Duncan Smith says in his speeches.

Targets may often be a necessary tool of management, but they have perverse consequences too, Janet says. 'Advisers are so busy knocking off easy cases, the low-hanging fruit, that they have no time to chase up devious criminal gangs and fraudsters who take much longer to catch.'

Most of the other staff are decent people, Janet says, but some have a real antipathy to claimants. Pressure is applied by senior managers. There is an almost hysterical tone of whipping up the staff to hit all targets, with a combination of threats and US-style motivational management techniques, oddly ill-suited to the work of Jobcentre Plus advisers.

Janet sticks it out for fear of not getting another job. 'What makes me sad is that I can't do some of the things that used to make this job worthwhile. For example, there's a woman who has been on ESA for over 20 years with such bad agoraphobia that she hasn't been out of her house ever in all that time. I was working on getting her out, with tiny steps. We were helping her to see how her life could be better, but it was going to be a long process. In the old days, I think we'd have got her there.' But another perversity of the targets is that once a claimant has passed the 65-week target for weaning them off benefits, then they are for ever a lost cause. They will never be a green number on the spinning plates and so there is no point in investing any more time on them. 'She became a dead loss to our success rates, so she was abandoned. She won't be bothered by us any more, but she won't be helped either.'

Undeserving Disability

Traditionally, politicians always regarded disabled people, along with pensioners, as the most 'deserving' of state support. But now Remploy, the government-owned company providing employment for people with disabilities, was closed down. The DWP wanted 600,000 disabled people off benefits by 2018, to make savings of £3bn. The method: everyone on ESA is to be put through tougher work capability assessments (which had begun under Labour). Proof that these work tests are crude comes from the strikingly low rate at which ESA claimants find work.

The payment to cover extra costs and transport, the disability living allowance (DLA), was cut in value by 20 per cent: 643,000 disabled people would lose out, saving £2bn. There was no rhyme, reason or research to suggest a fifth of disabled people could do without this help. The 3.1 million DLA claimants had tripled in number since it was introduced in 1992 by the Major government and the DWP knew the reason. The allowance had not originally been available to pensioners but, when they retired, those already on DLA could keep it, pushing up the numbers every year. There has been no increase in the numbers of people below pension age claiming for disabling physical conditions, despite population growth; back injuries have decreased with the decline of heavy industry.

On paper, the UK does look relatively generous in benefits for disabled people – in 2012–13 the DLA cost £13.7bn for 3.3 million claimants – but that's because we tend to give cash so that people can choose their own transport or care, while other countries spend more on direct services.

DLA for adults is now being replaced by a new, more limited personal independence payment (PIP), a non-means-tested benefit with components for mobility and daily living, paying between £21 and £134 per week and available to 16- to 64-year-olds. The qualifying tests are stiffer and new claimants go for assessment to private firms contracted to the DWP. Among them were the French-owned firm Atos, which formerly had been an IT provider, and Capita, adminis-trator of the London congestion charge. Atos testing centres became notorious as sites of humiliation and degradation for many. Delays built up, often leaving terminally ill claim-ants with no support, some dying first. Claiming required completion of a 55-page online form, beyond the ability of many sick people. The government panicked at the difficulty of putting existing DLA claimants through the tests, and deferred this expansion, leaving the victor at the next election a nasty legacy.

Macmillan Cancer Support was just one of the charities that saw at first hand the disastrous effect of administrative delays in the changeover to PIP. 'Heartbreaking, truly aston-ishing, I've never seen anything like this,' senior benefits adviser Emma Cross told us. Among her mountain of PIP cases is a mother being treated with chemotherapy for bowel cancer, whose operation left her with a colostomy bag. She gave up work and her husband had to give up his job to care for her and their two-year-old child, taking his wife to her frequent hospital appointments. Their claim had been lodged six months previously, since when they had heard nothing, no one answering their enquiries, just another case lost in the gigantic backlog.

Maladministration did not start with the coalition, but lack of capacity to handle multiple changes within the tightest of time-tables and a reduced DWP staff were a result of Duncan Smith's overweening ambition. Contracts signed by ministers showed more solicitude to the firms than the people they were making money from testing. The PAC found Atos's tender 'grossly misleading': it pretended to have hundreds of test centres inside hospitals, when in reality it had few, forcing people to travel miles, often to offices hard to access in a wheelchair.

Work is the Best Welfare

All countries across the western world were trying to move people off welfare, but the OECD found that UK spending on actively getting people into jobs was 'very low', adding that 'getting people off benefits without sufficient efforts to help them into employment could incur large societal costs in the long run'. As with Labour, the message was that work had to be the antidote to poverty (which it increasingly was not), so the unemployed and the disabled must be pressured into work.

Those out of a job for a year were enrolled in the Work Programme. Launched in June 2011, this replaced more than 20 previous welfare-into-work schemes. In it, the unemployed became a profit centre for private companies offering back-to-work schemes, though they would only get paid when a claimant stayed in a job for six months. It was meant to be win-win: the state paid little if the contractor failed, but if a claimant moved off the dole, costs would be recovered from savings on their benefit and their tax and national insurance payments.

The government's approach was grandiose and unempirical. No one ever quite explained what magic contractors would use in poor areas where jobs were still scarce. An unknown propor-tion of claimants on the programme were 'deadweight': of the 296,000 people on the programme employed by March 2014, many would have found work anyway. Without special help,

93 per cent of unemployed people usually find work within 15 months.

But profits failed to flow. The companies lobbied ministers to soften terms, unafraid to use the 'too big to fail' argument, since the DWP often had nowhere else to send claimants. The model was not magic after all. The NAO found that over its first years, the Work Programme accomplished no more than its predecessors; it found jobs for just one in six and was twice as successful in the south as the north: the state of the labour market, not the programme, was key. Contractors spent less on more difficult cases, often just parking them. In the case of disabled people, the Work Programme found jobs for just one in 20. By mid-2014 the numbers of people claiming ESA were starting to rise, because of problems with assessment. Atos decided disabled people were not profitable enough and walked away from its contract to assess ESA claims.

The government had cut off its nose to spite its face by immediately cancelling Labour's Future Jobs Fund, which had guaranteed a minimum-wage job to long-term unemployed young people. It had been one of the most successful back-to-work schemes: NIESR research showed that abolition tripled the number of jobless 16- to 24-year-olds. Another group likely to swell the numbers of applicants for benefits in future years were those temporarily sick while in jobs, perhaps becoming stressed or depressed. The government commissioned a study by Professor Dame Carol Black. The Fit for Work service she envisaged – intervening to help people before they became disabled and unable to work – would have required not just government backing but the engagement of employers. They, however, were 'conspicuously absent from the policy process', the OECD noted, also registering big regional variations in the availability of psychological therapies of precisely the kind that could bring tomorrow's benefits bill down.

Duncan Smith's Big Idea – Universal Credit

Here was a benefit system buckling seriously under the pressure of new policies, staff cuts and badly drawn outsourcing contracts. Hubristically, Duncan Smith made things even worse.

He arrived with Universal Credit, his master plan, but also took on Osborne's enormous cut in his budget. The two were irreconcilable. Universal Credit meant monumental resculpturing of HMRC's tax and the DWP's benefit systems, updating every citizen's changing income and circumstances each month. Six different benefits would be melded, so that when someone's income or family situation changed, their benefits and tax would be automatically adjusted up or down.

Nothing wrong with the aspiration, all parties agreed. Previous DWP secretaries had shared it. But the risk of upheaval and the costs of the IT changes were tremendous. We may never know whether the DWP's top civil servant, Robert Devereux, ever spelled them out to his imperious master; later, Duncan Smith sought to shift the blame and get him fired. From the earliest press conferences Duncan Smith showed his grasp of detail was strictly limited. But he alone would resolve problems that had bedevilled the Poor Law and defeated Lloyd George and Beveridge. To make sure work always pays, benefits have to be withdrawn gradually as people earn more, without steep cliff edges. But that requires going on paying benefits to people quite high up the earning scale before gently tapering them away, and that's expensive. Duncan Smith promised everyone would always be better off in work than out of work; hundreds of thousands would work because of better incentives and simpler processes, while administrative costs were reduced and fraud eliminated. In fantasy land, Universal Credit would produce a net saving of £38bn over the years to 2023 and cost only £2.4bn to implement. By itself Universal Credit would have been a tremendous achievement but the government also ordained the changes to disability benefits, caps and new child maintenance. All this was to be done with fewer DWP staff and cuts in departmental running costs of £2.7bn.

These dilemmas would not be resolved by better computer systems, even if HMRC and the DWP could construct them. Predictably the new IT kept escalating in cost, with armies of consultants recruited and deadlines missed. Eventually alarm bells rang in the Treasury and Osborne's aides started to spread the word that Duncan Smith was simply not up to it. Caught on the back foot, the DWP fought a fierce legal battle to prevent the publication of its risk register, the document that listed the likely problems. This provoked the Information Commissioner, but so far it has successfully managed to conceal the total cost.

As for claimants, merging six benefits does not simplify things, because they must still all be separately assessed. The application form for Universal Credit spills over 53 pages. Human lives are not simple or stable, so any just and comprehensive benefit systems will be complex too: an illness, a divorce, a new child, a new part-time job – circumstances change constantly. Add in Duncan Smith's new requirement: every claimant must apply online. The poorest fifth often had no internet at home; many are poor readers and the official forms spin the heads of even Citizens Advice Bureau experts. A cynic would say it's a recipe for preventing claims being made.

Making Work Pay

Mighty battalions are willing to push brooms, clean toilets, labour in call centres and care homes for not that much more than benefits would pay, and sometimes for less. Few people make nice calculations – they just work. Osborne frequently talked of the hardworking (it became one word in party political slogans) leaving home at dawn, only to see the drawn blinds of their lazy non-working neighbours. But those drawn blinds were far more often shift workers on zero hours.

The coalition pledged that work would always pay, but most Universal Credit claimants would only ever see minor improvements in rewards for work. Credits would be rapidly removed if their earnings rose. Under the old system many claimants lost 75p in tax credit out of every extra pound they earned. Under the new system most would still lose 65p in the pound. Better, yes, but a tiny margin to justify all the cost and upheaval.

In a JRF study Donald Hirsch said that under Universal Credit, families working full-time would find themselves with less money in hand than if they worked part-time. 'If a family with young children works more than 10 hours they will generally earn virtually nothing extra, and some will end up with less.'[3]

A father working full-time on the minimum wage would take home £346 a week (with credits). Let's say the mother in the family also gets a full-time job, five days a week. Their total income would improve by only £29, as credits are withdrawn. Their income would actually be greater if she only worked three days a week. So the system builds in an incentive for the man to be 'the breadwinner', depriving the labour market of the woman's skills, and ending up costing the system more in the long run.

A disincentive for mothers to work is dangerous, both for them and for the future costs to the state. A third of parents separate and mothers who lose touch with the workplace will be ill-equipped to become breadwinners for their children, and so will fall back on the state. Perhaps Duncan Smith, despite his visit to Easterhouse, despite his thinktank reports, simply did not understand people's lives on the edge. Perhaps his theoretical beliefs trumped quotidian reality. Whatever the reason, almost everything he claimed for Universal Credit proved false. It is, however, still nowhere near proper introduction. A million people, he said, would be on Universal Credit by April 2014: in reality only 7,000 single people with no children were then in a handful of pilot schemes.

As it dawned that for many families Universal Credit offered no incentive to work full-time, Duncan Smith brandished a new stick. For the first time people working part-time would be penal-ised – their benefits cut – if they couldn't prove they were seeking more hours. 'In-work conditionality' was the new jargon.

Low pay, zero hours, short hours and enforced self-employ-ment on low earnings were part of the story hidden behind the employment figures. Already an estimated 1.4 million part-timers were looking to add hours, but now these people, the underemployed, were to be treated as skivers too. Couples who couldn't find 24 hours of work between them were by 2013 suffering a £4,000 cut in benefit, leaving people frantic for extra hours of work and giving employers the whip hand.

Housing Disbenefits

Housing costs vary markedly, depending on space, family size and location, location, location; they are one reason why Universal Credit could never actually be 'universal'. The number of people in work drawing housing benefit is set to double between 2010 and 2018, pushing up its real-terms cost from £3bn to £5.5bn. Over 14 per cent of the total social security bill is now going to mostly private landlords. That's because rents are rising and because there are more people in low-paid work, who can't afford accommodation.

To stem the increasing bill, the government set benefit at a maximum of £290 a week for two bedrooms – which may sound a lot in Huddersfield, but doesn't go far for a family of four seeking a flat in Haringey or Hammersmith. This cap would force landlords to keep their rents to within housing benefits limits, said ministers, but demand was so strong that landlords had no trouble letting to those not on housing benefit instead.

To instil 'responsibility', rents would no longer be paid directly to landlords by the DWP, but monthly to tenants. Landlords took fright at possible arrears and many began to refuse to let to housing benefit tenants. (Duncan Smith thought one 'behavioural response' to less housing would be 'lowered fertility rates', an objective he presumably did not check with the pope.) Arrears have been mounting, among council and housing association tenants.

Bedroom Tax

To sweat the available stock of dwellings, the government resorted to a crude measure. Labour had worried about how to balance the number of people in a household and the available flats and houses; housing managers tried to ease older people out of family homes into local, specially built smaller homes – but there were few of these. The coalition, prejudiced against social housing, did no research and rushed ahead with a cut in housing benefit for all working-age tenants deemed to have 'spare' rooms. Pensioners – who had by far the most unused space – were again protected. The government tried to call it 'removal of the spare room subsidy' but inevitably it became the bedroom tax. It was a class measure, a demonstration of housing inequality, when most 'spare' rooms are in homes owned by their occupiers.

Half a million households in Great Britain, or one in eight social tenants, were affected. They were allowed a room per person except for couples. Under-10s and those aged 10–15 of the same sex could share. Housing benefit was cut by 14 per cent – an average of £12 a week – for one spare room and 25 per cent for two. Tales of injustice erupted everywhere. A mother was charged for the rooms of her two sons serving in the forces in Afghanistan; a Hartlepool family were billed for the empty room left by their 10-year-old daughter who had recently died. Disabled couples needed extra space for kidney dialysis equipment, a mentally handicapped child who shouted in the night needed a room of her own, a dying cancer patient needed a room apart from her husband. The government rushed to exempt forces families and foster parents with spare rooms to take in emergency children, but not the sick and the disabled.

As a way of shaking up the stock, it failed. Only 4.5 per cent of affected claimants downsized in the first year. The DWP's own research found people did not want to move because of their work, friends and family nearby – and above all their children's schooling.[4] Two-thirds of those affected were disabled, 220,000 had children. The average bedroom tax was £720 a year, a huge hit on low-income households. Very few took lodgers. Many scrimped, borrowed or went into arrears on the rent. If evicted, councils had no spare smaller flats and instead they had to be placed in the private sector: absurd, because their far higher rents had to be picked up by housing benefit, costing the state more. In theory, the bedroom tax was supposed to save £500m but no official account was kept to reveal the extra costs to councils, housing associations and the housing benefit bill. Here was a perversity: Stoke-on-Trent council's stock was almost all larger homes, and they now had three-bedroom houses left vacant, as young families couldn't afford to move in and pay the bedroom tax on the extra room.

At the Treasury, Danny Alexander was embarrassed when his father, chairman of the Lochaber Housing Association, protested that the bedroom tax was 'particularly unfair' as it penalised both tenants and landlords for 'not being able to magic up a supply of smaller properties'. In July 2014, the Liberal Democrats suddenly about-turned and announced they were now against it, too.

Did the Big Stick Work?

Better employment figures were claimed as proof the medicine was effective, and sent people back to work. Unfortunately, there was no evidence the unemployed were finding work more quickly than before the recession. When Duncan Smith claimed the benefit cap was why people in high-rent accommodation were taking jobs, he earned a reprimand from the UK Statistics Authority: jobs were, in fact, turning over at the normal rate and the threat of the cap had no measured effect. The OECD said sanctions, in various countries, did reduce the duration of unemployment but also drove people out of the labour force – the Duncan Smith regime knocked off benefits many who were not going into jobs, often the vulnerable, surviving penury through help from family, friends and food banks. It was the end of the welfare idea, that the state put a safety net under those who simply had nothing else.

Governments are always inevitably conflicted, with generosity at war with meanness, laxity with stringency, moral decency at odds with fear of moral hazard. But nothing stamps the character of the government as clearly as its assault on the welfare state and its campaign to turn public opinion against the needy. Its legacy is a cruel, less civilised country and a hardening of hearts.

7

Recovery – Pallid and Partial

During recent months George Osborne has barely been seen on television unless wearing a hard hat, surrounded by workers in high-vis jackets. The subliminal message is chancellor as saviour, rebalancing the economy towards manufacturing and construction. Unfortunately, the statistics didn't back up the TV pictures. You could also read another symbol into the photo ops: here is a Tory who, by upbringing and party affiliation, regards staff as decorative background, indifferent to the growing gap between their and their bosses' pay.

The chancellor's trips were adverts for reconstruction and renewal. But the storyboard had lost key pages: investment had not picked up. Adjusted for depreciation, private sector capital investment was £43bn in 2008 but only £14bn in 2013. The building site pilgrimages were also meant to dissociate the chancellor from class. When up late preparing his 2013 budget, he tweeted a picture of the hamburger he was eating at his desk to show how hard he was working for the people, only to be mocked for eating not a Big Mac but a Byron burger, an upper-class brand. The incident echoed his pasty pasting. Perhaps the budget's subliminal message was that our future lies more in low-wage burger flipping than in well-paid making and exporting things.

Wearing a blue hard hat made Osborne look distinctly like a Lego man, the *Daily Mirror* joshed. But he could take the brickbats if we really were now seeing the long-awaited recovery, and soon enough indicators were arrowing up to allow him to declare victory in time for the 2015 election. We will spend the next few years regretting how hollow it turns out to be.

Renewed Growth, For Some

The ONS said the decline in living standards finally came to an end in 2012–13, with median household real income about the same as in the previous year, but it remained 6 per cent lower than before the crisis. Growth had returned. Yet it was lopsided, dependent on services; manufacturing and construction were still below pre-recession peaks. Private house building had picked up with starts 21 per cent higher in 2013 than the preceding year, though it won't be until 2017 that construction reaches 2007's levels – and they were not so high. Office building steamed ahead in London and the south-east – aided by the public sector rail schemes – but had a long way to go to compensate for the 13 per cent cut in the volume of school, hospital and similar building work under the coalition. Pundits prescribed an investment boom to improve supply and increase the economy's capacity to export, as the balance of external payments was showing real strain. But instead growth was powered, once again, by consumer credit. Households are still burdened by debt, on average 140 per cent of disposable income. Mortgages that represent several multiples of the borrower's annual income were accounting for a higher proportion of new lending than ever before, not productive lending to small business. Plan Osborne was based on exports rallying; instead the UK trade deficit worsened.

Despite this weakness, fiscal policy was deemed to have 'earned credibility' in the phrase used by the OECD, reporting in 2013. Here is where economics borders on magic. How are confidence and credibility measured? Are they any more than one lot of rich people (brokers and investors) judging that a government that is less likely to tax them must be better than another government that might? When the chief executive of Deloitte UK says, 'All political parties need to be focused on ensuring they don't kill off an economic recovery', the incantation has ideological purpose: he is warning against policies that would affect the material interests of Deloitte's sources of profit.[1] The OECD typically tried to have it every which way. Despite lauding Osborne, it was worried about 'inequality'. The UK government, it said, covering all bases, should simultaneously pursue growth-enhancing and inequality-reducing reforms.

No one quite understood why, but total private sector employment increased at a remarkable rate, by an extra 1.6 million jobs between spring 2011 and 2014, without pushing up economic growth. The arithmetical answer was lack of productivity growth: more people in work did not add to the total of output. GDP expanded by around 3 per cent in 2014, with prospects of 2.4 per cent in 2015; unemployment was now 6.5 per cent and inflation was 2 per cent. But, still, in 2015 average household incomes are likely to be well below their 2009 peak. GDP is growing partly because population is growing. It's the amount of money individuals and families have that matters and GDP per head is still below its pre-recession levels.

Recovery was bound to arrive sooner or later; the ground on which to judge the coalition is its quality and sustainability. In Osborne's first budget he pledged to build a new sort of economic model, 'to raise from the ruins of an economy built on debt a new, balanced economy where we save, invest and export'. On that measure, over the five years, he failed. Instead of investing, FTSE 100 companies piled up cash on their balance sheets, reaching an all-time high of £166bn (the banks not included), much of it secreted away in accounts in tax havens. Pundits asked why it had all taken so long despite, as *Guardian* economics editor Larry Elliott caustically put it, revisiting 'the failed debt-sodden splurges of unsustainable growth Britain has seen in the past'[2]: easy money, shovel-loads of cash for the banks and mortgage help schemes surely would stimulate animal spirits.

British business hadn't exactly rallied to the flag, despite historically low interest rates, big cuts in corporation tax, receptions in No 10 and deathly silence around the cabinet table on the subject of boardroom greed and governance failure in companies. What if – plenty of evidence for this – British business was itself part of the problem, and it was getting worse? 'We're faced', said Peter Aycliffe, president of the Chartered Institute of Management, 'with a ticking time bomb of myopic management, with widespread underinvestment in the next generation of leaders.'[3]

Debt had been a cause of recession but more borrowing became the solution. As for exports, despite sterling's fall in value, foreign trade had not been galvanised. 'Disappointing', said Vince Cable, blaming his cabinet colleagues' views on Europe for creating investment uncertainty. In this chapter, unlike others, we have to evaluate the presence in the government of a senior Liberal Democrat, economically literate and apparently unhappy with its direction of travel – but whose pithy asides were rarely followed up. Cable had a habit of coming on like Cassandra, as when in a lecture to the Royal Economic Society he prophesied on the sustainability of recovery: 'We cannot risk another property-linked boom-bust cycle.' But he presided over a commercial landscape where house prices rocketed as households were 'dissaving' and borrowing more to support spending.

Shopping but Earning Less

And spending went on. Travelling around Britain and Northern Ireland over the past two years we saw shoppers queuing at the Tesco checkout in Mart Road, Dingwall, the Saturday bustle in the Victoria Square shopping centre in Belfast, the May evening throngs in North Laine, Brighton, the scrum at the German-style Christmas market on Centenary Square, Birmingham. No wonder that as the Scottish referendum campaign approached the wire, it was the respective pricing policies of Aldi, Tesco and Waitrose that excited voters.

But after five years of Osbornomics, shoppers are no better off. Once upon a time, each year's income would be a bit bigger than last; the family could afford a little more. But since 2008 real weekly wages have fallen by around 8 per cent, which amounts to a fall in annual earnings of about £2,000 for the typical (median) worker, a steeper fall than in comparable economies. A kind of breakthrough came in 2014 when average earnings finally started rising faster than prices, so real wages grew for the first time in six years, though on present trends it is going to take till 2020 before real pay gets back to 2008's level.

Jobs

Jobs were lost in the recession: unemployment rose by 2.5 per cent between 2007 and 2013, and at its peak one in 12 was workless. But the Tories' political fortunes rode on the back of a phenomenon neither Treasury officials nor analysts at large could quite understand. GDP contracted and then failed to rebound, but unlike previous recessions most people kept their jobs or could find other work if they were fired. The population was growing but so was the total number of jobs. By the end of 2013, the UK had its highest ever number in employment, 30.2 million, 1.2 million more jobs than in 2010, despite the cuts. Before the recession a higher proportion of working-age people had jobs, but the 1.4 million extra private sector jobs were undeniably a phenomenon. As Tory ministers had pledged, people being made redundant in the public sector could find work in the private. Outside the public sector there were no mass redundancies. Cameron's Thatcherism was not wreaking the jobs havoc of the 1980s.

In the year to June 2014, an additional 700,000 people found work, the largest annual increase for 24 years. But more than half were self-employed. A TUC report said self-employment accounted for more than two in five of jobs created since mid-2010 and now totals 4.5 million, the highest since records began in 1992. The new self-employed are often actually working for agencies or on contracts without an employee's protection. Not many were setting up businesses; the evidence is mixed on whether they feel liberated or condemned because they cannot find employment. There may be trouble ahead. Saving for retirement looks inadequate; what will they live on when they stop working?

Experts scratched their heads. People are working fewer hours than they wished, with more in what the OECD called involuntary part-time work (meaning they would rather work full-time). Yet many are working harder: average hours increased. Employers kept people on because they did not have to pay them more. Either staff did not ask or were refused and did not walk away. Trade unions exercised bargaining power in only a few sectors and, even there, remarkable moderation ruled as pay fell behind inflation year after year.

All this contributed to the productivity puzzle. Output per hour worked collapsed; in 2014 it was 4 per cent lower than pre-recession and, the Bank of England said, a mammoth 16 per cent below what it would have been if previous trends had continued – a quite different picture from other countries. Staff are doing the same jobs for less; wages have fallen, or rose by less than inflation, and across all industries and occupations. Tory nirvana: weak unions, Victorian welfare and a business class that preferred cheap workers to investing in machinery and skills?

But the upshot is that households are only just getting by, many returning to the pre-crisis habit of borrowing in order to stay afloat. Rising house prices foster an illusion of prosperity and inject some spending power into the market when people realise capital gains. Housing is central; it affects the distribution of capital, life chances and wellbeing across age groups and geographical areas. Osborne pursued short-term policies to enhance that old feelgood for homeowners and stoked property inflation.

A Programme for Growth?

Civil servants told us in late 2010 of scouring the cupboards for anything that could be tipped into the government's growth programme. It was indeed a ragbag of projects. Adult apprenticeships were expanded, pleasing employers who were then subsidised for training they would probably have done anyway, but no wider skills programme was advanced. Recession had reduced the growth capacity of the UK economy but no one quite knew by how much. The OBR worried about the 'output gap' – how far the economy could grow without supply running out and prices pushing up. The government could exult in high business profits and an economy where workers were cheap and prepared to accept low pay; but political success also depends on delivering growth and households' believing that next year incomes will rise.

The governing challenge for the coalition, as for all governments, was how to stimulate spending on new equipment, push organisations into better ways of working, regenerate those parts of the country where jobs were scarce and unemployment high, elevate skills and invest in infrastructure. But for the state to take responsibility for growth in that way offends pro-marketeers and neoliberal economists who believe, contrary to centuries of evidence, that markets will clear and find their way back to equilibrium, as long as the state backs off.

Osborne, like his neighbour in No 10, remained a vote-hungry politician as well as a dogmatic believer. State involvement in growth was never abandoned, but it wasn't exactly celebrated either. Another kind of Tory government might have found a way to join the dots between companies, investment, state enterprise and investment; it might even daringly have mentioned industrial policy and planning. One led, say, by the flamboyant Michael Heseltine, who kept hearing 'that the government had not got a growth strategy'.[4] His own unofficial plan, as we saw in chapter 3, involved regional planning, taxing, public corporations, all anathema.

When money is tight, the distinction between capital investment that will produce a future return and revenue spending becomes more important than ever. Cameron might have told a politically plausible story, as Labour had tried to, saying public sector jobs had to go, but the state had a mighty role to play in sustaining demand through securing infrastructure improvements leading to productivity gains. But something had flipped in the post-Thatcher mind-set. Osborne viewed all public spending as the same – all subject to cuts, capital first and deepest, because voters won't notice for years to come. The result, in the first few years of the government at least, was disjointed decision-making, when decisions were made at all. First, the upgrade of the A14 was abandoned, only to be reinstated later, by which time project costs for this vital east–west link had inevitably risen. The government cut road maintenance then allowed the cabinet clown Eric Pickles to create a 'potholes challenge fund' for councils to bid for, trying to prove he cared about an issue that locally provoked much concern.

The Great Growth Plan

What was labelled as the official 'growth plan' did eventually appear in March 2011, signed by both Cable and Osborne. The UK had lost ground in the world economy and needed to catch up by becoming more competitive. So far so banal. The remedy was passive-aggressive: cutting business taxes, removing barriers to enterprise but also (unspecified) changes in education and, again, infrastructure. Presumably reflecting the influence of BIS, the document went on to envision Britain becoming a world leader in advanced manufacturing, life sciences, creative industries, green energy and non-financial business services. The government would deploy its science budget, a green investment bank and apprenticeships to build on its 'flexible' labour market and exploit the asset of speaking English.

The overall scheme was: a) get the state out of business's hair and cut taxes; b) get the state to help small business by reforming the banks; c) a measure of industrial policy, involving grants and schemes for science, high street retail, IT hubs, motor manufacturing and so on. The labour market, vocational skills, migration and the spread of low-wage employment were not mentioned.

Setting Business Free

Freedom meant less regulation. The government commissioned the venture capitalist and Tory donor Adrian Beecroft to report on the way employers were prevented from sacking their staff as they liked. He demanded 'compulsory no-fault dismissal', allowing employers to get rid of 'unproductive workers' at will. It did not sound calculated to inculcate the loyalty and long-term commitment that would underpin the model through which the UK would conquer the 21st century.

The Liberal Democrats stirred and Beecroft was rejected, but the centrepiece of Osborne's 2012 party conference speech was another plan to lessen 'burdens' on business. Employers could offer their staff tax-free shares in exchange for them cashing in their right not to be unfairly dismissed and to mothers' maternity leave. He said the intention was that new enterprises would take on staff knowing they could be shed easily. It was a resounding dud. Virtually no businesses expressed an interest. Except one: Whitworths, the heritage dried fruit and nut company that had supplied the ingredients for Christmas and wedding cakes for 150 years. It had been gobbled up by private equity and the owners used Osborne's shares for rights as a brilliant tax loophole. They gave £50,000 worth of shares to eight of their senior managers, who could cash them in at a profit, exempt from the 28 per cent capital gains tax.

Freedom also meant less or no taxes: the government had already begun with a package of tax adjustments favourable to business said to be worth £11bn. Key was a cut in taxation of profits, with corporation tax lowered to 24 per cent and a further fall to 20 per cent by 2015. But letting companies keep more profits did not mean they would invest more. The excuse was finance, especially for SMEs. Quantitative easing was changing the relative weights of bonds and equities, financing the repurchase of equity, which pushed up share prices and fattened executive bonuses. No one could say with a straight face that the way companies ran themselves was either fair or effective, but Cameron the free marketeer saw no reason to intervene in the 'market for corporate control', the wild exuberance of mergers and acquisitions that yielded mammoth rewards for executives, bankers, consultants and lawyers, but not necessarily for the shareholders, let alone employees. Takeovers by US firms were often 'inversions' to avoid US taxes rather than create value. John Plender of the *Financial Times* noted: 'The incentive structures of all involved are dysfunctional and transaction costs are extraordinarily high.'[5]

He was writing about the attempt by Pfizer to take over AstraZeneca. The former is an American company insofar as the US is where most of its staff work even if its cash is secreted offshore. Its proposed victim posed as British because it owned laboratories in the UK and was listed on the London stock market, but it too was an international business, owing scant allegiance anywhere. Pfizer played the game badly and the proposed takeover provoked a storm of concern about the UK's life sciences base. When fellows of the Royal Society shout, ministers tend to listen even if their instincts are to side with the predators.

Building on what Labour had started, the Treasury allowed pharmaceutical and research businesses a much lower rate of tax – half the corporate rate – on income earned by certain types of intellectual property inside what was called the 'patent box'. Cable muttered ineffectually. We dug out interviews with him before he took office, rereading his dire warnings about lobbying and political interference by companies. But that was then. And no sooner had Pfizer retreated than AbbVie, another American drugs company, targeted Shire, the London-registered pharma company – bigger than Tesco, Rolls-Royce and BAE Systems in market capitalisation. Again, it showed how artificial were national tags – its management and research were largely American and its money came from drugs to treat attention deficit hyperactivity disorder in the US. Shire's tax domicile is the Republic of Ireland and its UK workforce under 500. The company is almost the definition of the 'mid-Atlantic floating entity with no allegiance to anybody except the lowest tax rate', said the *Financial Times.*[6] A prime minister and chancellor whose purpose in politics was to set markets free were never likely to intervene. The new entity would be run from Chicago, with London its domicile for tax purposes. In October 2014, this deal also collapsed, apparently because AbbVie couldn't guarantee the American government wouldn't clamp down on the tax deals that had made it all look so attractive.

When people protested at gross greed in boardrooms, the government's reply was that it was up to shareholders to rein in excess. But shareholders don't rebel. Many are foreign, or only hold a share for a micro-second; shareholders are pension funds living in the same financial stratosphere where these salaries and bonuses seem normal. But the deficiencies of corporate governance did not much interest ministers. They had even cut the length of time private equity companies had to hold investments to exempt their gains from sale from capital gains tax.

On the proclivities of investors, the government had fresh evidence to hand. John Kay was asked to review the equity markets and, not for the first time, found prevalent short-termism, taking the form of underinvestment in assets and employees' skills. Here was a deficiency in markets that only government had the perspective and capacity to correct. But that implied a skills strategy and, more than that, some kind of vision of matching firms, people and places.

In 2012, 60 per cent of Sir Martin Sorrell's shareholders rejected his pay package – an almost unprecedented rebellion. He had a rough ride again at the WPP Group annual general meeting in 2014 when shareholders protested at his £30m a year. As ever, such objections got nowhere. 'Corporate governance' amounts to a day of ritual embarrassment for the mega-earners; nothing changes; remuneration committees proceed in their own sweet way.

Sorrell is not even one for embarrassment; this captain of industry doesn't hide. He is one of the very few willing to go on *Newsnight* or the *Daily Politics* show, defiantly ready to talk about himself, his world and the Tories. Most top bosses refuse to appear anywhere confrontational, walled beyond challenge in their glass towers and gated seclusion.

Although they wield enormous power over jobs and incomes, their voice is rarely heard; they appear to have no opinions on matters of national interest or, if they do, they get expressed only in the corridors or dining clubs. They play no part in national conversations, despite their salience. Are they likely even to emerge over Europe? Only late and under political pressure did business panjandrums take a public position on Scotland and the UK.

But Sorrell is different. He talks. That £30m? 'I put most of it back in the company, I buy shares. I keep two to three million for myself.' He makes it sound like small change. But Sorrell is exceptional; he is an entrepreneur and builder, and doesn't just exploit what predecessors made. Rare among FTSE 100 executives, he built this company out of nothing, swallowing marketing and advertising agencies and PR companies, in 110 countries. In a series of enormous hostile takeovers, he ate up

J. Walter Thompson, Ogilvy & Mather, Young & Rubicam, Grey, and GroupM, the largest media-buying company in the world.

He's a shark, and on tax affairs too. He moved his company registration to the Republic of Ireland in 2008 in order to pay less, making a political point in blaming Labour's plans to double-tax foreign earnings, which never actually happened. WPP returned to the UK in 2012 because (Sorrell said) the government was looking benign. For all that, he does criticise Osborne for cutting tax rates: 'It was too early to cut the top rate of income tax. Income tax isn't important. He should have cut capital gains tax and corporation tax — those are the tax cuts that stimulate investment.'

As for the EU, he strongly criticises Cameron for offering a referendum. 'The uncertainty is very damaging. A small UK, out of the EU? We could be an offshore island, like Switzerland — though their banking industry is crippled now by transparency rules. Nissan, Renault a lot of companies would go.' But company chief executives wouldn't swing public opinion even if they spoke up. 'Do people listen to toffs in London? I don't think so. There are no industrial heroes any more. When people are asked to list business idols, all they can think of is names from long ago — Arnold Weinstock and so on.'

Otherwise, top marks for the coalition. WPP grew during the recession. Employing 12,000 in 2010, it now has 15,000 staff; 2011 to 2014 have been 'record years', and the UK has done well in the new world of digital advertising. 'Osborne has arrived exactly where he intended, pulling up the economy in time for the election. Look where we are now — high growth, unemployment falling, inflation down.'

As for the public finances: 'There has been no cut in public spending,' he says. You challenge him, saying no, the overall figures didn't fall as expected — but that was the cost of failure as Britain suffered three years more in recession than Osborne had forecast, meaning more unemployment pay and tax credits. He says, 'Well of course we've all had to go through some hardship.'

And there you have it, a voice from the other universe that can use that casual 'we' without self-consciousness.

So is there anything wrong with a society where the top and the bottom stretch further apart from one another and inequality keeps growing? Sorrell, so active and dynamic in his business life, suddenly turns into a fatalist. There's nothing to be done, it's just the way the world is. 'We move in great 200-year cycles and we are going through one now where there will just be no work for a lot of people.' Growth is booming in Asia, Latin America, China, India and the US, but 'it is increasingly capital that matters, not labour'. He calls for better skills, more high-quality apprenticeships, which his own company does offer. But what of the great growth in low-paid service work, with no ladders out, even for many graduates? 'There are always risks. For my company, for example, the risk is that Google might disintermediate us – cut out the middleman and deal with our customers direct.'

In his dystopian world where capital is king and technology devours ever more jobs, doesn't he worry about resentment against people like him or indeed against capitalism? 'No.' A mob of the disinherited and disenfranchised isn't massing at his gate. For him, globalisation is our fate still, as much as before the crash. Governments matter, but only as minor players in a world driven by forces beyond their or anyone's control, where red-blooded entrepreneurs swim hard and seize their chances when they can. Ayn Rand lives.

———

A less flattering analogy is the casino; wheels spin, chips fall. Sorrell accumulates companies abroad; Americans, Chinese, Russians eviscerate the UK. The City even uses a gaming metaphor. ITV is 'in play'. It's to our credit, says the culture secretary, that American predators should want to buy up *Downton*. That's the marketeers' line; they don't connect the quality of a programme (in this case an ITV hit) to a broadcasting culture in which regulation, stable ownership and public sector quality standards from the BBC and Channel 4 underpin acting, directing and so on. Four out of five pounds spent on original commissions from UK TV producers in 2013 came from public service broadcasters. The total of commissions was £1.7bn; in the same year Murdoch's BSkyB paid shareholders £750m.

Of course the 'market in corporate governance' helped explain UK economic underperformance. But the government was never likely to seek to understand, let alone act. Martin Sorrell could get on with it, as he indeed did. Beyond a few ineffectual asides from Cable, the government had nothing to say about governance or the relative power of executives and shareholders or the operation of capital markets' fixation on the short run.

Industrial Policy?

But it was never the Wild West. All governments, even this one, have an 'industrial policy' even if it is inversely expressed as *laissez-faire* neglect of company takeovers. Besides, after the bank crash and nationalisations of RBS and other banks, the government had to have a policy for one sector of the UK economy – finance. But could a government prejudiced against state enterprise ever reconstruct a banking system that would serve business and remedy the multiple defects exposed by the crash?

Banks

The banks presented the coalition with its toughest test of both philosophy and governing competence. It feels like they failed it. The finance system has not flushed small and medium companies with lavish loan finance: the Confederation of British Industry (CBI) joined the chambers of commerce in blaming the banks. We've spoken to many companies, including a Derbyshire steel stockholding firm, one that makes flues for Aga stoves and a microbrewery; we spent time in the bankruptcy court hearing angry tales of woe about banks calling in small loans and sending viable businesses to the wall. The banks that caused the crash delayed recovery.

But by 2014, the impetus for bank reform was fading, without resolving basic problems. UK banking bonuses sparkled like bubbles in a flute of Veuve Clicquot, up £600m in the year to April 2013. They bought no extra investment, precious little enhancement of UK growth potential or balance of payments improvements.

'The banks are still too big to fail', concluded Justin Welby, the former banker and now Archbishop of Canterbury.[7] A choir of respectable voices sang in unison behind him. We cannot afford to go into the next business cycle without the protection of ringfencing retail from investment banking, said the Tory chair of the Commons Treasury committee, Andrew Tyrie, referring to a central recommendation of the clean-up commission chaired by Sir John Vickers. 'We need to get on with it,' he said – but in the same breath added that the government should attend to the voices of the bankers who are saying the 2019 deadline for the ringfence is too soon.

Perhaps ministers believed their own propaganda and did not think the collapse of banks was the responsibility of anyone but profligate Labour ministers. That played into the bankers' extraordinary claim of innocence on the grounds that Labour had failed to stop them doing what comes naturally, which is taking exorbitant risks with other people's money and thereby threatening the fundamentals of the economy. That Cameron was not a deep thinker is not necessarily a black mark. But what if the crash had proved a major tenet of conventional economics wrong? The Bank of England quietly published a paper that painstakingly subverted the textbook view that banks were somehow neutral intermediaries in the money economy, using our deposits to lever productive investment by firms. Banks created money out of nothing, the paper explained. They lend cash they don't own; they have a licence to print money, which is why banking supervision and regulation needs to be corset tight.

These were structural not cyclical problems. Calls for 'ethical behaviour' by bankers were naive. The Tory MP for the City, Mark Field, who should know, said fears that 'robust regulation' would send banks scurrying off to jurisdictions with lower standards were 'overblown'.

With the banks as with the energy giants, the government could never quite decide whether the problem was caused by a profound failure of competitive markets, which demanded permanent regulatory scrutiny. Indecision was compounded by the Treasury's determination to fatten up RBS and Lloyds so they could be sold. To cut quango numbers the Office of Fair Trading and Competition Commission were merged from April 2014 into the Competition and Markets Authority. The new body had a £60m budget and 'sweeping powers' (said BIS) which would allow it to stand up for consumers – but where were the fierce initiatives on, say, the dominance of Google or Amazon or other quasi-monopolies, and why is the fledgling body spending so much time enforcing destructive competition in the NHS? The competition authority is now inquiring into the big banks' stranglehold on small business and personal accounts, where the big four – Barclays, Lloyds, HSBC and NatWest – have three-quarters of the market.

The obvious remedy was to split the behemoths, so avoiding any future 'too big to fail' bailouts. But that would – the old, familiar cry – reduce the City. As the banking lobbyists wormed their way into Downing Street, regulatory reform was watered down to homeopathic scale. Recommendations were shaved and sidelined – for example, that big banks' equity capital should be enough to absorb losses so that shareholders feel the pain of boardroom incompetence and greed rather than taxpayers. As the housing boom ignited, banking culture and assumptions were shown to be unchanged, despite tighter regulation. As for talk about capping bonuses, whether heard in Brussels or Westminster, the bankers complained furiously and the government backtracked. No legislation came forward to ringfence retail lending or formalise a hierarchy of risk; no blocks stopped the banks concentrating their assets in government debt and mortgage lending, precisely where the problems had arisen before.

Small Business

If money was cheap small businesses weren't able to afford it. The commercial banks, including those nominally under government control, wouldn't lend to them. Instead of addressing this basic problem, the government dreamt up a welter of separate schemes. As well as rates relief they included small loans to would-be entrepreneurs, a bounty if SMEs took on apprentices and encouragement to get them to adopt new technology. Small companies were most concerned about business rates. This was where the Tories had come in. Thatcher's downfall can be dated to her attempt to 'do something for our people' by doctoring local property rates: she ended up with the disaster of the poll tax. The 2013 autumn statement announced consultation on simplifying the tax system for firms with a turnover of less than £77,000. Business rates were capped at 2 per cent for the year from April 2014, to rise after that by no more than retail prices. Meanwhile, the government insisted there be no updating of the register of property values on which the tax is based, which had been due to take place in 2015, despite multiple changes since the last valuation in 2010. It is now supposed to happen in 2017.

Small- and medium-sized business lives in its own world, deaf to political talk about regulation or burdens, focused on getting by. Some drop dead. Draka cables in Derby lies empty and derelict, its 100 workers laid off when it closed down in 2012.

But the warehouse next door belongs to a going concern with 46 employees, a family firm, which Richard Hewitt successfully steered through the rapids of recession.

Since 1809, the company that is now Eggleston Steel has been handed down from son, to niece, to cousin. Hewitt is managing director of the steel stockholder, his mother company secretary. The chairman, his father, took him on in the 1980s, and his two children will probably follow in his footsteps.

He's a cheerful man in his mid-40s, jovial with his staff, consumed by the company and every detail of its operations. He arrives at the plant at five o'clock sharp every morning, driving the two miles from his nearby home in his BMW with personalised plates. He never leaves before five, and often stays later in the evening. The business, in a modern warehouse with a two-storey office block, stands behind steel railings on the road to Alfreton. It's 12 years since Eggleston Steel moved from where it was founded, on a picturesque setting beside the river Derwent opposite Derby Cathedral. Soaring property prices made the land too valuable and on the old site rise expensive flats with an ecclesiastical view.

In the warehouse his stock of steel is laid out in racks and rows, all shapes and sizes – flat bars, rounds and squares, L-shapes, C-shapes, with overhead gantries and cranes ready to lift them for cutting and shifting. This is steel for small things, for gates and fencing, lintels and beams, imported and collected from the docks. His men work through the night, loading lorries for next-day delivery, bound for Rotherham, Newark, Chesterfield or Ilkeston; Hewitt reckons that instant personal service is what kept them going.

'When the recession hit, construction and housing went first, so steel wasn't far behind. No one was moving house, no one doing DIY, no need for steel. We fell six months behind. I had sleepless nights. I didn't want to do it, but I had to let some go, and it was very painful.'

But Eggleston is on the up again, borrowing to invest in an expensive new laser cutter to do on site what customers used to do for themselves. He's proud of Derby and its technological capacities, expressing outrage at the coalition's failure to award the £1.4bn contract to build Thameslink trains to Bombardier, the Canadian firm with plant in the city; it went instead to Siemens in Germany. Many were laid off before, the next year, the government awarded Bombardier a smaller contract for Crossrail carriages. 'Real damage was done,' Hewitt says, shaking his head. 'The knock-on effect you could see everywhere, with local shops and sub-contractors. Someone high up in government should have said no. It wasn't patriotic or right.' For the government not to buy British looked to him like insanity.

The night before we visited, he had to collect a framed certificate commemorating Eggleston Steel's 85 years as a member of the Derby Chamber of Commerce. They were all talking, he said, of a speech the governor of the Bank of England had made —like other borrowers he fears rising interest rates, knowing they must come, but not when or how high.

Hewitt doesn't have time for small-business cliches. 'Red tape' is not a problem and he regards health and safety regulation as essential and sometimes not tough enough. 'This is a very high-risk business. In my view there are not enough inspectors. When I do deliveries sometimes myself on our lorries, I see the state of other companies and I don't know how they get away with it.'

But if he doesn't sound like a standard-issue small business Tory, his patience for politicians is strictly limited, seeing them as obstacles not helpers in his task of keeping his business going. Now it's thriving, taking on staff, and he's mostly optimistic, give or take a steep rise in interest rates.

———

The coalition did intervene in the economy, but quirkily. A local government minister asked residents to nominate their high streets for an award. Meanwhile, BIS published a strategy for retail, extolling firms that were investing in 'omnichannel' ways of reaching consumers. Since these are focused on deliveries to customers' doors, their contribution to the survival of the high streets was not clear. Free enterprise, as favoured by the coalition, has not sprinkled vitality. Despite pop-up shops and, in some towns, ingenious council schemes to bring people back to their centres, high streets have gone on declining. Coalition ministers flirted briefly with the TV retail guru Mary Portas, inviting her to lead a review on the problem, but it has been charity shops taking the space vacated by closing businesses.

The government seemed to welcome takeovers but then bemoaned the consequences. The supermarkets had become a cartel. In 2013 the government set up a groceries code adjudicator to stop them squeezing their suppliers. This fed into an odd initiative, which involved 50 big companies demonstrating their 'corporate responsibility' by tracking the value added by their small suppliers. Cameron had even appointed a special adviser on corporate responsibility, whose public utterances personified the vacuity of modern corporate social speak. If our staff feel good, so will our customers, and so will our shareholders. Apparently, corporate social responsibility does not cover companies' most important responsibility – to pay tax in the country where they made their profits.

Exports

All governments, however pro-market in theory, make mercantilist noises over exports. The Tory 2010 manifesto had said 'a sustainable recovery must be driven by growth in exports'. The UK's share of world trade continued to decline. John Cridland of the CBI came on like Billy Bigelow in *Carousel*, barking in the customers. 'They want British insurance, British coats, British handbags, British music, British architects, British cars, a whole range of consumer goods and products and we've got them.'[8] But economists unhelpfully suggested that a booming export market might depend on a strong domestic market: products need to thrive at home first, to succeed abroad, but GDP growth and home demand had been choked off by the austerian policies.

Although sterling had fallen by 30 per cent after the crash, trade was sluggish. The government fantasised that exports would double by 2020, which implied their value would have to grow by 10 per cent a year between now and then. In 2013 exports grew 1.4 per cent. Then, one of the UK economy's zombie problems returned, the external trade deficit. Sterling rose 10 per cent during 2013 and by the summer of 2014, the IMF was warning that it was 'overvalued' by 5 to 10 per cent, impeding the efforts of exporters. The CBI hyperventilated; promising increases in production at Vauxhall and other motor manufacturers were in jeopardy.

Of course, the government had no control over economic conditions in major export markets. Ministers talked about breaking into the BRICS (Brazil, Russia, India, China and South Africa) and toured the world, on embarrassing cap-in-hand trade missions. Targeting sales to the 'emerging middle classes' required government to be both *active* in organising support, and *passive* by keeping shtum about Indian rapes, Chinese civil liberties or Russian invasions. Instead, it suited Osborne to blame the eurozone, where half of UK exports still inconveniently went. The UK government's position was barely coherent. The Tory line seemed to be that the eurozone should not exist; since it did exist, it should pursue policies that boosted trade. But the European Central Bank, under German pressure, was following Osborne's own recipe for austerity or, as *Observer* columnist William Keegan mocked, 'growth friendly fiscal consolidation'. The OECD estimated that between 2010 and 2013 the attempt in various countries to cut spending and balance their budgets sucked out 4 per cent of GDP on average – medicine that kills rather than cures. No wonder UK exports weren't growing.

Rebalancing the Economy

Rebalancing the economy, the government's new aim, has to mean reinvigorating manufacturing and lessening reliance on finance. At private dinners, the likes of Martin Sorrell said the future lay in very high-value manufacturing, 3D printing, super-materials. But that pointed to state enterprise and generous grants for graphene, the wonder material from the University of Manchester. Instead, the government made a series of uncoordinated interventions, none of which quite added up to the necessary reshaping.

As the election neared, Osborne put on his high-vis jacket to visit Manchester with suspicious frequency. But his assent to ambitious super-city plans for the Liverpool-Manchester-Leeds/Yorkshire corridor is watery; the party tactician is not going to make gifts to Labour-controlled cities in a hurry. Osborne the ideologist insists it's a trade-off between infrastructure and 'continuing to spend on welfare payments that are not generating a real economic return'. His prejudice is telling. In fact, social benefits sustain people's ability to spend; tax credits subsidise the labour market.

An ambitious plan for infrastructure, we saw in chapter 3, might have been predicated by a vision of economic development across the regions and territories of the UK. But it would necessarily involve second-guessing the market. State intervention did pick up – requests to the EU for 'state aid' approval increased during 2013, though at 0.3 per cent of GDP the UK remained below the EU average of 0.5 per cent. A programme to install high-speed internet connections was typical of the piecemeal approach. Three separate projects went ahead: for rural broadband, improving mobile signals and connecting in cities to get 'the best super-fast network in Europe by 2015' (the Tories had been infected by Blairite hyperbole). Some £530m was allocated to rural broadband, in what became a vast programme of outdoor relief for BT. Broadband speeds had been increasing but the government could not decide whether it should be a handmaiden for EE, Telefónica, Three and Vodafone, or a far-sighted visionary for how improved access to the internet would push up productivity.

Industrial intervention, never to be called that, could be whimsical and personal. Cameron complained about mobile phone coverage while canvassing for the Tory candidate at the Newark-on-Trent by-election, adding to his discontent over coverage in his own constituency, Witney. Cameron did manage to get the culture secretary on the phone and announce he was going to persuade phone companies to share masts. They said no, pointing out they had invested in their own masts. That's the competitive market. As for 'national roaming', didn't the government realise that network differentiation – better signals from some companies' zones than others – was basic to their business model?

Manufacturing has undergone welcome revival in some places and sectors. Ministers hailed Nissan's expansion in Sunderland, where it was spending £250m on factories and increasing its workforce by 1,000. Public money was dispensed; intervention was not entirely eschewed. Aerospace was awarded £154m of public funds for new technology, such as 3D printing of aircraft parts; subsidies went to Airbus-related projects and to the French company Thales for airborne telephony. The revival of the 'British' car-making industry was signalled by Indian-owned Rover's investing in a £500m engine plant in Wolverhampton, creating 1,500 jobs and expansion at its Solihull plant. It's an exciting time for the UK automotive sector, says the industry body: car production is up 3.5 per cent in the first half of 2014. But truck production fell. It's a matter of niches, for example the hub around Silverstone in Northamptonshire, where engineering companies linked to Formula One racing and performance vehicles formed supply chains and networks: small but prosperous. Government support helped car production, plus the decision by Nissan and General Motors to make the UK their European Union base – all investment decisions now contingent on those firms' estimation of Tory intentions in Europe: several warned they'd be off if Britain left the EU.

In pockets, clusters and concentrations, elements of a future-oriented, science-based economy are visible. Google rates the UK as a tech hub, home to a fifth of European developers of smartphone apps, generating a third of all revenues from mobile software in Europe in 2013 (yet again mostly in London and the south-east).

In Rochdale a company is finding commercial applications for graphene. In Nottingham 75 companies and 650 people are clustered in the life sciences centre, a joint venture involving Alliance Boots. But the old chemist business was now owned by private equity traders, who in the past had shifted their capital around short term: they paid their minimal taxes in Switzerland. Why should they stay the long course needed if Nottingham BioCity was to prosper? Still, regional omens were good: the Nottingham economy grew at 1 per cent in the first quarter of 2014 against 0.8 per cent for the UK as a whole. By then the east Midlands regional economy was bigger than at its pre-recession peak – most of that thanks to manufacturing. The market for the aircraft engines built by the 12,000 staff at Rolls-Royce in Derby is buoyant. Other sectors came good, drink among them, but international market conditions for steel were dire, as the 4,000 employees of Tata Steel at Port Talbot discovered when in 2014 it began a redundancy programme that may end with the entire plant closing. Jürgen Maier, the UK chief executive of Siemens, reckons the UK faces a huge challenge if it is to reinvent itself as an industrial leader on German lines, blaming the banks, business insularity and absence of strategy.[9]

Privatisation, the Old Aim

Since growth by the coalition's definition sprang from private ownership alone, it insisted on dispersing what remained of the national stock of assets. The Tote was sold to Betfred, for £265m, half the proceeds going to horseracing. When the government sold the company supplying blood plasma to the NHS to the private equity company Bain Capital, the business secretary was left asking the health secretary for assurances that patient safety would not be compromised in the search for profits. This sale was doubly symbolic: NHS blood supply was being sold to Mitt Romney's predatory private equity asset stripper, the owner of Burger King, Dunkin' Donuts, Domino's Pizza and much else. The government kept a minority stake. Bain protested it would not materially change the nature of the business – conjuring a fascinating if implausible picture of it reinventing itself as a benign, long-term holder of stock.

Labour had tried to fatten up Royal Mail for sale. The coalition transferred its pension liabilities to the public account then proceeded to a speedy sale, not even bothering to pretend, as the Thatcher government had, that it was interested in creating a people's capitalism by spreading share ownership (though 10 per cent of shares were reserved for staff). It secured nearly £2bn for selling a 60 per cent stake. On the first day of trading, shares were worth 38 per cent more than the offer price, and subsequently traded in a range nearly 200 pence per share higher even than that.

The privatisation had been rigged in favour of 17 City and foreign investment banks and funds, which were given pole position on the understanding they would hold the shares for a while 'to form a stable long-term and supportive shareholder base', said BIS naively. Half the shares allocated to them were sold within a few weeks of the flotation. Lazard Asset Management was allocated 6m of the 13m shares reserved for banks advising on the deal, and sold immediately, making a £8m profit. Lazard & Co had previously been hired as the government's lead independent adviser on the sale. But of course, old boy, there are 'Chinese walls' between the two Lazards.

The state, as with the banks and the utilities, will be left holding the baby if Royal Mail should collapse and the delivery of letters and parcels throughout the country be threatened – something even the Victorians recognised as a pristine public service. Within weeks Royal Mail wanted the state back, appealing to Ofcom to protect it from competition. TNT Post is cherrypicking lucrative door-to-door services, leaving Royal Mail with rural areas where it could not make so much profit.

After this botched sell-off, Cable seemed to lose his bottle. Plans to sell the Land Registry were abandoned – it was to have raised £1.2bn, though the idea involved replacing the Land Registry with a new quango to ensure the private owners did not gouge estate agents (to some homebuyers an enticing prospect). Cable then asked the ubiquitous Lord Myners, former Labour minister and scourge of bad management at the Co-op, to examine alternatives to public share sales in disposing of state assets. Take your time, he probably added.

8

Infrastructure Undermined

The UK is an old country. It relies on bricks laid by Victorians and tunnels dug in the 1930s. Buried pipes, tubes and wires get forgotten. Also in an old country, patterns of land use get fixed. Green belts become inviolate; neighbours vehemently object to new homes and 're-densification' of sprawling suburbs becomes impossible. Impossible, that is, if you hate the only agency capable of breaking through these logjams – the state (meaning councils and the Homes and Communities Agency).

The Tories arrived with no vision of urban Britain's future shape. A wise government would try to match necessary infrastructure in the prosperous south-east with stimulus in the Midlands and north. Instead, support for Crossrail and other London projects amounted to £5,500 per head of population spent on Londoners compared to £223 spent on infrastructure for the denizens of the north-east. The comparatively high figure for the north-west, £1,248, looked good – but that turned out to reflect the expense of decommissioning nuclear plant at Sellafield, hardly constructive investment for local people, even if necessary and inevitable for the country.

A theme of this book is that Cameron was a lot more ideological than his public persona suggested; another is that ministers were not up to it. Margaret Thatcher was a lot less effective than her reputation implies: her policies were at times shambolic and major social and European legislation passed without her realising what it said. The Tories' reputation slid as Norman Lamont fruitlessly searched for those green shoots and the railways were so disastrously privatised, but recent years have hammered a final nail into their reputation for competence.

This chapter is about infrastructure and its subtitle should be 'dogma and disarray'. Transport, housing and energy policy were bungled and mismanaged. Yes, these fields are complex. Technology, time horizons and commercial and consumer interests collide and compete. The public – you, us – cannot escape censure. We may worry about climate change but, as drivers, we don't want to pay more for fuel. We deplore building new roads across the fields and houses on green belts then moan about road congestion and our children being forced to rent. Our expectations are contrary.

Appreciating Expertise

The art of politics is, as always, how to align exiguous means and ambitious ends. With austerity the coalition decreed the former; lacking the latter in environment and transport, the job should have been easier. But it takes effort, not just resources, the Tory chair of the Commons energy committee said on looking at the failure to support low-carbon technologies. And as well as strategy, you need expertise. It's a sad sub-theme of the book just how little the government seemed to appreciate professional nous, except when it came to finagling market margins and making money. Downing Street advisers said the state was overstocked with overpaid officials, so why should the transport secretary bother to check the department still had enough experienced staff to conduct basic business? It didn't – so amateurs and administrative underlings tried to let the contracts for the West Coast line, only to be seen off by Richard Branson's highly fee'd barristers.

National Infrastructure

The Tories had a philosophical problem. A driver stuck in a queue on the M5 or a householder seeing gas bills going up might care little for theory, but practically, in the car, switching on the lights, a pro-market government is always likely to make their lives a bit more difficult. To generate electricity or move people and goods around (or speed up internet downloads), you have to believe in a 'developmental' or investment state. Government might not own infrastructure but it has to be closely involved in planning, regulating and adjusting the interests of customers, users, shareholders and managers.

In 2010, Britain (Scotland had its own plans for trams and a controversial new Forth road bridge) needed grandeur, both to renew and replace ageing infrastructure and to pick up Labour's plans for bold investment to spearhead recovery. Labour had even bequeathed a decent set of precepts, in the 2006 report from Sir Rod Eddington. The coalition vacillated. Its infrastructure plan took two years to appear, and its 500 schemes worth £500bn turned out to be a scratch list of projects under way, urgent updating (such as the M1/M6/A14 junction, a notorious bottleneck) and private investment that customers would end up paying for. Ministers talked of mobilising the private sector, as if mates would stump up as a gesture of support. Insurance companies had promised to invest £25bn but then said changes to annuities ruled it out.

As the recovery went on, private investment did expand. By summer 2014 Costain, the infrastructure company, said it had record forward orders worth £3.2bn, but this was a drop in the bucket for projects Osborne had assumed private developers would pursue when he slashed and burnt public spending. Crane jibs swung giddily in particular places, London of course, and certain sectors; *Construction News* told its readers of a £9bn bonanza in university projects. This might be seen as welcome expansion except payback could only come from the debt being piled on young shoulders through student loans.

The same Queen's speech that included Osborne's plans to tin-open pensions promised an infrastructure bill, making it easier to drill for shale gas, even in national parks. Fracking, if it worked, would drive energy prices down. But that would affect the complex subsidy schemes for new nuclear reactors and renewables, in order to meet commitments on reducing carbon (which fracking would increase). How did it all fit together?

There was no plan but plenty of ribbon-cutting photo opportunities. By spring 2014, 200 projects were supposedly due for completion that year but, again, the list was a hodgepodge, including an extension to the Nottingham tram – an ironic choice, given the criticism showered on (Labour) Nottingham city council by Pickles; the rebuilt Terminal 2 at Heathrow, an investment made years before; and the Gwynt y Môr wind farm in Wales – safely offshore. Pickles had rushed to abolish Labour's scheme for speeding up big investments by overruling local objections. Offensive to localism, they said in opposition. Once in power the Tories realised they too needed to cut through local (often Tory) objections. At one and the same time Pickles created an infrastructure commission remarkably akin to Labour's and pushed legislation ostensibly allowing councillors to put local considerations first. Confusion reigned. Or, as the OECD diplomatically put it, 'Defining a more precise strategic planning framework would be desirable.'[1]

Trains, Roads and Planes

There's no integration, MPs moaned, repeating their call for more joined-up planning of passenger and freight transport. To prove their point, the grand-sounding 'National Policy Statement on National Networks' ignored regional railways and east–west connectivity (meaning getting a container off a ship at the Seaforth terminal on the Mersey and on one on the

Humber). Yet only a few months later, Osborne discovered the urgent need to join Hull and Liverpool, sometime in the 2030s.

Roads

The coalition seemed to be saying that no new roads are needed. Transport secretary Patrick McLoughlin told the Institution of Civil Engineers (ICE) they would manage by controlling traffic better and would 'no longer need to build an entirely new road or widen an existing one'. The coalition had, however, come in like Jeremy Clarkson, saying they wanted to raise the speed limit on motorways. Experts predicted deaths on Britain's motorways would rise by 20 per cent if the limit increased to 80mph. 'I think 95 per cent of the country will think "great",' opined the then transport secretary Philip Hammond. Sense prevailed.

Between the on and exit ramps, the government funked the big road questions. 'A Fresh Start for the Strategic Road Network' in 2011 could have been exactly that – building maximum agreement from where Labour had left the debate. The M6 toll road in the West Midlands was in trouble, and that was newly built. But technology would allow sophisticated congestion charging on existing roads as an alternative to tolls – provided you were prepared to think honestly about the costs and benefits of inter-city journeys versus the old couple next door trundling down to the shops in their low mileage saloon.

Instead of planning, the government was preoccupied with parking. Pickles (the localist) forced councils to provide more space for cars outside newly built dwellings and stopped them enforcing parking restrictions. Cameron's also became the pothole administration. ICE estimated that one-third of local roads are in urgent need of attention, though the figures were hazy because, in the name of lightening 'the burden', less data is collected.

Amid all this, the government mooted the sell-off of the entire 4,300 miles of the major roads network looked after by the Highways Agency. This was dogma at work. The only way firms would buy is if they were guaranteed a return. That either meant a hugely expensive private finance initiative (PFI)-style deal or (again) tolls. The government backed down, turning the agency into an arm's-length company.

Buses and Bikes

One in eight people rely on a bus to get to work, and travellers make three times as many journeys by bus as by train, yet ever since Margaret Thatcher had maliciously declared that anyone over the age of 25 who took the bus was a failure, the Tories paid this mode of public transport scant attention. They believed Thatcher's Transport Act 1985 had cured all ills by enforcing competitive contracting of services. Of course, it didn't. It had not even created a competitive market: only 1 per cent of bus services outside the capital faced competition over all or most of their routes. Except in London, where buses had mass appeal thanks to subsidies and generous timetables, private buses meant fragmented services, leaving hapless councils to try to join up stations, passengers and routes. Now, fares are rising and passenger numbers falling, affecting shops and employability. The Institute for Public Policy Research pointed out that the poorest fifth now took more taxi journeys per year than others because buses were unreliable.

Alternatively, if you could afford one of the machines sold by Andy Brooke (below), you could cycle, though you now ran the risk of being run over by hype. The Tour de France, the elevation of Sir Bradley and Sir Chris and the downhill descents of Chris Froome and Geraint Thomas, did wonders for the popularity of a sport. Now, as well as increases in the total distance cycled, some 2.1 million adults in England cycle at least once a week, up from 1.6 million in 2005–06. But so much more could be done to encourage mums, children and grandfathers to cycle day to day, without having to wear Lycra. The coalition's contribution consisted of appointing a junior minister with an enticing name, Robert Goodwill MP, but not much else.

Talk about livable cities, children and active travel made coalition ideologues uncomfortable: Oliver Letwin decreed that local enterprise partnerships should not allocate any money to cycling. The result was a disappointing gap between potential and present-day limitations. British Cycling said the activity had to be made to look as safe as it really was, and that 2.75 million people wished to cycle more but were fearful. Public spending on cycling of £2 per head a year is lower than elsewhere and the Department for Transport shows no sign of joining up regulation of heavy goods vehicles, traffic speed control, changed road layouts, cyclist education. Vainly, MPs called on it 'to show leadership'.

The Bespoke bike shop is on a busy road near Derby station, just down from the Crown and Cushion. Or at least it was busy (its owner complains) until London Road was closed to mend a railway bridge, a repair that has been long-delayed in the cuts. The middle of a recession seems an odd time to start up a new business, but Andy Brooke is doing quite well. Bike ridership has been rising. Bespoke is high end; its bikes start at £1,000 and soar on upwards, machines for serious and well-off contenders, triathletes a speciality. 'We're a destination shop, people come from far and wide.'

Among them are those who have barely been affected by slump or austerity. But Brooke says some did take to pedal power after the crash, saving on the expense of a car. Personally, he was dramatically affected. After university he went into the family damp-proofing business. 'It was going terribly because damp proofing depends on people moving into new homes. When no one was buying or moving, the business went right down.'

He started out on his own, adjusting bikes to fit their riders, before launching the shop. He is well-sited. Derby's Labour council is building a gleaming new velodrome up the road at

Pride Park. 'It was planned after the Olympics. There was a wobbly moment when the council ran out of money and threatened to pull the plug, but there was such a big local row, protest from cycling clubs and a local press campaign and loads of other people in Derby, that we got it going again.' Like other small businesses he had trouble with the bank, though his overdraft is low. He employs four part-timers: 'We would have expanded much more, if it weren't for the bank. Our industry is not in recession.'

Brooke is not a typical small businessman. He studied political economy at Newcastle University before taking a second degree in sports science at Nottingham. He has views on economics and they are not those taught on orthodox courses. 'Austerity was not the way to end recession,' he says. 'The government and local councils should have invested in jobs and infrastructure. If there'd been more projects like the velodrome, the country would have had a less hard time and the recession would have ended sooner.'

Rail

Rail factories in Derby may get to build its rolling stock but the city is well away from the route of HS2, which feels increasingly like the coalition's infrastructure fig leaf.

Rail just did not fit the Tories' political commitments. The 'market' did not work – it would not build high-speed connections. UK fares are the highest in Europe per passenger mile and set to get higher still – thanks to the sheer complexity of arrangements. Network Rail, successor to the failed private company Railtrack, had £34.2bn of public debt that was not recorded on the public balance sheet: had it been outed as a nationalised company, it could have borrowed far more cheaply. The Office for National Statistics insists it must be honestly registered. The ONS won – only for the Tories to promise that if they win in 2015, they will find a way of obfuscating rail finance once again.

Confusion, however, is profitable. Fares rose by a quarter between 2010 and 2014, when, nearing the election, free market principle gave way to expedience and the government intervened to cap commuter fare increases at inflation. In fact, many fares are continuing to rise, as train companies ruthlessly manipulate tariffs. Passengers are paying for cuts in subsidy, which has fallen 40 per cent per passenger mile, and for returns to shareholders. Angel Trains, a leasing company, made £372m profit in 2013 alone. (Train operators don't actually own carriages or engines. Two of the three leasing companies are headquartered in Jersey and the third in Luxembourg; tax avoiders have no obvious interest in manufacturing trains in the UK.)

Disarray first, then dogma. Pursuing 'competition' the Department for Transport transferred the West Coast franchise to FirstGroup. Incumbent Virgin challenged and not only won expensive refunds but got to keep the line. (The part owners of Virgin are Branson family trusts located where else but the Virgin Islands, a notorious tax haven.) An independent report blamed amateurism, caused by the exodus of experienced officials. Procurements were being run by a 'stretched department', the PAC sniffed. One result was that existing franchisees held on regardless of their service: FirstGroup is set to continue on the Paddington–West Country lines till 2020, despite dodging £800m in premium payments.

For an example of dogma, take the East Coast franchise. Moved into public ownership in 2009 when the private operator upped and walked away from the contract, having failed to make sufficient profit, East Coast was well run and five years on producing a handsome surplus for the Treasury. As if angered by such success the government has dashed to privatise it before the election. It goes without saying that among likely replacement franchisees are consortia formed by the (publicly owned) French, Dutch and German railways.

Here's a vignette on a kind of madness. Northern Rail, running about 2,500 trains a day, was pressed by the government to increase fares so its subsidy (covering 69 per cent of its costs in 2012–13) could be cut; the subsidy also covers an annual payout of £36m to shareholders. The main bidders when the contract is re-let in 2016 are Arriva (owned by the German government) and Govia (part-owned by the French government).

In the broader scheme of things, HS2 is a giant anomaly, evidence that political leaders, however dogmatic, can never quite resist the lure of glory or, more prosaically, the sense of achievement that large-scale state action can bring (which is why they often plunge into military adventures abroad). It's also hugely wasteful, not least because the private sector is making no contribution, even though the line will create value at stations and at the railheads in London, Birmingham and – in the far distant future – Leeds.

The plan was inherited and opposition Labour's man was an archetypal trainspotter: Andrew Adonis's enthusiasm blinkered both political and fiscal judgment. Business executives' alleged wish to travel to Birmingham half an hour faster has so far outweighed other evidence, which favours longer trains on existing routes, better capacity management and fewer first-class carriages. Boosters of the project seem to forget that quicker to New Street (except the railways won't run to that hub) is also a quicker exit from the West Midlands towards London. As with roads, what was missing was strategy. Would a line starting in the capital help regions where transport investment had been disproportionately less, the north-west and Yorkshire and the Humber? The vanity of HS2 is its vacuity.

Airports in the Long Grass

Would HS2 subtract numbers from the inter-city road network or even airlines? Why did the coalition announce, before Heathrow's future was decided, that the new railway would no longer go anywhere near the air hub? It seemed, to mix transport metaphors, to be putting the cart before the horse. The government's equestrian is the former chief of the CBI and LSE director, Sir Howard Davies, but his report on expansion at Heathrow won't be appearing this side of the election.

What his brief lacked were any brush strokes for the bigger picture. How did concentration of airport capacity in the south-east square with the prospects of Manchester as a growth node, which had airport capacity to spare, or Birmingham for that matter? What was the balance between air transfers and destination flights, a critical question if the demand for extra capacity was to be met by building a second runway at Gatwick? How far was expansion being driven by the interests of the airport owners, out to maximise profit?

Once owned by the public in the shape of British Airports Authority, Heathrow is now controlled by FGP Topco Ltd. If Heathrow was, as frequently claimed, vital for the UK, it is also vital for the Spanish giant Ferrovial, Qatar, Canadian investment funds, the Singapore and Chinese governments and, home-grown at least, the UK universities' pension scheme – which are FGP Topco Ltd. Cameron, ever short term in outlook, had opposed a new runway to gain west London votes in 2010. In office, to the dismay of business, he prevaricated.

Air travel in the UK is projected to increase by between 1 and 3 per cent every year over the next decades, which amounts to an increase in passenger numbers at UK airports from 219 million in 2011 to 315 million two decades on. Such projections are often presented as if facts of nature rather than the result of commercial considerations and policy choices; by the way, there is little direct evidence linking air miles to export or import sales.

Broken Markets

At some deep level of consciousness the Tories believed that markets will always self-correct. It isn't true of transport and, across the world, energy and water – the stuff of life – are intensively regulated. By the second decade of the 21st century it is high time to rethink the regulatory scheme set up by Thatcher era privatisations: Labour had failed badly here, too. Flat-footed Ofwat, Ofgem and Ofcom were being circumvented by clever manoeuvres and takeovers, or had themselves been captured by the industries they were meant to hold in check. Some people say, what does all this matter if the lavatory flushes and potable water comes out of the tap? The answer is: totally. For example, Thames Water planned a mega-sewer to run from Hammersmith to Barking – with increased bills for decades to pay for it. Engineers were sceptical, ecologists argued for long-term water saving as an alternative. A key question is the company's rate of return from the surcharges it proposed to levy on customers. The profits accrue to the owners of Thames Water, who include (to the tune of at least 9 per cent) the China Investment Corporation, the sovereign wealth fund that answers to the State Council of the People's Republic of China, which is controlled by the Chinese Communist party. In eastern seas, Ofwat was wading out of its depth, but dogma forbade any thoroughgoing rethink of water regulation, let alone ownership structure.

The average UK household has been spending 8 per cent of its total budget on energy and water. But households on the lowest incomes spend 15 per cent. Bills have been rising faster than incomes. With median incomes flat or falling, energy costs have begun to bulk menacingly large, which gave Labour an opportunity to score a big hit in the 2013 conference season by promising a freeze followed by breaking up the cartel of energy companies, separating their generating from their retailing arms. That forced the coalition to call in the Competition and Markets Authority to investigate the big six.

Climate

Householders – us – energy producers and ministers cannot avoid two uncomfortable truths, though we all try to. One is that the planet is warming because of manmade emissions. In his husky-hugging, cycling-to-work phase, Cameron had said so. The Tory manifesto talked about being 'the greenest government in our history'; in power, he not only chose not to disown the band of Tory climate deniers, their 'charities' and the money behind them, he even appointed one as his environment secretary, Owen Paterson. 'People get very emotional about this subject,' he soothed. 'I think we should just accept that the climate has been changing for centuries.'[2] Later, he proclaimed that temperatures are not rising at all. By then Cameron had long thrown off the disguise, telling aides to 'get rid of all the green crap' in a panicky response to rising energy bills.[3] Tackling climate change came second to making industry competitive.

The other truth is that one way or another the price of energy has to rise both to choke demand for carbon and to encourage renewable alternatives. The policy challenge is how to manage energy prices up while sustaining prosperity, mitigating the effect on poor households, preventing excess profit by the cartel of domestic energy suppliers and channelling surpluses into energy efficiency. Because only an active interventionist state could begin any of these, this lot were fated to lifeless indecision.

Carbon

The government showed its colours early and they signalled prevarication. Labour had put into law a promise to cut emissions by 80 per cent (on 1990 levels) by 2050 – one of those nice round numbers well beyond the planning horizon or longevity of the politicians who would enact them. Now, green commitments and decarbonisation would not be abandoned, but slowed right down. In the next decade, somehow, car emissions would fall, buildings become super-efficient and electricity generation decarbonised. Like St Augustine they would be good, only just not yet.

Cutting emissions by 50 per cent by 2025 is going to cost at least £110bn of new investment – but that's for later. Meanwhile, MPs said progress towards the new miracle technology of carbon capture is 'frustratingly slow', adding that pushing targets into the 2020s undermined credibility. Labour's 'feed-in' tariff had worked. South-facing roofs on both old and new houses offered an impressive array of solar panels, with an average of 18,000 photovoltaic installations per month by 2012, producing 1m kilowatts. This was not much – enough for one million microwaves – but still too expensive, the government decided, cutting the incentives. Support for solar farms was crippled when subsidies were withdrawn earlier than promised, despite reductions in unit costs and rapid growth (though total solar energy output of 2.7 gigawatts was less than the potential capacity Germany installed in the single year of 2013 alone).

Less heating is needed if homes are insulated and modern boilers installed. Energy can be saved: Cameron's predecessors had wanted 800,000 cavity wall insulation schemes completed each year, as a win-win for carbon reduction and job creation during the recession. After 2010 the target fell to 100,000 and energy efficiency dropped as a goal. The coalition's Green Deal offered loans and energy companies promised 'social price support' rising to £310m in 2014. But marketing was costly; ambitious targets were discarded and, by autumn 2014, MPs pronounced it a disappointing failure, with only 4,000 households signed up. Builders and plumbers caught up in the energy department's prevarications complained of its 'roller-coaster' approach.

Not daring immediately to cut Labour's successful Warm Front scheme to help poor households insulate, the government had scaled it back before administering the kiss of death by absorbing into the Green Deal.

Energy

That seeming indifference to the costs and (dis)benefits of infrastructure investment, especially as they affected poorer households, marked the era. The NAO found 'failure by the government to assess the impact on consumers', as two-thirds of the £310bn it claimed as investment to come ended up on bills paid by consumers of energy, water and telecoms. Paying for infrastructure by padding household bills is more regressive than using the proceeds of taxation: those on low incomes end up paying a far higher proportion of their income for new pipes, sewers, masts and reactors.

The EU directed that, by 2020, 15 per cent of UK energy should come from renewable sources, that is 30 per cent of electricity. But Labour's scheme for paying renewables generators a premium over the market price was thought too generous. The Department of Energy's alternative was to place even more fervent faith in the market mechanism. Contracts would be let to generators to supply the grid at a set (strike) price. If, as domestic suppliers shopped around, the market price ended up less than the strike price, then big profits for generators; if more, they lost. Complicated is an understatement, and made even more so when the government, anticipating the 2013 Energy Act, rushed to let big contracts for wind power and biomass. (Was it 'green' to grow trees to fuel power stations, after you added in the environmental cost of getting the pellets to Drax and other power stations to be burnt?) Separately, Osborne went ahead in the 2014 budget to cut the carbon tax levied on generators using coal and gas, which had the effect of cutting wholesale electricity prices and increasing the subsidy that would be claimed by the generators. Buzzing around, working for both sides (but not necessarily the public interest) were the companies that seemed always to make money, the big consultants, notably KPMG.

Domestic customers were always likely to get a raw deal. The big retail suppliers looked more and more like a cartel:

in a competitive market, average retail profits could not have risen from £233m in 2009 to £1.1bn in 2012. Consumers were, the Competition and Markets Authority said ruefully, 'inactive'. Too few could be bothered to navigate the comparison websites and actually switch supplier. Ministers toyed with the idea of forcing us to switch, but the practicalities and the politics defeated them.

Domestic suppliers such as EDF and Centrica were also energy generators, opportunity galore for sharp practice. The fact that EDF is owned by the French state was not going to stop it making money from a UK setup no Parisian politician, left or right, would ever have tolerated. French nuclear might be an *amour fou* but it gave our neighbours energy security. By contrast, the UK was vulnerable. Ironically, the Tory donor Guy Hands, director of Terra Firma, reminded the government that energy is not like other markets: '[It] is not just another commodity but the lifeblood of an economy. No responsible government can step away. Security of supply as well as affordability are critical.'[4]

Nuclear

A quarter of electricity-generating capacity is nuclear plant that will be closing during this decade; the reactors' wheezing condition was exposed when, in summer 2014, EDF shut four to check boiler parts, cutting a sizeable portion of potential electricity from the grid. Following from where Labour left off, the government's list for replacement nuclear plant turned out to be Bradwell in Essex, Sizewell in Suffolk, and Hinkley Point in Somerset, all existing nuclear sites, where in principle many locals would welcome development and accompanying jobs.

The line is that new reactors cannot go ahead unless operators submit 'robust plans' for decommissioning. The bill for disposing of yesterday's waste is mounting, from an estimated

£49bn future cost in 2010 to more than £60bn now. The Nuclear Decommissioning Authority spends its time writing cheques to contractors, mainly at Sellafield, to deal with leaking ponds and irradiated plant. Everyone wants the product, continuous electricity, but few want those ominous reactor cupolas in their line of sight.

After haggling, the government agreed that EDF would undertake new nuclear generation at Hinkley Point. The tricolore was unfurled. 'As two great civil nuclear nations, we will strengthen industrial partnership, improve nuclear safety and create jobs at home,' Cameron said. But what exactly was the UK contribution? The deal also involves the China General Nuclear Corporation – nuclear policy, like the flow of water in London taps, is a reminder of how the UK's very vitals are being eaten away. If EDF eventually brings new nuclear power to the grid, its strike price will be just under twice the current market price of electricity and index-linked. Consumers, both poor and better off, will have to cover the gap through increased bills.

Wind and Rain

Nuclear electricity is supplied continuously, but in these windy islands renewables can and must form a significant additional sector. Promotion of wind generation had been agreed policy for two decades. Now, deferring to rural Tories, the government swung against wind and cut support for the onshore turbines that are now generating about 5 per cent of electricity; a regime for offshore wind remained, but support has become less generous. A barrage to harness the Severn estuary's huge tidal flows, promoted by the former Labour minister Peter Hain as an emblem of Welsh energy sustainability, fell foul of the protectors of fowl. Government was lethargic. Experiments did go ahead in Ramsey Sound off Pembrokeshire, where Tidal Energy Ltd trialled a useful but small-scale device only capable of powering 1,000 homes.

The government quailed, hoping the problems of climate change, energy cost and security would be miraculously dealt with by companies. Similarly, when the rains came and the waters rose during the winter of 2013–14 – the wettest in England and Wales since 1766 – the government was oddly passive. Since the floods in 2007 the Environment Agency had worked hard and defences were built to protect 1.3m additional homes and businesses. But savings had been forced on the agency, along with cuts to departmental staff preparing the UK for the impact of global warming.

Record rain in December and January was another sign of the unpredictable extreme weather we can expect due to climate change. The Somerset Levels, between the Mendips and the Quantocks, were inundated for weeks. Though mostly farmland, long ago reclaimed from the marshes with state-provided drains and pumping stations, a few hundred houses were flooded, too – and residents succeeded in protesting so loudly that reporters in waders filled the nightly news for weeks. Prince Charles arrived in green wellies and pronounced it 'a tragedy' that more had not been done: his charities donated £50,000. Locals blamed the Environment Agency for not dredging the river Parrett. Local Tory MP Ian Liddell-Grainger attacked the chair of the Environment Agency, who conveniently was the former Labour minister Lord (Chris) Smith – saying he would 'stick his head down the loo and flush'… the sort of thing a public schoolboy would do.

The people of the Levels should be especially attuned to global warming, you might think. But the opposite is the case. Ecotricity had proposed erecting four turbines, enough to power 6,769 homes, saving 9,606 tonnes of CO_2 a year. A vociferous local campaign protested, though Somerset has only one wind turbine in the entire county.

Black Ditch was the site chosen for the wind farm and it's an apt name. Beside the busy M5 motorway, it is next to a demolished ordnance factory and the Huntspill, a manmade river that had been dug to service wartime munitions-making. This dreary strip of the Levels is crisscrossed in all directions by enormous pylons, carrying electricity from nearby Hinkley Point. Fields look as if they are growing black plastic, with so many shrink-wrapped hay bales littering the landscape. There are no local protests about farmers' eyesores or pylons, but wind turbines stir something much deeper. For or against, they have become symbols in the warfare between green campaigners (left) and climate change deniers (right). Beauty is in the eye of the beholder – and to the *Mail/Telegraph*/rural/Tory MP faction, they have become monstrosities, while environmentalists see those great slow-turning white sails as symbols of hope for the future.

Roger Lucken, a retired veterinary vaccines expert, is the man who kicked off the local anti-wind farm campaign. When we visited, he drove us round in a green Land Rover, which chugs along at 28 miles to the gallon. 'Yes,' he volunteered, unasked, 'they do say I'm putting out a lot of CO_2, but I think methane does more damage.' He doesn't believe in climate change; if there is any change it's part of a millennial cycle, a natural alteration. Nor does he believe wind power generates power efficiently: 'It's intermittent and it always needs other sources for when the wind doesn't blow.'

Organising the campaign was 'like herding cats', he says. Making sure everyone understood the legal grounds for objection, he had to explain to them ' that you can't argue about how useless windmills are, or about the noise or the flicker shadow that can affect some epileptics. We could only put in an objection to the site.' The campaign argued that although the turbines wouldn't be up on a hill, they were still going to be visible for miles around. Also, birds fly down this stretch of the Huntspill – though they seem to be able to navigate the pylons with their thickets of wires.

Sedgemoor district council's planning officer didn't find this convincing and agreed Ecotricity could use this eminently suitable site. But Tory councillors rejected the advice. When Ecotricity appealed to the planning inspectorate, Pickles intervened to take over the process: he turned the application down. He did not consider 'the harm the scheme would cause to the landscape and its visual impact would be outweighed by its benefits'.

Pickles was acting for a minority: polls show a clear majority in favour of onshore wind. And however vocal the locals, dredging the river Parrett is wasteful and unnecessary and the Environment Agency could better spend its cost elsewhere. The coalition had no sense of an overarching common interest.

Paterson's predecessor, Caroline Spelman, had disappeared after a little local difficulty involving expenses, but not before she produced what was billed as the first major statement on the environment for decades. Anxious at loss of habitats and species, it proposed (with minimal spending) partnerships and improvement areas, creating heaths, woods and wetland on, for example, brownfield sites in Birmingham and the Black Country. When it comes to the coalition's record, the official advisory body, the Natural Capital Committee, is not impressed. England is 'not yet on a trajectory to meet the white paper's ambition that this would be the first generation to leave the environment of England in a better state than it inherited'.

It was never clear how biodiversity would be served by selling off the Forestry Commission. The ensuing protest united farmers, bird lovers and the National Trust, and the plan died. However, a subsequent attempt by the Woodland Trust to promote legislation protecting the nation's forests in perpetuity went nowhere and selling the trees remains an option.

Agribusiness carried a lot of weight, as the badgers found out, before (as the asinine Paterson put it) they tried 'to move the goalposts'. Eminent scientists such as Lord Krebs called the cull crazy.[5] Apart from proving that ministers, like their predecessors, had only the haziest grasp of risk or probability, the subsequent culls showed that the government sided with farmers and commercial interests against tourists and urban dwellers, who have every right to love the striped snouts.

Plans had been announced to control buzzards, for the sake of owners of shooting estates. The Royal Society for the Protection of Birds deplored a 'scandalous waste of public money', forcing the government to back down. Over the exhibition of animals in circuses, the government refused to carry forward its own proposal for a ban. Tory love of freedom did not extend to liberating mangy animals cooped up in travelling vans.

Housing

At least being cooped up meant a roof. For humans they are in increasingly short supply. Thatcher's political heir shattered her great dream of universal home ownership; owner occupation was falling for the first time since the war. The coalition spawned a confusion of small temporary schemes doing the wrong thing – raising prices – but failed to address affordability, overcrowding, excessive land costs, rental insecurity and the inadequate supply of dwellings of the right size given the changing structure of households. Basic insecurity rose: Shelter said that during 2013–14, 215,000 households in England were at risk of eviction or repossession. The average age of buyers is rising and is now 37. A fifth of 25- to 29-year-olds are still living at home with their parents.

Labour had been seduced by the lure of inflating house price rises, filling Treasury coffers thanks to stamp duty and other taxes: the OBR detected that public finances 'may have been flattered in the runup to the financial crisis by the impact on revenues of buoyant housing and equity markets'. Home ownership in Britain is not about roofs, but family fortune; a house is a bank for borrowing, a source of university fees, a deposit for children's first homes, a pension for retirement and care costs for old age. All was predicated on prices rising forever, a one-way bet. For that, it was worth mortgaging yourself to the hilt and beyond. We are a nation (the Scots, Welsh and Northern Irish by no means averse) addicted to housing bubbles, fixated by daily reports on every twitch in house price indexes. Not even the great crash, originally caused by banks' wildly reckless lending on a never-ending stairway to property heaven, has cured the addiction. All this antedated the coalition; they made things worse.

The new Bank of England governor took 11 months to discover that the UK housing market posed a huge risk to recovery. There are 'deep, deep structural problems', he said. Part of the solution had to be the word Carney never uttered, at least not in public. Tax. How property is taxed in the UK is a dysfunctional absurdity – and everyone knows it, but no party dares touch it. Capital gains from homes went untaxed, yet to mention it brought apoplectic *Daily Mail* splutterings about an Englishman's home (ditto an Irish/Welsh/Scotswoman's).

Council tax, hastily cobbled together by John Major out of the poll tax fiasco, had been left with its valuation bands untouched, so properties still counted as what they were worth in 1991 and the top band was too low. Osborne opted for raising less visible stamp duty: property transactions crossing the £2m threshold would pay 7 per cent on the entire sum, and 15 per cent on deals through a company. High-rolling oligarchs, foreign bankers, Chinese and Arab investors looking for a safe investment took it on the chin; the market frothed and whole streets in Mayfair and Belgravia went on emptying, becoming morgues of moth-balled houses.

Pumping Up Demand

Carney soon caught the British disease. By endorsing Osborne's scheme to subsidise mortgages as a way of stimulating economic activity (and winning votes), he approved a bubble of precisely the kind that had burst in 2007–08. The mechanism was Help to Buy, introduced in April 2013 as a state guarantee for 95 per cent of a mortgage. At first, it was tied to newly built homes. But a bold promise to create 100,000 new homes ran on empty and Osborne soon made it a general subsidy on any mortgage including existing properties right up to homes worth £600,000 – no longer a new build encourager but a house price inflator. Many beneficiaries were not even first-time buyers.

The impact turned out to be as much psychological as practical. In fact, its scale was not great – during 2014 it was supporting only about 1 per cent of transactions, using £12bn of guarantees to back £130bn of lending. The Treasury claimed the scheme was backing sales at the lower end of the price range, in places such as Leeds and Glasgow, at values of around £150,000, well below the average house price of £252,000.

But it had sent a signal. Martin Wolf in the *FT* said the government conspired to sustain a nation of property speculators.[6] He was not the only commentator to note the political thrust of a scheme that appeared to help the victims of house price inflation while in fact serving the interests of banks, existing homeowners and, as a housing bubble inflates, the government itself through stamp duty and related tax revenue. Most of generation rent, in whose name it was done, found house prices moving skywards, further from their grasp. Housing debt has been rising but, if fewer people are now homeowners, that could only mean prices going up, year on year at nearly 11 per cent under the coalition – leading to a situation both economically dangerous and socially damaging, as well as failing to house growing numbers of people.

The Failure of Supply

In Carney's Canada, with half as many people as the UK, twice as many houses are built every year; the UK has a 'chronic shortage of housing supply', he reminded the assembled dignitaries at the 2014 Lord Mayor's Banquet. Among European countries only Switzerland and Luxembourg, restrictive and

tiny respectively, have built fewer homes per new head of population during the past decade. Yet Tory chairman Grant Shapps
declared that extra homes were the 'gold standard upon which
we shall be judged'. House building did start to pick up as part
of the recovery. In the year to March 2014, work started on
108,400 dwellings, a big rise on the previous year but still well
short of the 207,000 in pre-crash 2007. Subsidies for buyers
helped the likes of Taylor Wimpey, which started paying out a
'special dividend' thanks, it told shareholders, to its 'ongoing
strategy of prioritising margin over volume' – in other words,
building a cash pile not homes. Developers were sitting on
enough land with planning permission to construct half a
million homes, but they made more from sitting watching land
prices rise.

Old shire Tories demanded 'localism' so that Nimby councillors could refuse building. Younger neoliberals regarded
planning restrictions and the green belt as antiquated and anti-
market. The government twitched. Before the election Tories
had denounced Labour's ambitious (but under-financed) plans
to foster growth in corridors in the south Midlands and the
Thames estuary. They replaced these with nothing. It's unclear
whether the green fields are really needed for building; England
has 61,000 hectares of brownfield land, half of which has been
identified as developable, allowing for 1.3m dwellings to be
built, plus the 400,000 with planning permission but not yet
built. Such figures are, however, meaningless in the absence of
a determined, energetic state that believes in planning.

Pickles invented a bribe to councils if local areas accepted
development, worth £2bn by 2014. The NAO sniffed that
the scheme lacked 'discernible impact' on the number of
new homes: councils benefiting would have permitted some
building anyway. The next ploy was to blame councils and the
NHS for not releasing land for housing, regardless of whether
they might need it for future development of schools or clinics.
Developers jumped for joy, as it often meant handing them

land at knock-down prices, which helped them conserve their own land banks.

For years too little had been built. The result was growing subsidy – housing benefit now costs £24bn. Either you could subsidise bricks and mortar and build council or non-profit housing association homes, or you would have to give cash to people towards their rents – the more of the former, the less, ultimately, of the latter. The coalition redefined 'affordable' rents as 80 per cent of what was charged in the private sector – but that meant rents wildly out of reach for many, especially in the south-east. Even so, the government set housing associations' new lettings at this higher rate.

Councils used to have the right to demand that affordable dwellings be included in new developments. Under the so-called Section 106 agreements this 'planning gain' had provided about half of all affordable homes in England. But the coalition now weighted the odds in favour of developers, cutting the requirements. The National Housing Federation warned it would lead to the loss of 35,000 affordable new dwellings a year. A firm developing a scheme of 211 homes in Bletchley had agreed to include 63 affordable dwellings. With an eye on the new rules, the developer resubmitted plans with no affordable homes at all, saying that including them would mean they made no profit.

Getting Bricks Laid

The job of housing minister was downgraded after Shapps moved on, but not before he ran into trouble in his Welwyn and Hatfield constituency when it emerged that he tried to block plans for a housing estate on an airfield where he kept his Piper Saratoga. (Surveys showed, however, that because people could see how bad housing supply had become, opposition to new building was diminishing, even in the most Nimby of areas.) Another scheme failed: loan guarantees for investors did not encourage pension funds to invest in housing for rent. Even if they had, they would have demanded higher rents in order to secure their dividends. Developers found it easier to build for sale or, their usual perch, to sit on the land they owned and watch its value rise.

Cameron himself now entered the fray with a vague speech about 'garden cities'. Within weeks they were disowned when shire Tories realised it meant cities in their gardens. All that was left was to resurrect an old John Prescott scheme to build 15,000 homes in a disused chalk quarry at Ebbsfleet in Kent, near the high-speed railway line to the Channel Tunnel. It wasn't Eden.

As recovery took hold and applications for planning permission increased, developers and ministers talked big numbers. But getting bricks laid involved several further stages. The government said its liberalisation of the planning framework should speed up development. But the local planners who were needed to process applications had been fired in the cull of council jobs; councils were required to listen to residents and their objections. In the year to June 2014, 137,000 new dwellings were started in England; to accommodate likely growth in the population, 250,000 new units will be needed each year into the 2030s. There is a lot of ground to make up, says Grainia Long of the Chartered Institute of Housing.

Right to Buy Revisited

A public sector (never private) tenant's right to buy was Thatcher's way to aspirational working-class hearts. The Scottish government, concerned about the 185,000 on waiting lists for social housing and fearing the loss of a further 15,500 council properties over the next decade, ended it. The Tories, in reverse direction, offered additional bribes to buy and deplete the stock of affordable rental dwellings. Discounts to tenants buying a property increased to £77,000 (£103,000 in London) and are set to rise further.

Two million council homes have been lost over the previous three decades, a third of them now owned by private landlords who lease them at higher rents to tenants on housing benefit, inflating the benefits bill. During 2014 right-to-buy purchases rose sharply. Over the past five years only one new social home has been built for every seven sold.

Here's a Camden family, housed in a hostel as homeless, who collected enough points to be offered a 16th floor flat, near a tube station. They are winners in the housing lottery. All they need to do is live there for three years and then they can buy this flat worth some £400,000, with their tenant's discount knocking £103,000 off the price. If they can't find the money to purchase, there will be plenty of vulture agents knocking on their door who will put up the cash to buy the flat for them. The tenants take their share of the proceeds and move on to where they can buy their own home outright outside London; the vultures let the flat at a far higher rent than the council, adding to the housing benefit bill. Across London, Harrow council is spending £500,000 a year renting back from extortionate private landlords 35 ex-council properties sold under right to buy in a desperate attempt to find dwellings for its homeless.

Councils could not even build when they had resources. Camden has land to build on, and a stock of housing against which to borrow. But the government rejected its bid to increase its borrowing limit by £29.5m, capping the increase at £190,000, enough to construct just two extra homes. Pure ideology was preventing councils from borrowing and building.

The Return of Private Landlords

The party of home ownership presided over its decline, to its lowest level for 25 years, at 65.2 per cent, compared with a 71 per cent peak in 2003. Under-35s simply could not afford to buy and over half of people aged between 25 and 44 are now tenants. Households living in the private rented sector overtook those in social housing and now account for 18 per cent of all tenures. In 1982, 57.5 per cent of homes in the London borough of Hackney were rented from the council, but by 2011 that had sunk to just 23.8, while privately rented homes rose from 17.8 per cent to 29 per cent. Private rents now take up 40 per cent of tenants' gross income compared to the 20 per cent owner occupiers spend on housing costs.

In a flight of fantasy, betraying its own lack of understanding of the new shape of the market, the government claimed that capping housing benefit for private renting would squeeze rents down. In fact, rents have continued to escalate and tenants on housing benefit in the south-east have often been forced to move.

The only way to cut the rising bill paid is, of course, to increase the supply of homes. The government duly announced grandiose targets. But who would build them? Housing associations – 'social landlords' – now owned 28 per cent of all rented homes in the UK but could only build if they increased rents to pay back the commercial loan finance on which they increasingly depended. In 2011, the coalition cut the grant it paid them for building new homes from £3bn a year to a paltry £450m. This plan was 'cobbled together on the back of a fag packet' according to David Orr of the National Housing Federation.[7] Lower-income households that housing associations used to exist to serve could not afford the higher rents. The upshot was that for the first time in a generation the total number of homes to rent for social tenants fell each year, and fell below even the low targets set by the government. In 2012–13 alone, social housing shrank by 35,000. Even so, the housing benefit bill has risen 20 per cent from 2010, money that could have been better spent on building homes tenants could actually afford.

A Very British Bubble

By June 2014, the Treasury was at last officially worried about the housing bubble the government had deliberately inflated: the IMF was warning that the widening ratio of house prices relative to income denoted a bubble. Any upward tweak in interest rates would hit household non-mortgage spending hard, warned the Bank of England. The Resolution Foundation said 1.1 million households are living 'unsustainably' because of their housing debt.

Thanks mainly to London (where prices rose nearly 22 per cent in the year to August 2014), average English house prices climbed to nearly their November 2007 peak, at £177,824. The devil lay in regional differences. In the north, Scotland, Wales and Northern Ireland prices remained below their 2007 peak. The recovery, with low wages, low productivity, real incomes still below 2007 levels, was looking like the old British sickness – built on high household debt and ballooning house prices in the south.

Underlying this were old verities, spelled out by Professor Danny Dorling in his book, *All That Is Solid*. The housing crisis was another manifestation of extreme inequality. The bedroom tax was brought in, ostensibly, to move smaller households into smaller council properties to make space for larger families to move into larger homes. But if that principle were to be applied to all housing then, he said, there is no shortage. Half of all owner-occupied dwellings are under-occupied; the 2011 census counted many more bedrooms in Britain than people to sleep in them, some 40m bedrooms unslept in each night. Plainly no one was going to order the fairer division of large houses, but a well-crafted property tax could provide some reapportionment. The bedroom tax applied to the poorer third of dwellings, not to where the likes of us live.

Schooling the Nation

When Gordon Brown opened the rebuilt Wright Robinson College in late 2008, it was among the biggest in the country, with over 1,800 students aged from 11 to 16. The Gorton school specialises in sports and arts. It is endowed with a 25-metre pool, multiple sports halls, fitness suites, dance studios, a weights room, tennis courts and football pitches, alongside eight information technology labs, drama studios, music recital rooms and a fine auditorium.

Neville Beischer has been head for 23 years and we visited not long after the rebuilding, for our book *The Verdict*. East Manchester is not well off. A fifth of the school's children are classed as having special needs, two-thirds come from single-parent households and nearly 70 per cent from homes poor enough to qualify them for free school meals. He tells how he has managed, so far, to avoid being strong-armed into a chain of academies, a flagship coalition policy.

Here's one reason. 'Listen,' he says. He throws open his door and the corridor is silent, no stray children. That's explained by the presence on site of a dedicated police officer, whose salary the school pays. Beischer says the extraordinary orderliness of a school in a tough area is testament to her skills. The building remains pristine, no scuff marks, no graffiti, 'zero tolerance of vandalism', he explains.

The school won accolades for students' behaviour and safety, and Ofsted praises the teaching at Wright Robinson. But it's not enough. The crunch is Ofsted's 'requires improvement' for student achievement. 'The rule is three strikes and you're out, and I'm on two. If we don't get the improvement in this year's GCSE results, I'm out.' Outgoing, cheerful, bounding with energy despite his years in the job, his extrovert demeanour doesn't match his alarming words. 'Ask any head, we're all under such pressure.' No surprise they're having trouble recruiting headteachers up and down the country: deputies are refusing to step up and take the endless flak.

Pupils are micromanaged. He takes out the charts. Graded on entry, 70 per cent must rise three levels in their five years here, the other 30 per cent must rise four levels. Wright Robinson has progress coordinators who chase every child, each of whom is assessed six times a year, checked on their milestones and their 'flight paths'.

Coalition policies have helped. Beischer welcomes the £1m added to Wright Robinson's £11m budget by the pupil premium. He puts the extra to use in diagnosing and treating any sign of falling back. If a child can't do algebra, they're taken out of class and given intensive coaching; teaching assistants are not 'wasted sitting in classes', but taking the students out for special help.

Beischer's criticism of the coalition is not this intense pressure on standards. It's the rigidity, the insistence that every child, regardless of background or ability, has to take the academic path, as if they were at an old grammar school. In the government's new GCSE, coming in 2017, English and maths get double points. Fair enough, everyone needs those. But so few points are given to music, arts and drama that they will have to be dropped, however well children do in them, because they affect a school's overall score and threaten to plunge it into the darkness of special measures.

Wright Robinson specialises in the very subjects that will do it down. Sports and arts will go the way of its vocational courses.

Its purpose-built salon, used for the BTec vocational qualification in hair and beauty, closed last year; the school stopped offering qualifications in hospitality and health and social care, despite those being fields where employment in Manchester is on the rise. They are subjects that can keep the attention of students who may otherwise be marked as school failures.

The beat does not go on, and this in the city once called Madchester. Music has taken a heavy hit. A school with no music has no heart, Beischer laments. A subsidy from Manchester city council for specialist music teachers has gone. Subjects that used to sustain the interests of disengaged students are being axed. Take drama, which works wonders for articulacy, self-presentation and the discipline of public performance, bringing reluctant students to culture and literature. It offers the soft skills employers want, so why, he asks, did the government come down on it so heavily?

On education Cameron himself had no fixed ideas, no vision for teaching and learning for young people in an area such as Gorton; perhaps it's too much to expect Etonians to understand or care much about the 93 per cent who don't attend fee-paying schools. But Cameron knew someone who did. Gove.

A Good Childhood

Education was what Blair famously promised three times over. According to an LSE audit, Labour had 'articulated a wider vision of a good childhood, through Every Child Matters and the creation of a department embracing children and families as well as schools'. But Labour had funked the reorientation of A-levels and secondary schooling to create respected pathways into vocational and skills training, and too many were still leaving school without the basics.

In 2010 a calm and measured government that cared about the country's future prosperity could have built on a rich legacy, while paying attention to the neglected areas of vocational education and passage into the labour market. Successes included the London Challenge, Aimhigher and Reading Recovery, all positively evaluated in studies. A visit to Germany might have been a good idea, to see how vocational skills training and apprenticeships could work. International league tables such as the OECD's Programme for International Student Assessment (PISA) risked turning schooling to what could safely be measured across cultures, not what employers value or what underpins a fulfilled life. This triennial test of 15-year-olds showed in 2013 that the UK was no better than average in reading, science and maths. What English schools needed was a consensus builder with fire in the belly to push schools further along the path to improvement.

Making Sense of Gove

Instead, they got forceful, obstinate Gove, determined to use his perch to pursue partisan preoccupations. He showed his colours at once by immediately renaming his job: no longer families, it was solely about education ... as if schooling could be separated from family background: here was one of their great policy errors. Ministers, including the Liberal Democrats, talked about social mobility and economic achievement as if they could be injected into poorer children at school, playing down all the evidence saying life chances are largely determined by background and especially by household income.

Gove wanted children from poor homes to do well, but his ideal was a 1950s grammar school, which of course had excluded the majority of children; for him, educational success was defined solely by getting into a university. Tory backbenchers wanted actual grammar schools, to add to the selective schools surviving in the state system. But the political attractions of the 11-plus shrivelled once ministers realised they would be telling the millions of voters whose beloved children did not pass that they are lifelong failures.

Cameron treated Gove as he did Andrew Lansley, the health secretary, letting them get on with toxic and politically dangerous policies. From the start, Gove picked fights. To improve schooling you need to win the hearts and minds of Neville Beischer's colleagues, to stimulate, motivate and pay them. That's what all the PISA evidence said. But Gove sneered at them, cut their pensions and denigrated their training. They, together with civil servants and even Ofsted inspectors, formed a malign establishment he called the 'Blob', against which his freedom fighters would be launched. (In a 1958 horror movie the Blob had been a man-eating metaphor for communism; Gove was a believer in global conspiracies.)

A reactionary strain was unmistakable. On what schools did for less able pupils Gove was uninterested, if not actively hostile. He attacked what he called the 'careers lobby', whose offence seemed to lie in a wish to ease young people's move into the labour market. Little wonder inspectors found four out of five schools were failing to provide adequate careers advice to pupils during the critical years between ages 11 and 16, when ambitions are formed and vital choices made.

Though it's never quite clear what employers do want from the schools, it's odd that the coalition made no special effort to find out, for all its tenderness towards corporate interests. Studies showed that employers were after the very things the government has been trying to expunge from the schools. For them, team working, emotional maturity, empathy, and other interpersonal skills are as important as good English and maths.

Teachers are now 96 per cent graduate, but Gove insisted theirs is a craft best learnt 'on the job' rather than a profession based on academic training. Overall the number of unqualified teachers grew, with 17,000 in the English schools system in 2013 – one in 25 in all schools but one in seven in the new 'free schools'. The General Teaching Council, the body set up under Labour to enhance the vocational standing of education, was abolished. Gove talked wildly about parents going into classrooms and assessing teachers – imagine the provost of Eton allowing his teachers to be downgraded in that way. It was also a political misjudgment. The public ranks teachers along with doctors, and parents like and trust the teachers they know. The evidence (again) undermined Gove: the OECD said the success of education systems such as Shanghai's came from investment in training and developing teachers.[1]

Public Schooling – Silence as Usual

The provost of Eton happens to be the former Tory minister William, Baron Waldegrave of North Hill (one of whose achievements in office had been the poll tax). It was never likely that he and his fellow public school heads would come under any pressure from a government comprising as many former pupils. All the talk about social mobility was never going to affect schools whose very reason for existing is to endow advantages over state school students in entering universities and getting top jobs.

In a rare moment of intellectual honesty about the social dynamics of modern Britain, Gove called the number of Etonians in the cabinet 'preposterous', adding: 'I don't know where you can find some such similar situation in a developed economy.' His aim was a public sector school with 'standards so high that you should not be able to tell whether it's state or a fee-paying independent'. What a glorious vision, said the education writer Peter Wilby. Let's try it out on, say, Marlborough College (founded 1843), which we saw at the start of the book is the alma mater of the wife of the governor of the Bank of England.[2] Equality between Marlborough and a state secondary would mean dealing with the small matter of the £27,420 cost of a year's teaching, plus £5,000 for boarding fees. For 870 pupils, Marlborough has 150 teachers and assistants, a ratio that, if applied to all England's 8.2 million schoolchildren, would require the teaching workforce to be tripled to roughly 1.3 million. A seeker after equality, said Wilby, would wander the grounds and register 11 rugby pitches, eight cricket squares, 14 cricket nets, 12 tennis courts, an eight-lane swimming pool and .22 rifle range, and games facilities that, if extended to every state school, would require 33m acres, or more than half the English countryside.

Deconstructing Schooling

Gove ignored all that and instead attacked weakly defended ground. Labour had taken school budgets out of the hands of local authorities, and now state schools were to be bribed and bullied away from any formal council responsibility by becoming 'academies'. In front of MPs, minister Lord Nash said out loud that removing democracy from education 'is partly what the academisation process is all about'.

International evidence does link higher performance to school autonomy, provided schools connect with one another in 'self-improving networks'. The coalition ignored the proviso, which councils were anyway starting to organise. Philosophically, the approach was of a piece with the government's bastard-Hayekianism: if you remove the state everything will spontaneously order itself for the best, which in health and education became pretty much 'it'll be all right on the night'. The Department for Education's own research said you couldn't take collaboration between schools for granted. The coalition answer was to encourage chains, which are to be run by unaccountable sponsors or mysterious charities, which Ofsted was forbidden to investigate or assess.

One result was the death of any education 'system'. No one now had any responsibility for getting schools in a local area to cooperate and no one had oversight of the way they were run, especially when they belonged to a chain. As a consequence, there has been no planning for the fast-growing number of children. A fifth of primary schools were full or over capacity by

May 2012. But the capital pot to provide them with Portakabins and new classrooms had shrunk. Councils were left with the legal responsibility for ensuring all children had a place but they had no power to require academies to increase their size, no say in whom they admitted and no capacity to open new schools.

Academies

By 2014, one in 20 primaries and half of all secondaries were academies, totalling about 3,610 – a 15-fold increase on the number inherited from Labour. Labour's idea had been to use the special status to push improvement in poorer areas. The coalition wanted every school to convert, and channelled public money to a charity run by a former aide to agitate for transfer. By September 2013 the government had paid it £1.5m to put out propaganda. The Charity Commission kept its eyes tight shut. Later, the charity's director became a Tory peer.

Academies were given money previously spent by councils on back-up services, including careers advice, exclusion units and special needs. The coalition rush to convert them incurred additional costs (so the NAO said), at the same time as the DfE was cutting civil service numbers. No wonder the Comptroller and Auditor General 'qualified' the education department's accounts. In prevailing style, Gove never thought through potential issues such as how to stop heads pocketing the dinner money; what to do about special needs and other vulnerable children, now at risk of being excluded or forgotten; where to find competent governors and, critically, what role for inspectors. The number of schools getting their money directly from Whitehall rather than passported through town hall accounts increased by half by 2015, yet successive reports said Gove's own department lacked the systems needed.

Here's a piece of accounting magic. In 2011–12 councils transferred to academies land and buildings with a book value of £6.5bn; the academies' accounts showed additions of land and buildings to be worth £12.3bn. Nobody, the Treasury sheepishly admitted, quite knows what the academies' balance sheets look like – and in a few notorious cases fraud was detected. Multimillion-pound enterprises relied on high street accountants. Academies were exempted from various controls, including the edict that no public officials are paid more than the prime minister, and some academy heads are now on £300,000. Some had identifiable governors, others were run by shadowy boards. Even the Tory chair of the Commons education committee expressed his surprise at 'the ease with which school trustees can personally profit'. E-Act, a chain running 31 academies, was reprimanded for 'a culture involving prestige venues, large drinks bills, business lunches and first-class travel'. Its director general resigned.

Academies are supposed to adhere to a national admissions code to ensure a comprehensive, mixed-ability intake, but with no effective scrutiny the shadow of selection by ability has grown. Some are using their autonomy to exclude 'difficult' children, leaving other schools to take hard cases. The coalition kept Labour's ban on academies interviewing children or parents, or favouring those whose parents offer financial or practical support. But there are ways round all this, such as holding social events with prospective parents.

Are Academies Better?

Does any of this matter if these schools are better? Unfortunately, academy status has been no panacea. A Royal Society of Arts review found no evidence that academies are transforming life chances.[3] Their status matters less than whether a school has an inspiring head, committed (and trained) teachers, and is backed by a catchment community's will to succeed. Academies have not been especially innovative. The Sutton Trust said schools in some chains had improved by more than the national average between 2011 and 2013, as measured by how well disadvantaged students did at GCSE. But others are doing badly and, according to Professor Becky Francis of King's College London, 'risk becoming part of the problem for their disadvantaged pupils'. So far, so inconclusive – and little justification for major upheaval and loss of public accountability. Inspectors found improvements but also ordered sponsored academies to improve and placed some in special measures.

The OECD said that to blossom, schools need freedom but also a common administrative and legal framework. That common identity is under threat. It's not just that in many areas parents now face a bewildering array of different types of secondary schools. The welfare of the 'whole child' gets lost: academies are exempt from the nutrition standards that had become compulsory in state schools since the campaign against Twizzlers and chips.

The more freedom, the more financial autonomy, the more academies looked like stalking horses for privatisation. Companies were starting to supply the educational infrastructure formerly provided by councils; in Staffordshire, for example, contractors are now responsible for disabled children. Some chains, such as Academies Enterprise Trust (75 schools) and Kemnal Academies Trust (38), began to look like candidates to be packaged as companies and their shares offered for sale. In the background remains the idea of vouchers, an old rightwing ambition: make all 'state' schools charge, then let parents choose them or top up the voucher and send little David to Eton. The state would become merely a transmission mechanism for cash, which would be as available to private schools. 'Hopefully,' said Gove's special adviser Dominic Cummings, 'recent reforms will push the English system towards one in which parents can spend in any school they wish, thus breaking down the barrier of private/state school.'[4]

Free Schools

The ultimate academy is the 'free school', which groups of parents, teachers or sponsors can set up when and where they want, regardless of the need for new places. Right-of-centre thinktankers had been to Sweden and proclaimed the future lay with autonomous groups coming together harmoniously to do it themselves. (The discovery was made before Sweden suffered a precipitous fall in the PISA rankings.) This was policymaking by faith. Parents' interest is, of course, a factor in how well children do at school but their income is much more relevant; besides, there was no evidence their involvement in running a school has any causal weight. The most eminent public schools exclude parents from any role in school life, beyond paying fees and applauding on speech day.

By 2015 some 331 free schools providing 175,000 places were open or in the pipeline. To them went a generous slice of the severely reduced budget for building and repair. In a rational world, Gove would have sat down with councils, looked at population projections and plotted new schools where demand was highest. The location of free schools was not entirely random, but in half the areas known to need more places, no free schools were opened at all. Only 19 per cent of secondary places in free schools were in areas where need was growing, the NAO found. But enthusiasm has its own geography.

———————

Outside the station in Feltham, in far west London, a moment's head scratching followed our asking directions for Reach Academy. 'Oh yes! That's the new one in the old jobcentre.' The setting for one of the coalition's flagship schools may be inauspicious, but after just two years it has won Ofsted's top rating and is set fair to succeed, if the spirit of these heady first days still burns bright in terms to come.

A £10m building is rising on a site bought by the Department for Education and given to the pioneers. They are young educational professionals. The Gove experiment has given Reach Academy's principal, Ed Vainker, and the head of its secondary school, Rebecca Cramer, total freedom to create the school of their dreams – and market it to the parents of Hounslow. Neither has been a school leader before. Both are graduates of Teach First, the scheme that places those with top degrees from elite universities into schools in deprived areas; both have previously taught in tough schools. All but one of their staff are also from Teach First; they have recruited no one without a first or a 2.1, even their teaching assistants are graduates. At 32, Vainker is the oldest.

Free schools have tended to emerge where pushy middle-class parents or sponsors fancy, not where they are most needed, which is why half have sprung up in London. Vainker and Cramer went out of their way to choose an area where new places were needed. There's a deficit in several London boroughs but Hounslow was the only one that was positive about their plan, pointing them to central Feltham as the area most in need. The Labour-controlled council already had nine putative free schools approach them, but all were faith-based and were given the cold shoulder.

Vainker and Cramer say they were not looking for a middle-class catchment in order to boast of their good results. 'We want to show what poor children can achieve. That's the whole point'. Half the children at Reach come from homes poor enough to qualify for free meals, above the Hounslow average of a third. Seven out of 10 come from homes where English is not the first language. 'We have a lot of immigrant kids, poor, but with highly ambitious parents who push them hard.'

Vainker is no grammar school zealot and mocks the free schools with fancy blazers started up by parents demanding that teachers decline *amo, amas, amat*. He is a member of the Labour party and like the former Blair adviser, Peter Hyman, who has opened a free school in Newham, Vainker wants to prove a good school can close the attainment gap between social classes. 'That's our moral imperative,' he says.

Local politics are delicate. 'We have been careful not to market ourselves aggressively in the area,' he says, as some free school advocates have put the noses of existing local schools out of joint. 'Instead, it was word of mouth as we went round to parents and begged them in their front rooms to send their children to us.' Because free schools are so controversial, Labour-controlled Hounslow has never quite supported Reach in public. But there has been encouragement behind closed doors: after all, councils are not allowed to set up new schools, however desperately more places are needed.

The school takes students from four to 18; so far, it has filled just the first two primary years and the first two classes in secondary. The idea is to grow the school with its own pupils, avoiding the cliff-edge jump from primary to secondary that is often associated with regression and a falling-off in results. Reach wants eventually to open a children's centre, to become a hub for neighbourhood children from birth onwards, in the knowledge that the earliest years matter most.

The Reach ambition is for each class to achieve the results that Ofsted would expect from students aged a year older. They say they are nearly there, with only four of 60 five-year-olds approaching the end of year one not graded in advance of their chronological age. The school offers intensive speech and language therapy and support for those falling behind. All this, they say, is paid for on the same per capita budget as other schools.

Every aspect of school life has been planned down to the micro-moment, every element of teaching, progress and behaviour is studied and discussed by this hyper-enthusiastic cohort of dynamic young teachers. Vainker looked at all the dysfunctions of the schools he had worked in and is determined not to repeat them. 'I used to teach 450 students in a week, and I couldn't get to know them. But we will know our students well, not shifting them between too many staff.' Teachers visit families at home: they have got to be involved – an ambition easier to reach in a small new school.

So there it is, a founder's dream. They want to start more Reach schools in poor areas, and to train and send out to other schools teachers who will become excellent new heads, at a time of acute national shortage.

But there's the rub. Is this wonder school replicable, in places such as Gorton? Will this school really be exceptional, once it's running full with less select teachers and less motivated pupils than in these first heady days? Already the school is struggling to find teachers: only eight applied for seven vacancies last time they advertised. If Reach succeeds in the way Vainker described, it would become oversubscribed, with the result that deprived children would find it harder to get in.

Reach may be exceptional. By April 2014 only 38 free schools out of the 174 had been rated by Ofsted: 6 were outstanding, 21 good, 8 require improvement and 4 have been found inadequate. Measured by pupil numbers, half are being taught in free schools Ofsted says are inadequate or need improvement; several received scathing Ofsted reports and closed. That's despite their disproportionate share of capital spending and the opportunity they have to bend admissions through setting their own catchments, choosing their own 'feeder schools' and guaranteeing places for the offspring of their founders. Free secondary schools have the chance, an early academic study noted, to create 'intakes which are less balanced in terms of socioeconomic status, ethnicity or religious affiliation'.[5]

Inspection and Autonomy

To head the inspectorate the government chose Sir Michael Wilshaw, celebrated former head of Mossbourne Community Academy in Hackney. A Roman Catholic and moralist, Wilshaw sent out all the required signals on discipline and improvement and Gove saw it as an outstanding credential that he was distrusted by the National Union of Teachers. Yet, Wilshaw was an uncomfortable bedfellow. He deplored Gove's sacking Baroness Sally Morgan as chair of Ofsted – a Blairite advocate for academies, who had given Gove the veneer of bipartisanship. Her successor, appointed under Gove's successor, was David Hoare, former chairman of a company (owned by a holding company based in the Cayman Islands) and trustee of an academy chain.

Wilshaw was critical of how the outsourcing of inspection to private firms had gone and he proposed renationalising the training and conduct of inspection. Perhaps most offensively, he insisted the secretive chains and the background of academies did need to be inspected. A zealous regulator chasing failure in academies was the last thing Gove intended. Then a crisis in Birmingham showed the limits and costs of the new non-system. Ofsted's ambiguous role, somewhere between independent inspector and ministers' lackey, was exposed.

Over the years concern had swirled around electoral corruption within ethnic minority communities; a new allegation was that certain schools had been 'taken over' by Islamic extremists, who had exploited the opportunities of academy status (but had also mobilised as governors of schools still connected to councils) to push a sectarian curriculum and browbeat, and even dismiss, teachers.

Because the allegations involved Muslims, Gove was compromised. As a *Times* columnist and author of *Celsius 7/7*, an apocalyptic 'clash of civilisations' novel, he had presented himself as someone unafraid to name 'Islamic rage'. Why then, the Home Office tartly asked, had he not done something about Birmingham? Schools there had been regularly inspected. Now Ofsted was ordered back and Gove appointed Peter Clarke, a former counter-terrorism police officer, to examine 25 schools in the city, causing consternation at the city council at the danger of sending out the message that conservative Islam was always synonymous with terror.

Tory ministers had wound up the Prevent programme started under Labour, which had subsidised 'moderate' Muslim groups. On taking office, Gove had talked tough, yet he had agreed to more faith schools – Muslim and Christian. To his embarrassment, Clarke concluded that academies were the problem: in theory accountable to the minister but 'in practice the accountability can amount to benign neglect'.

Ofsted reinspected and dramatically revised its views of the affected schools, though puzzlingly found what was taught in one of them would have been appropriate had it been a 'faith school'. Evidence emerged of an organised campaign by certain Muslim community figures in Birmingham and five schools were placed in special measures, three of them belonging to the same academy chain. Ofsted was now to inspect without warning, which was not exactly a ringing endorsement of the autonomy that the government had favoured. Nor was the subsequent appointment of a sort of schools Gauleiter in the shape of the former chief inspector, Sir Mike Tomlinson, to supervise the city's schools. Localism, anyone?

What Should Be Taught?

For an enthusiast for school freedom, Gradgrind Gove took an obsessive interest in what they taught – except free schools and academies, which were exempted from Whitehall edicts as long as they taught 'a broad and balanced curriculum'. He knew what he liked and in an early, self-indulgent gesture dispatched a copy of the King James Bible to schools under his personal signature in order, he said, to direct them to a source of reputable English. Perhaps Aberdeen-born Gove, still Scottish accented if now transplanted to suburban Surrey, subconsciously identified with King James VI and I, the wisest fool in Christendom.

Primary schools were instructed in minute detail how to teach and test, a rigid system that has children reading out nonsense words to make sure they are not guessing from the sense of a sentence. All six-year-olds are now tested in maths and all 11-year-olds are made to sit spelling and grammar tests. Ministers (echoing their predecessors) made speeches calling for higher levels of mathematical competence – but their extravagant praise for classroom practice in Singapore and Shanghai ignored obvious differences and the fact that the east Asian crammers were increasingly looking for a more rounded approach.

Curriculum-drafting is never easy or particularly useful, since there is little or no international evidence on what works best to promote learning, especially for disadvantaged children. But Gove indulged himself by setting out his own, simplistic heroes-and-villains view in such subjects as history. He ordained a new national curriculum heavy on factual knowledge and the basics of grammar, spelling and multiplication tables. Taking an unashamedly traditional view, he promoted rote learning and swotting up. Gove's prescription for GCSE English specified 'high quality, intellectually challenging, and substantial whole texts in detail', which should include at least one play by Shakespeare; at least one 19th-century novel; a selection of poetry since 1789, including representative Romantic poetry; and fiction or drama from the British Isles from 1914 onwards. All works should have been originally written in English. Exam boards and schools could add any extra books they saw fit, but the new rules caused a storm, with Gove being accused of anti-Americanism when the school favourites *Of Mice and Men* and *To Kill a Mockingbird* were dropped, and neocolonialism when Mary Seacole, Crimean war nursing heroine, was dropped from history – after a rumpus, she was restored.

Exams

Results in GCSE and A-level can never be ascribed to a single set of ministers. They come and go; the education system is not some transmission belt, and measurements keep shifting.

Pushed by Ofqual, the exam regulator, the government said it was clamping down on 'grade inflation' to restore public confidence. Gove had said he wanted to bring back O-levels, but since this would mean bringing back the despised lower grade CSEs as well, the Liberal Democrats put their foot down. Instead, GCSE resits were banned. Instead of course work, it was back to traditional written exams for 60 per cent of marks available in GCSE English. He had to drop a plan for English Baccalaureate Certificates too, a rigidly prescribed list of academic subjects every child must take, because it was likely to exclude from the exam stakes the bottom 40 per cent of pupils. New GCSE and A-level syllabuses will be taught from 2015, with the first new exams in 2017.

Reform was necessary, claimed Professor Alison Wolf of King's College London (now a peer), in a report for the government. She found that 3,000 different qualifications had been recognised as GCSE 'equivalents', but were not welcomed by universities or employers. Bright pupils were sometimes misled into taking these semi-vocational options. However, instead of reforming them and creating a respected set of vocational exams, Gove abolished almost all, causing Wright Robinson College to close down decent facilities.

Money

In the 2010 spending plan, the total budget for English schools was to be protected, meaning funding would increase each year at the annual inflation rate. But the child population was increasing; primary school admissions were bulging; the per capita spending fell. To keep up with demand, the government needed to find an extra 240,000 school places by 2015. If not, schools had to be squeezed, and they were. Class sizes grew and the ratio of teachers to pupils shrank. One in eight primary school pupils in England are taught in classes that exceed the statutory maximum of 30 children: 12.5 per cent of pupils are now in classes over the limit. In 2014, nearly 3,000 infant classes breached the 30-pupil limit in the crucial learning-to-read years. About 94,000 are being taught in classes bigger than 30, three times more than in 2010.

Gove gave up Labour's £55bn Building Schools for the Future programme. This was more than obedience to austerity: Gove wanted to prove that schooling was about teaching, needing only pen and paper and desks, another whiff of nostalgia for chill no-frills pedagogy. But amid loud protests from Tory MPs who found much-needed repairs and new buildings for constituency schools summarily stopped, the DfE was within weeks surreptitiously trying to reverse the error. It made a string of subsequent announcements about 'priority schools' and complex schemes to bring in private finance.

A similar spirit hovered over playing fields. Like drama or vocational subjects, sport is an irrelevance and a distraction from schooling. Gove allowed fields to be sold, abolished Labour's £162m scheme in which well-equipped secondary schools lent PE teachers to primary schools. Later, following a damning 2013 Ofsted report on school sports, £150m was hastily earmarked, about £9,250 per primary school, for 2014 and 2015. Here again was a typical pattern: wilfulness then hasty regret at what had been destroyed.

The Tory instinct was to play down social needs: Gove wanted a fixed amount per pupil, regardless of home background or need. The Liberal Democrats complained, and fought to introduce a 'pupil premium' for students from poor households. Nick Clegg was the latest would-be reformer who hoped a relatively small amount of extra money in schools could miraculously compensate for the very large differences in resources between the social classes. An extra £488 per pupil eligible for free school meals was allocated in 2011–12, rising to £900 by 2013–14 in secondaries and £953 in primary schools. But this extra amounted to only 4 per cent more income for a primary school with high levels of children on free meals, and barely 1 per cent extra income for a secondary in a relatively comfortable catchment. Some schools used their ingenuity and tried to game the system, encouraging parents to sign up for free school meals.

It's too early to measure its effect, though extra money usually makes some difference to what a school can offer. One study produced a formula linking an extra £1,000 per primary pupil eligible for free meals to a term's extra progress at key stage 2. Much depends on what happens to the money inside the school and whether it is used to buy more or better teachers, or support staff or books. LSE researchers spelled out the larger truth that school income never compensates for lack of income at home. 'We estimate that closing the income gap between households with children eligible for free meals and other households with children (an increase of £6,000 a year) might be expected to halve the average school achievement gap between children on free meals and others.'[6]

Universities

Despite fees and loans, more students from disadvantaged backgrounds are applying to and entering higher education than ever before, even if those not eligible for free meals remain more than twice as likely to go to university. By accident, design and fiscal subterfuge, the coalition has presided over something of a higher education golden age. Numbers of 18-year-olds have fallen but applications from them are up two percentage points over the four years from 2010, with 412,000 students accepted on courses in 2014.

For all the building work and cranes swinging over campuses, and the continuing success of UK universities in international league tables, with Imperial and Cambridge appearing in the global top five, not many academics share that rosy view. The university pension fund is in deficit; pay under pressure, the gap between professors and lecturers growing; and the passage from PhD into secure employment fraught. Academics feel oppressed by the strain of adapting to growth, creating a mass system in which elite institutions have become ever more rarefied, conditions for the average academic have worsened and now, thanks to a deliberate move by the coalition, private sector colleges are snapping at their heels.

The government put a new funding regime in place, after amending a bipartisan scheme proposed by Lord Browne, the former BP executive. One element required the notorious policy somersault by the Liberal Democrats that irretrievably damaged their reputation. After a solemn election pledge to oppose an increase in tuition fees, to agree to raise them, let alone to £9,000 a year, will remain a political millstone. The block grant that had paid for teaching was withdrawn and the universities now relied on fees, to pay for which students qualified for state loans; these were also to cover living costs (with grants available for poorer students). It wasn't clear the government quite knew what it was doing. Fees of £9,000 would be 'exceptional', said higher education minister David Willetts. Five years on, only two of 123 universities are charging less.

For the first time, loans were extended to students at private, profit-making colleges. Thatcher's support for the new free-market University of Buckingham (a charity) today looks staid and unambitious. Now, fly-by-night firms and American corporates smelled opportunity. Students at what the coalition calls 'alternative providers' – private companies – now receive £1bn in public loans and grants.

Older universities started behaving more like businesses, paying their vice-chancellors fabulous sums and opening campuses in lucrative overseas markets such as Qatar. University College London acknowledged it had no control over how workers were treated on its site in the Gulf, which prompted the question whether it or other universities could really enforce academic standards halfway across the world.

For universities, indeed, this turned out to be an odd kind of austerity. They had received what Willetts called a 'surge' of cash but under the counter. Students were taking on huge debts, up to £67,000, and the average teacher could still owe £37,000 in 2014 prices by the age of 40. At first the government conceded a third of students would not pay back, but now it's thought three-quarters may never repay the full amount. By 2044, BIS said sheepishly, outstanding debt would be an enormous £330bn. The government started muttering about universities themselves advancing loans, so acquiring a good reason to teach subjects that would maximise students' future earnings.

The former vice-chancellor of the University of Sussex, Alasdair Smith, noted wryly that the government had 'paid surprisingly little attention to the problem of how to collect loan repayments from graduates'.[7] First, it tried to control student numbers, then allowed universities free rein. The government was effectively committing to at least £5.5bn of extra spending after 2015 and untold amounts to cover the cancellation of debt in future – which sounded neither austere nor prudent.

To pay for extra student numbers the Treasury planned to sell the loans to a company, which would pay to take over a notional debt total, then profit by collecting more than this amount from students. The calculations were fraught, and made more complicated by the fact that students from elsewhere in the EU could get loans but there was no way of chasing them if they returned home on graduation. The privatisation stalled, over Liberal Democrat objections. Student finance is a mess.

Ditto entry for non-UK students (and, within the UK, disparity in undergraduate fees and loans between Scotland and the other countries). As we discuss in chapter 11, Tory instincts on migration pushed a fall in the number of overseas (non-EU) students registering, for the first time in 30 years, a disaster for a sector that sees itself in contest with other countries for their fees.

Conclusion

In 2014 a record number of university places were available, which meant that, although A-level performance dropped slightly, for the first time in three decades most aspirants got a place somewhere. At GCSE the proportion getting A* to C grades rose despite the tougher regime instituted by the coalition, even if there was a slight fall in A* numbers and variation across the subjects. However, the proportion of students entered fell, and fewer 15-years-olds took the exam, which explained a lot, said the exam boards.

Neville Beischer was crowing, an extraordinary 64 per cent of his pupils getting A* to C grades including passes in English and maths. Wright Robinson is the most improved school in Manchester, doing better than the academies it was supposed to join, as measured in the scores for added value.

He has no simple formula. What really makes the difference is 'tracking and monitoring every student all the time, with a report sent home every half-term showing exactly where they are. It's incredibly hard work for everyone, working with every child, with absolute attention to detail, but it's a whole school attitude. We have 96 per cent attendance, by keeping at it all the time, never letting go.'

With downturns in 2012 and 2013, GCSE results have continued on the fairly steady upward path as under Labour, the social class attainment gap at GCSE lessening at the same slow pace, according to official figures. Poor children are doing better, the government claiming that 250,000 fewer pupils are now taught in 'underperforming' schools and 800,000 more in schools rated good and outstanding. Such measures depend on (variable) judgments made by Ofsted.

Their reliability accepted, they back this verdict on the coalition and English schools: unspectacular progress, relying on spadework under Labour. All Gove's sound and fury signified not a great deal. Never before had a minister united the moderate and less moderate unions; all passed votes of no confidence in his policies, complaining of a climate of fear and intimidation in their schools, as well as deteriorating pay and conditions. Academies and free schools have not caught the public imagination. Within sight of the election, the focus groups giving him a unanimous thumbs down, Gove was ejected. Once he had set in motion a tumultuous upheaval and attracted appropriate opprobrium, he was dispensable and was dismissed. Like Andrew Lansley, to whose disastrous assault on the NHS we now turn.

10

Health Re-disorganised

Watford general hospital has seen a procession of important political visitors, and not because they wanted to catch a game at Watford Football Club, its neighbour on Vicarage Road. The reason has been Samantha Jones, its forthright chief executive. She has made a reputation for her 'onion' meetings every morning at 8.15, where any staff member can come and talk about risks they see, peeling away the layers to get at the truth: transparency is her mantra. Over the past decade six chief executives have come and gone; over four years six finance directors have walked away or been ejected. Now her, a paediatric nurse by background. Health secretary Jeremy Hunt spent a day as a healthcare assistant; Ed Miliband shadowed her for two days; Norman Lamb, the Liberal Democrat minister, made the pilgrimage to the Hertfordshire town.

Watford's problems typify a growing number of NHS sites. Its buildings are 'a challenge', Jones says with a wry smile, 'inherently inefficient, not conducive to patient flow'. She manages a haphazard collection of shabby departments, difficult to navigate. The hospital belongs to West Hertfordshire Health Trust, which itself is awkwardly split across three sites, with hospitals at Hemel Hempstead (which has an urgent care centre) and St Albans, where patients go for elective surgery and diagnostics.

Watford A&E, like everywhere else, is under intense pressure; it may well be where the 2015 general election is decided.

Jones's budget covers only 30 per cent of the cost of emergency admissions. They are up, partly because of the rapid increase in numbers of the old and frail in its catchment, not something Jones can control. It's not just emergencies. Across England 68 per cent of outpatient appointments and 77 per cent of inpatient bed days are for those with long-term conditions.

Under the coalition the NHS budget has been flat. It kept up with general inflation, which is less than inflation in health service prices. That fixed amount has had to pay for the care of a growing and ageing population. The consequent squeeze has been unprecedented. Since 2010, mismatch between budgets and demand has grown: by 2014 the NHS was 'falling off a fiscal cliff', according to the Nuffield Trust, an independent thinktank. Bungs and bailouts ensued, to prop up wheezing trusts until after the 2015 election, as A&Es prayed for mild weather, for no outbreak of norovirus leading to ambulances queuing outside and cancelled operations. Whoever wins at Westminster in 2015 inherits a catastrophic shortfall.

Watford general is inspected by the Care Quality Commission (CQC), a quango grown so fat it now hires coaches to ferry its regiments of inspectors from hospital to hospital. Its 2014 report on Watford was grim. Jones claims not to resent the heavy-handed CQC inspections, which on slender evidence can damn the entire hospital: a single blood spot on a wall in A&E makes it dirty; one nurse off sick in a hospital of 600 beds and the whole place is deemed dangerously understaffed.

The CQC itself was deemed to have failed, by not detecting bad care and needless deaths at Stafford hospital, run by the Mid Staffordshire NHS Foundation Trust, and Furness general, run by University Hospitals of Morecambe Bay NHS Foundation Trust. Now inspectors are as afraid as those they examine, and pursue a deliberate policy of blaming and shaming. Any manager who protests risks sounding as if they are defending bad practice.

Here we try to explain the deep paradoxes in Cameron's treatment of the NHS, how halfway through the Tories tried to suppress their own mega-reform plan and, without putting any extra money in, deliberately stoked up pressure on trusts to spend more. After Mid Staffs, the National Institute for Health and Care Excellence (NICE) set guidelines for the number of nurses on wards – encouraged by Hunt and the government. As a result, nurse numbers have been rising sharply, pushing up trusts' pay bills. Watford general hired 160, recruiting from Italy, the Republic of Ireland, Spain and Portugal, in absurd and expensive competition with other hospitals. The extra numbers added £4m to Jones's mounting deficit.

Yes, things can't go on like this, she says, and 'there has to be a debate with the public about what they want to pay for and how. The public need to be engaged with the future of the NHS.' By the 'public' she really means the parties, which have to come clean with voters on the true cost of decent healthcare available to all.

The two great practical challenges of healthcare are the same now as they were in 2010: how to unify health and social care while rationalising community and acute provision, and how to pay for it. Instead, in the memorable phrase coined by Dr Sarah Wollaston, the Tory MP who took over the chair of the Commons health select committee, the effect of their legislation was 'to throw a hand grenade into the NHS'. Watford general is among the walking wounded.

In Good Shape

The coalition inherited a health service in better shape than at any time since its foundation – and so it should have been, since Labour had doubled spending on it, increasing at an average 5.6 per cent a year. Public approval rose, 51 per cent in 1997 to 71 per cent by 2010. Over 90 per cent of those leaving hospital declared their treatment good or very good. NHS waiting times for surgery, which used to stretch to two years ahead, had been abolished. Labour increased the number of doctors by two-thirds and nurses by a third. The UK reflected international trends: in all OECD countries health spending rose, often faster than economic growth, pushing up the ratio of health spending to GDP to an average 9 per cent by 2008.

Labour had also fragmented the NHS by creating Foundation Trusts, semi-autonomous bodies to run hospitals, mental health and ambulance services. Blair used private cataract and hip units to treat NHS patients, though, by 2010, only 2 per cent of NHS treatments were conducted in private beds.

By the election, Sir David Nicholson, NHS chief executive, had announced that £20bn in 'efficiency savings' would have to be made over the next four years, just to pay for natural growth in the numbers of the elderly and new technologies. Preparing for tougher times meant amalgamating hospitals and services. And controversy.

Still, nothing augured the assault on the finances and the structure of the NHS that followed. On the contrary, from the day he became leader of his party in 2005 Cameron strenuously reassured the public of his devotion to the NHS, even invoking his disabled son as evidence of his understanding of its value. 'I'll cut the deficit, not the NHS', said the posters. 'No more tiresome, meddlesome, top-down restructures.' He even joined a picket line, brandishing a 'Hands Off Our Hospitals' placard outside the A&E at Chase Farm hospital in Enfield. It's now shut.

The Great Deception

The ex-Tory minister Michael Portillo later said simply 'they did not believe they could win if they told you what they were going to do'. Behind the scenes they saw the NHS as a Chinese army-sized statist monster, to be broken up, privatised or reduced to a hollow insurance scheme. Hunt was only one of the young Turks urging radical surgery. His co-authored 2007 book, *Direct Democracy – An Agenda for a New Model Party*, spelled it out: 'Our ambition [is] in effect denationalising healthcare in Britain.' The NHS was 'a 60-year-old mistake' and 'a fundamentally broken machine'. The minister for policy, Oliver Letwin, had long been calling for more 'joint ventures' with firms, softening up the introduction of credits or vouchers allowing patients treatment in private clinics.

The Tory shadow health secretary was Andrew Lansley, Cameron's former boss at Conservative central office, an accredited policy wonk whose own wife was a GP. He had been brewing a grand plan since 2006 and, given the health job, he went straight at it after the election, with a white paper ominously subtitled 'Liberating the NHS'.

We puzzle over this prime minister so often. Disruptive and ideological, yes, but also diffident, perhaps lazy. His signature in welfare or transport was policymaking by doctrine, with impatient implementation left to chance. Here he was, risking the political capital acquired from his pre-election love-in with the nurses and doctors. Former chancellor Nigel Lawson had famously warned that the NHS was 'the closest thing the English have to a national religion' – Scotland, too, as they later learnt when threats to the NHS powered the surge in yes votes. No better reminder was needed than the popular delight in Danny Boyle's emotional evocation of the NHS at the 2012 Olympics opening ceremony. Cameron seems never to have assessed the risks in Lansley's scheme and certainly never gave a moment's thought to how the Scots might perceive the dash to outsource. The broad intention was to shrink the state and render what remained 'weightless', but to operate on the NHS with a rusty, contaminated knife ... Lansley had worked on gas and electricity privatisation of the 1980s: just as Thatcher had 'liberated' nationalised industries, so he gave the Tories a chance to butcher the last remaining emblem of what they had come to see as the great disaster of the mid-20th century, the election of the 1945 Labour government.

Lansley's Revolution

Lansley called his plans 'revolutionary' and for once immodesty was justified. Hospitals, clinics and ambulance services would only exist if GPs (in new autonomous groups replacing the primary care trusts) chose to commission them. Or buy something else: commissioning was to be marketised. In principle, private firms could be brought in, replacing NHS providers and even, Lansley having forgotten to take his sedatives, private firms actually doing the commissioning itself.

The government could be confident that most people knew little about NHS management; they would not ask how money would be allocated or why they were being shunted into a brand-new bureaucratic setup, the clinical commissioning group (CCG), the boundaries of which would not match those of councils or other bits of the NHS. Under the Tory plan, 212 of these CCGs replaced 152 PCTs. It went ahead without pilots or modelling. GPs weren't asked; they had not chosen medicine to spend their surgery hours negotiating with scores of hospitals, mental health teams, district nurses and podiatrists. Some were eager and the government won protective cover from a minority of entrepreneurial GPs who seized their chance to share profits from clinics they referred their own patients to. This was a clear conflict of interest, banned even in the US. One GP cheerleader in Surrey was caught dumping scores of unprofitable frail patients from his list.

Putting GPs in the shop window was clever marketing, but the plan had no easy passage. Its key was the bill's Section 75, which ordained that every element of the NHS had to be competitively tendered. The NHS was exposed to the full force of competition law: any company that felt it had been excluded from the chance to bid could take a CCG to court and sue if its bid (even a loss leader, deliberately undershot) had been refused. Lawyers swarmed; CCGs were soon being sued by private hospitals for referring patients to the NHS.

Competition was a theory. In health it didn't work, even in the market fanatics' textbooks. Bill McCarthy, policy director of NHS England, was quoted telling his board: 'We're committed to being a system that works on evidence and in this area, even taking from international experience, the direct evidence of where competition and choice works to improve outcomes is fairly limited.'[1]

Lansley was a fantasist. For patients, he coined the slogan: 'No decision about me without me'. The new law gave patients no say in running the CCGs. Besides, how could they choose the NHS if Virgin, Circle or Serco won the bid to provide a service? 'Liberating the NHS' was a joke: it turned out to mean enhanced powers for a central regulator, Monitor, its remit to enforce competition. From 2011 its chair and chief executive was an ex-McKinsey consultant, David Bennett. Monitor's chair was a former Tory health minister and leader of Kensington and Chelsea council, Baroness Hanham; so much for independence. At the head of the Care Quality Commission arrived another Tory, former MP David Prior, who preferred to have his hip done privately (in an NHS hospital) then consummated his love of the NHS by calling for American firms to take over its hospitals.[2]

Anyone in doubt about the plan should have harked to Mark Britnell, a No 10 adviser and head of health at KPMG. As the bill was getting a pasting in parliament, he urged equity investors in New York to swoop on rich pickings in the NHS. 'The NHS will be shown no mercy,' he said. 'In future the NHS will be a state insurance provider, not a state deliverer.' The NHS would be a Kitemark, a shell where competitive forces are played out.

Late in the day, the government panicked. In an unprecedented move, a month-long tea break was called bang in the middle of the bill's parliamentary progress. Compliant health professionals pored over its clauses and alterations were made – serving to make an already complex organogram almost unreadable. But at its core, nothing changed: instead of 'promoting competition', Monitor's job became 'preventing anti-competitive practices'.

Realising they had forgotten public health, disease control and infection labs, the Tories cobbled together a new quango; then, as a sop to the Liberal Democrats, who wanted more democratic oversight, public health was given to local authorities. Within a couple of years the British Medical Association was protesting about 'councils who've taken a large amount of money [from the public health grant] and spent it on services they would have been providing anyway'. Coordinating anti-obesity campaigns, let alone the fight against growing microbial resistance to antibiotics, had suddenly got a lot harder.

Having been excluded from the CCGs, patients were to be represented on obscure new local bodies called Healthwatch, 'raising issues of concern'; and, another scrap thrown to the Liberal Democrats, councils were to establish health and well-being boards. The theory was better coordination; practice was often another talking shop. Later, CCGs started to merge (growing to the same size as the PCTs they had replaced) with councils' health role as obscure as ever. Soon, elsewhere in the crazy paving, the commissioning support units (CSUs) the government had glued on the CCGs were in trouble. Mostly private and run by management consultants, they simply did not deliver. By now, the NHS had become a squirming spaghetti of boards and quangos.

Formerly, ministers and the Department of Health had more or less 'run' the NHS. Now, in an elaborate pass-the-parcel, the department gives 90 per cent of the £110bn annual health budget to NHS England – the super-quango – which parcels it out to CCGs, councils and GPs. Though its board meets in public, NHS England is secretive and opaque, especially over how it divvies up the money place by place; it does not even have a physical existence, merely an obscure forwarding address in Redditch. Malcolm Grant, its chair, impotently complained that the NHS (over which he apparently has no control) is spending the same on a single A&E attendance as a GP gets to care for someone for a whole year.

NHS technocrats lacked the will to stop the Tories' petty political vengefulness in uprooting anything to with the NHS brand as a matter of tribal principle, regardless of its effectiveness. So NHS Direct, a phone and web-based diagnostic service to give advice and channel people away from A&E, was chaotically replaced by a botched NHS 111 service provided by a cheap, non-medical call centre. High street NHS walk-in centres, designed with the same purpose, were closed.

A Service in Dire Straits

Spending on the NHS was touted as Tory generosity until at last the watchdog snapped. The UK Statistics Authority wrote to Hunt denying the claim that NHS spending was rising; it cited the Treasury's own figures showing that real terms spending was approximately the same in 2011–12 as it had been in Labour's last year, and that is how things would remain till 2015, despite increased numbers of patients to treat.

The NHS needs a minimum yearly uplift of 3 to 4 per cent in real terms: under Thatcher and Blair it needed emergency resuscitation when it briefly fell below that. As well as coping with flat real terms cash, the NHS is supposed to be saving 4 per cent a year from the cost of providing services in order to furnish a reserve to meet the growing costs of new technology and ageing. Something had to give – and from 2013 foundations that were supposed to be financially sound started reporting deficits. In contracts from CCGs, the Cinderella services such as mental and community health and school nursing suffered most. In the three years to 2014, mental health nursing staff fell by 6 per cent and psychiatrist numbers by 2 per cent, at a time when social and economic stress was high and, putting pressure on local authorities as well as the NHS, a sharp rise in diagnoses of dementia.

Elementary planning packed in. In England the birthrate had been ticking up. In its wisdom the government had cut funding for maternity care in half of England's regions. In 2012, there were 32.8 births per midwife against a national standard of 29.5, implying an extra 2,300 midwives were needed. In the year to 2013 spending on maternity services in London fell by 6 per cent, despite the rising birthrate. 'There is not one midwife practising today who has seen this level of births and demands on maternity services,' said Cathy Warwick, chief executive of the Royal College of Midwives. Service quality deteriorated. A fifth of all mothers were not receiving advice following the birth that might help ward off depression; the number of midwife visits after returning home from a birth fell.

Enter Hunt

We've wondered before in this book at Cameron's political intelligence, sharp one moment, awol the next. He allows Lansley to create mayhem, then Hunt is appointed to implement the 2012 Health and Social Care Act softly, softly, in the words of an expert witness 'to foster competition and increasing private provision, while keeping the NHS largely out of the public gaze'.[3] But Hunt in turn is a disaster. He ramps up public criticism of care standards, then fails in his effort to blame Labour, nurses and NHS managers and finds the public pins responsibility on him and underfunding by the coalition.

As the act was being buried in PR terms, the government hoped it would conceal the £3bn cost of rebadging, repainting and forcing 90,000 staff to reapply under new nameplates or be made redundant. By 2014, 4,000 of 38,000 redundant managers had been rehired. Hunt tried to reposition himself as the patients' and carers' friend, breaking his lance against uncaring clinicians and bureaucrats: to sour the idea that a public health service could be safe or kind.

NHS executives tried to ignore the act. The NHS needed 'integration', implying coordination between primary care, hospitals, mental health and concentration of resources and skills in a smaller number of high-performance A&Es, leaving local hospitals to do urgent care. Labour had taken important first steps, creating specialist 'pathways' for stroke and cancer treatment, showing that close integration, not competition, was the way to improve services. But the new structure makes this difficult, if not impossible. Bournemouth and Poole hospitals sought to merge both to save £14m a year and, clinicians concurred, improve services by pooling skills. No, said Monitor, making common cause with the Office of Fair Trading and Competition Commission – organisations that formerly had had no place in the NHS. Merger was 'anti-competitive'.

Chaos ruled. Members of the cabinet such as Hague, Duncan Smith and Grayling, all enthusiastic marketisers, put constituency interest before principle and stood on picket lines making sure local media captured their opposition to local closures. Lewisham hospital became a cause celebre, when the insolvency of a neighbouring trust (caused by a PFI-induced haemorrhage of income) led the government to try to switch profitable units from one hospital to another. Campaigners took their case to court and won. Hunt hastily changed the law to allow such top down reordering, never mind what patients thought.

The arrival of Simon Stevens in April 2014 to take over as the new head of NHS England made forgetting about the Lansley act harder. He had been its advocate, praising 'the decision to extend competition law across the health sector and treat the NHS as a regulated utility'. Since 2004 he had held a senior position at UnitedHealth, the big US health insurer, which had been moving into NHS contracts; he told interviewers he wanted hospitals to become more independent and to compete more, like Gove's free schools. After a few months, however, the tone changed. He veered off message, saying councils should be empowered to ban the sale of tobacco and sugary products, to stave off an obesity crisis: such market interference was not part of the plan.

Private Interests

Now the private interests that had backed Lansley's act wanted their pounds of flesh. Billions of pounds actually. During 2013–14, the act's first year, private firms took NHS work worth £8bn. Firms won't win all tenders but the direction of travel is unmistakable.

Barely noted in public debate, the Transatlantic Trade and Investment Partnership (TTIP) being negotiated between the EU and the US looked set to prise open the health service, giving American companies the unfettered right to bid for any NHS function that was put out to tender. Labour called for the NHS to be excluded from the deal, but BIS said the NHS would not be affected, for the good reason that the NHS was already open to all-comers. American firms were winning work. The state-of-the-art cancer centre at the NHS flagship University College Hospital in London was astounded at losing a contract to treat brain tumours; NHS England decreed that patients now be referred to Hospital Corporation of America, a company that has given cash to the Tory party – and had been accused of price gouging in previous NHS contracts. American pharmaceutical companies have long wanted to dismantle the centralised NHS procurement of drugs. They particularly resent NICE, which tests the efficacy of their products with such rock-solid evidence that a quarter of all state purchases of medication worldwide use NICE guidance and NHS reference prices.

But Hunt had learnt a lesson from his secret dealings with Murdoch and kept his distance from the lobbyists. Instead, his tactic was to open the door to alternatives to the NHS by doing it down. He was determined to 'look under the bonnet' and unearth bad treatment. He showed us a giant noticeboard in his office listing 'never events', medical calamities that should never happen. Where, we innocently asked, was the board showing where the NHS had performed well? He characterised the NHS by sweeping generalisations about quality and practice.

The long Mid Staffs inquiry played into his hands. He ordained crude measures of worth, notably the 'friends and family' test on service quality, used by regulators and ministers to name and shame. Usually these surveys of patient opinion were statistical abominations, but a low score led to ominous warning signs appearing on government websites accompanied by big exclamation marks.

Forget Lansley's claim that commissioners and markets would run the NHS day-to-day, cutting the politicians out. Hunt was hyperactive, summoning NHS England directors and civil servants, interrogating chief executives of local hospitals over their A&E waiting times. The CQC was heavily leant on. For Hunt, it seemed the worse the inspection results, the better pleased he was. Tory commentators and MPs took up the refrain: the NHS was a failure, by its very nature.

Hunt devised a 'duty of candour' for NHS staff, requiring them to speak up when the care they saw around them was below standard. The new duty was not, of course, accompanied by financial commitments to improve the supply of services (which was most often the basis of complaints). Nor did it empower senior managers to tell uncomfortable truths to ministers. This was an era of fear and cowardice, when managers and civil servants only dared say off the record that targets, waiting times and high-quality care were not achievable on the available funds or that the Lansley commissioning model simply did not work.

Hunt's tactics chimed with Tory radicals, but by 2013 Downing Street became anxious. Election adviser Lynton Crosby could see from polling that dissing the NHS was rebounding on those in charge of it – themselves. The word went out that Hunt should pipe down. Even though the Tories remained keen to accelerate the NHS's demise through commercialisation, first an election had to be won.

Populist gestures and bungs became Hunt specialties – anything to tide the system over, while impressing electors with crocodile tears over patients. The secretary of state became a parking attendant. All hospitals must give free or cheaper space to the vehicles of relatives. It made a good headline. But freestanding foundation hospitals could not be instructed. Many had already outsourced their car parking to companies or would have to compensate their PFI company for loss of parking income.

The minister donned his chef's hat. Hunt would crack down on poor hospital food, threatening legally enforceable standards for meals. His interventions were utterly ineffectual.

The *Daily Mail* had led campaigns for various drugs that prolonged life by a few months and Hunt suddenly found an extra £160m for the Cancer Drugs Fund, set up after the election and already spending £200m a year on treatments that had been assessed by NICE and rejected on grounds of cost-effectiveness. Sir Andrew Dillon, head of NICE, said tartly that it made no sense to second-guess him. 'It's inevitable if you allocate more money to one condition, other conditions are getting less.' Neither the *Daily Mail* nor the coalition went in for probability or quality-adjusted life years.

Election Panic

The nearer the election, the more panic at being blamed for lengthened waiting lists and A&E queues, let alone distress in primary care. What was the point of commissioning if surgeries were closing? Some 500 GP practices have shut since 2010, with one opening for every five closures. Hunt tried to subvert the structure, bypassing CCGs, shunting money to trouble spots. Hospital trusts with bulging deficits were given one-off payments to speed up treatment and shrink waiting lists. The Foundation Trust Network said Hunt now recognised a 'direct link between funding and performance: you get what you pay for'. No, this was a sticking plaster, signed off by a chancellor wanting to staunch electoral bleeding.

Social Care Crisis

The cry echoes through the NHS; we heard it from Samantha Jones at Watford general. 'We need stability from now on. No more organisational change.' But she is wrong, on two counts. One has to do with why acute services are under siege, and how care for older people is structured – it has to change. The other is the need to switch from treating ill health to tackling its causes, with all that implies about markets, profitability and the state. Much disease is strongly linked to income. It's poverty and inequality that are associated with multiple ills, from diabetes to higher rates of cancer, depression and heart disease.

Root cause analysis never interested the coalition and it was never likely to take an all-round view of social and healthcare for older people. Community care is never going to be the cheap solution proffered by some, but for many patients and their loved ones home is always going to be preferable to the wards of acute hospitals, let alone residential care. So when Age UK reports that patients are blocking hospital beds for an average of 27 days while waiting for grab rails and ramps to be installed at home, it encapsulates the problem of strategy and coordination in social care that has bedevilled governments before – but, as the UK ages, the cost of failing to address it will only increase.[4]

In a given week, some 77 elderly patients occupy beds at Watford general, even though they need no further medical treatment. There's no plan for how they might be looked after at home. Some need four visits a day – a responsibility of the local authority. The coalition claimed it was addressing the question with its Better Care Fund, which is stripping £2bn from Watford and similar hospitals to provide a pool from which local authorities and the NHS are to create a joint system of care. In the long run, investing in good community services should mean fewer hospital admissions. 'Keep our nerve, and it could work. It must work,' Jones says. But in the short run, the government is taking money from A&Es and acute hospitals – the assumption is that Watford general could cut 15 per cent of emergency admissions – that are barely clinging on. As NHS finances worsen, the government has already been raiding its own fund to bail out hospitals.

Thinking of Retiring?

If you are thinking of retiring to Brixham or Bideford – attractive south-west towns both – you need to know that Devon county council is closing 20 of its care homes, and half its day centres, handing them over to the private sector. Devon is Tory controlled but the picture is not much different in Labour Durham, which also began shutting down its remaining stock of council care homes. Residents in five of its homes are all being moved on, potentially breaking up communities of friends.

The plan had been to push the NHS down the road already trodden in social care, where in some parts of the country care provision is almost entirely private and the 'market' is now worth £15bn. The *Financial Times* reported American investors flooding in to buy care homes and reap yields of 7 per cent in places like Bournemouth, for example. These would take only clients paying their own way. Homes that took in those funded only by the state were struggling and many closed.

Plymouth House outside Bromsgrove sits beside a canal that most of its 23 residents can see from their bedroom windows. Frank and Margaret Ursell have run this nursing home in a converted coaching inn since 1983 – and say the financial squeeze has never been harsher. Most of their very frail residents are paid for by Worcestershire county council at £538 each per week, a relatively low rate for people with dementia and other high needs. Dryly, Frank Ursell notes that you would pay £73 a night at the local Premier Inn, only £25 a week less than the council pays for Plymouth House residents and they get round-the-clock care. He is chief executive of the Registered Nursing Home Association, its members struggling.

Councils report that in the two years from 2011 there was a 13 per cent rise in 'safeguarding referrals' – instances where the public, police or inspectors say vulnerable people are at risk. Everything in care is done on the cheap: some 220,000 people working in care earn less than the minimum wage. Problems, and the failure of privatisation as a solution, are not new. The prevalence of dementia will double over the next 20 years. The number in care homes in England, 425,000, has been stable despite population growth, which shows more older people are staying in their own homes. Those in care are older and their condition more acute than 20 years ago. Typical residents have combinations of disability, frailty and cognitive impairment, and they need to take combinations of drugs. The mantra that everything can be done in people's own homes is often wishful thinking; care can be complex and expensive.

In 2013, councils spent some £14.6bn on adult care, the same as the previous year in cash terms, meaning a real terms decrease; the NHS spent an estimated £2.8bn, while the DWP spent some £28bn on adult incapacity, disability and injury benefits. In aggregate, it's a lot, but covers a multiplicity of needs and capabilities. Most caring is done unpaid by family members and neighbours and friends, including some 2.2 million people who have given up work in order to care for loved ones. Costs have been rising, although in absolute terms the care costs are modest compared to those of health and pensions – just 1.3 per cent of national income – but as the numbers of the very old increase, spending on long-term care is growing, taking another 0.5 per cent of national income between now and 2040.

The week we spoke to Ursell, the CQC had closed the inappropriately named Agape House in Chatham. Love of humanity was found to be absent in a home – not a member of his association – failing on every count, one of whose patients had died after being admitted to hospital with multiple pressure sores. As with health, the government toughened the regime, sending the stormtroopers of the CQC into more care homes at precisely the moment cash-strapped councils are driving down the rates they will pay. Ursell's home gets a tick from the CQC on every indicator, but he protests at rising expectations and shrinking funds, noting the inspectors never dare say council fees are simply inadequate.

All the old fault lines are cracking open. If you are categorised as having an 'NHS condition', it's 'continuing care' and treatment is free. If, however, you are merely dependent (or have a condition such as dementia which isn't an NHS condition) you need 'social care', provided by the local authority and charged for unless you are classed as poor and own no significant property. Coalition ministers talked of integrating the two budgets. The King's Fund commissioned a report from a panel led by Dame Kate Barker, who said an extra £5bn is needed to create a single system – treading into political no man's land by suggesting tax might be raised.

But we all have to go over the top. There is just not enough money to set up an effective new community care service that could keep the very frail at home; eventually, in theory, savings could be made from hospital admissions but the interregnum could be long and costly. Closing the old Victorian mental hospitals showed that money had to be found to build up community services first, with double funding for a while before removing beds.

How (Not) to Finance Social Care

In a few areas services have been blended but the exemplar, Torbay, crashed into the coalition's plan for the NHS, which tends to fragment services. They had no strategy for social care but were not averse to pretending they did. Councils used a means assessment as the gateway to residential care; paying for care sometimes required the sale of assets, which in most cases is a house or flat. The rightwing press frequently took up the cause of families, ostensibly outraged because Mum was having to leave her long-time home, but aggrieved at seeing an inheritance slipping away.

Labour had devised what was effectively a compulsory insurance scheme. On retirement, all those with property or significant savings would be required to pay in a lump sum (£25,000); the money would be pooled to pay for those who subsequently needed care, even long years in a home. The Tories and their journalist supporters ripped into 'Labour's death tax'.

But in his turn Cameron had to pay attention to the stories from MPs' surgeries, even affecting well-heeled party members: the care system was failing. He played for time by asking Andrew Dilnot, the unimpeachable former director of the IFS, to report, but on a narrow brief to do with protecting inheritances not raising extra care funds. It was an impossible task. The only options remained what they had been under Labour, taxation or compulsory insurance – a welfare state extension the Tories could never contemplate.

Dilnot did some careful arithmetic and worked out that the cost of *care* for any individual could be capped, with relatively small consequences for public spending. This sounded too good to be true, and was. Dilnot's cap didn't include accommodation costs; residents in care homes would still have to fork out from their own money to pay for their bed, food, cleaning and so on, around £12,000 a year. Even then Dilnot was regarded as too generous. The coalition raised the cap higher than he suggested and, with fanfare, announced £72,000 as the upper limit on what anyone would ever pay for care, even if they were as rich as the Queen. Once a property owner had spent this much of their money, remaining costs would be taken on by the state. They would, of course, have to live long enough to expend £72,000 – the Institute and Faculty of Actuaries predicted the cap would benefit barely one in 12 men and one in 6 women, who tend to live longer. Most entering care would still end up paying the full costs themselves.

The cap is to apply from April 2016. The government hoped that once there was a firm limit on care costs, insurers would offer policies. So far, none of the big insurers has played ball, saying total costs remain too vague; it's yet another example of the strict limits of markets. Then Age UK spotted another flaw. The clock would only start ticking towards the cap once an elderly person was officially designated as having 'substantial' needs. But councils are defining 'substantial' much more tightly; means testing is getting meaner.

Local authorities' total spending on adult social care fell 8 per cent in real terms in the three years to 2013, and the NAO said this meant 'spending on individual packages of adult care services of home care, care homes with and without nursing, and day care has fallen significantly'. Age UK reported that 800,000 fewer frail people were receiving any home care since 2010, despite rising numbers in need.

Cynically the coalition imposed a new duty on councils to assess and support carers, from April 2015. The Local Government Association says they have been given too short a time to implement 700 pages of regulations and guidance; but that is a minor problem compared to the money – councils won't have enough. A survey by directors of adult social services finds nine out of 10 councils in England no longer offer social care to people whose needs are deemed 'moderate' or 'low'. These are loose categories, allowing councils lots of wiggle room. Take Julie-Ann Baker from Crawley in West Sussex. Tory West Sussex county council fixed her needs as 'moderate', even though she is totally blind and has hearing aids. A council-paid carer came in for just four hours a week to take her shopping, change her bed, sort out bad food in her fridge and vacuum her home. Then West

Sussex abolished care for those with 'moderate' needs and she lost that small but vital help. How much worse would her condition have to be for her to have 'substantial' needs? Until that point, whatever she spends on care does not count towards the £72,000 cap.

Councils have also been cutting support for the charities that otherwise might step in with help. Southwark Circle was a showcase membership and mutual support group. For a joining fee of £20 a year, it offered isolated older people practical help from neighbours with domestic tasks. In his big society days, Cameron lavishly praised it and an evaluation said it might help reduce unplanned hospital admissions and non-essential GP visits. In 2014 it collapsed, for lack of funds.

Final Thoughts on the NHS

UK health spending has been falling as a percentage of GDP since 2009 and even penurious Portugal now spends a higher proportion. As planned, the ratio falls from 9.2 per cent of GDP to just 8.5 per cent over the next 10 years. During this time the number of over-80s will rise steeply. Not all will be vulnerable or sick; increased longevity is a great blessing for many families. But the population is also rising, by some 3.5 million between 2010 and 2018. The result has to be less money for health per head, about 9 per cent over the decade, says the IFS. If it cost £550 a day to look after an adult with learning difficulties in 2010, £495 will notionally be available in 2020 – which translates into fewer nurses and occupational therapists, less time and attention, a harsher life.

Forward projections are tricky. To avoid cuts in service or a reduction in the quality of healthcare, and to accommodate the growth in population, the NHS in 2020 would need up to £54bn more; if it made productivity gains, between £28bn and £34bn more. Those figures assume that the NHS budget would be protected after 2015: if it had to take a proportionate share of the aggregate spending cuts in Osborne's plans, the pressure would be that much more severe.

Monitor looked ahead at that gap and called in McKinsey to see how it might be bridged. The consultants came up with the same old chestnuts, moving care into the community, treating the chronically ill at home not in hospital, selling off NHS property, cutting doctors' and healthcare assistants' pay – which would cut quality of care and end today's effort to reach post-Mid Staffs standards.

Such savings don't plug the black hole. We already face a crisis over the shortage of GPs, and hospitals with lowest staff ratios have the lowest standards. Maureen Baker, chair of the Royal College of General Practitioners, said that, in 2013, 60 million people were having to wait a week to get a doctor's appointment, which was 'a national disgrace': so much for putting GPs at the heart of the NHS. At Watford general, Samantha Jones wants the politicians to be more honest about money, but she too needs to tell her clinicians, cleaners and patients the hard facts. If more money is not found, health and care services will decline. But more money has to mean more tax. The coalition cannot be held responsible for ageing, cost pressures or the structural divides between community and acute care. But Cameron can and must answer for failing to address these existential questions, and for the disastrous reorganisation of the NHS in England while putting it through the worst financial squeeze in its history.

11

Britannia Unchained

We borrowed the title of this chapter in ironic spirit from a peculiar book that's essential reading. In 2012 appeared *Britannia Unchained*, written by a group of Tory mates, several of whom were later promoted to sit round the cabinet table. They are the Tory party present and future. What's peculiar – dig out a 50 pence piece – is Britannia; she is equipped with trident, shield and lion, the accoutrements of 'old' statehood. They point to naval, military and diplomatic strength (and, of course, to the unity of the realm, which is now in jeopardy).

To the book's authors, the state is the enemy. Their 'chains' are welfare spending, taxation and regulation. Strike down those shackles and Britannia will rise again, trading and enterprising. But not, it seems, running an army. This is new Toryism. 'We may not have many gunboats any more but we hardly need them,' said Boris Johnson in a telling intervention, 'because we are already fulfilling our destiny as the soft power capital of the world.'[1]

Leave aside his breathtaking arrogance, given the failure of the City and the mediocre performance of British business. Our question is what Cameron's coup implied for all that traditional Tories used to hold dear: order, and power, guarding the borders, protecting citizens at home from crime and terror, and defending national interests across the globe. For them, Britannia needs shield and trident. But does she wield them to fend off immigrants, who free-market Tories must surely welcome as they set up businesses and help cut wage levels?

Britannia's sibling is Leviathan. A state with aircraft carriers, drones and Trident nuclear submarines or, at home, police boots on the streets or a fleet of new water cannon trucks doesn't feel 'weightless'. It's also not cheap. The contradiction confronts Tea Party republicans and the right everywhere: how does a low-tax, marketised, hollowed-out state still flex the strong arm of the law at home and project influence abroad?

We can't pretend to have found some golden thread of coherence in their approach. Cameron's ministers talked creative destruction and anarchy in government, but real anarchy, on the streets of London and Birmingham in the August 2011 riots, was something else – the kind of thing 19th-century Toryism came together to suppress. The state cracked down hard. But the riots were a one-off; austerity damped rather than excited revolt. For the party of the *Daily Mail* and *Daily Telegraph*, cuts to police, courts and prisons were high risk, all the more so because ministers did not simultaneously wind down the old rhetoric of punishment and retribution.

Crime Falls

In March 2014 crime hit its lowest level in the UK for 33 years, according to the ONS Crime Survey for England and Wales – including violent offences and theft. Sexual offences reported to the police had, however, been rising, perhaps because victims were encouraged by public discussion of celebrity scandals, including the Jimmy Savile case. Crime-free utopia had not arrived. One estimate put the cost of unrecorded crime at £24bn plus the £50bn the NAO estimated for known criminal and fraudulent transactions. Police forces reported that shoplifting for food was up. Half of all offences went unsolved, including three-quarters of thefts. One in 20 credit cardholders fell victim to fraud; internet crime was rife and cyber law enforcement was inadequate, the Commons home affairs committee complained.

Labour had thrown the kitchen sink at crime, expanding police numbers, creating the support officer role, legislating hyperactively, expanding prisons. However, the political return was paltry and the Tories were ahead on law and order in 2010. As ever, the public thought crime was rising. Theresa May, the rightwinger who became home secretary, spotted cover for cuts. 'There is no simple relationship between police numbers and the level of crime,' she said. 'Across the world police numbers have gone up and crime has gone up, or police numbers have gone down and crime has gone down.'

Tories and the Police

The Tories used to be the police party. Sir Robert Peel, who created the Metropolitan police in 1829, was the man who went on to save the Tory party from self-destruction in 1846. Now May was determined to put the bobbies in their place. The former chief constable of Gloucestershire, Tim Brain, called it deliberate de-professionalisation, noting the attack on the police had been extensively planned before the election in Policy Exchange seminars. May implied she would personally hold the stopwatch as constables were being put through their fitness paces in running the 100 metres in the Home Office-approved time.

It was a torrid time: the Met was accused of smearing Stephen Lawrence's family, and the South Yorkshire force were accused of presenting false evidence in order to blame Hillsborough on the victims of the disaster then of ignoring the sexual abuse of hundreds of children in Rotherham. The Police Federation gave May the silent treatment at their conference, later to find Tory MPs gunning for them, supporting investigations into the Met (after the 'plebgate' affair) and approving the appointment of a desiccated lawyer as chief inspector of constabulary rather than a decorated police officer.

But even he was concerned at £2.5bn of cuts since 2010, with another £656m to come in 2015–16. The workforce fell by over 34,000 in the five years to March 2015, including 8,500 uniformed officers. May had promised to 'end centralisation, targets and ringfences' and put an end to Labour's attempt to rationalise the 43 separate police forces in England and Wales. (In Scotland, a single force now covers the entire country.) She promptly tried to centralise the purchase of helicopters and IT – even constables' shirts and shields.

Police and Communities

The police became party political. The coalition engineered constitutional shifts. On the one hand the Police Reform and Social Responsibility Act 2011 made the police subject to elected commissioners; on the other, the 'Strategic Policing Requirement' in July 2012 strengthened Whitehall control. But having legislated, the government seemed to lose interest in its new-fangled commissioners. Elections that year were called for dark November, not the best month to get people out to the polls. Turnouts were derisory, ranging from 11.6 per cent in Staffordshire to 19.5 per cent in Northants, and averaging 15.1 per cent across England and Wales. An inquest by MPs concluded that most people neither knew what they were voting for or (the Home Office having refused to pay for election flyers) even that elections were happening.

After, awareness rose marginally, as commissioners were accused of nepotism and high salaries. Some were accident prone, notably the Kent commissioner who appeared to be mystified about her functions. A film company specialising in mockumentaries met Ann Barnes and left viewers unsure whether she cleverly played the television game by pretending not to know she was in a spoof or, more likely, hadn't a clue what was going on. When the incumbent commissioner for the West Midlands died, the consequent by-election attracted fewer than one in 10 of the registered electorate.

Yet local policing was vitally alive…

Inspector Damian O'Reilly of Greater Manchester police remains an effective officer. His job now is policing Manchester airport, but the citation for the MBE he was awarded in the 2012 New Year honours noted services to the community of Gorton.

That's where, five years ago, we talked to him for *The Verdict*. Policing an area where he himself had been born and bred, he had been in charge of 'community reassurance' across three tough wards, as important as crime reduction itself.

Then, he had been patrolling the patch since around 2000, during a decade of plenty. Police resources swelled. He had a team: 55 staff, police and support officers working in partnership with social workers and council officials. One was based in the local housing office. This was what neighbourhood policing should be, he said, intertwined with every other service.

Ears to the ground, they knew every problem household. They had just broken up a gang, the Ryder Brow Soldiers, who had been terrorising a local estate – 15- to 17-year-olds, hoodies up, had set on a community support officer. One went to jail, the others were fined and asbo'd, banned from assembling in groups of more than three. End of problem. 'Crime reached an all-time low, by our hard graft.'

Then, he bounded with enthusiasm, eager to show off his remarkable Key Individuals Network. KIN was 1,200 residents willing to help the police stamp out crime and antisocial behaviour: an army of curtain-twitchers and an intelligence network. Four hundred locals would turn up to a community meeting: in those days, O'Reilly even had petty cash to pay for a cup of tea. Surveys showed that 75 per cent were confident the police were getting to grips with local problems.

It's different now. Since 2010 the Greater Manchester police force has been cut from 8,200 to 6,400. Gorton was downgraded to a satellite station. O'Reilly's team was moved five miles away, to cover all of east Manchester. 'Often officers are called somewhere else. We became reactive, not proactive, no longer a team. We raised Gorton up and I was just so sad to see all that we had built being lost.'

And yet the figures for recorded crime don't seem to be rising. Not yet, or not officially. 'But Gorton people see fewer police on the streets. Families we know are now getting the message: they can get away with stuff.' People don't report crime the way they did. Residents are pessimistic. 'They see services running down. They don't blame us, they know it's the cuts, but you should hear the choice words they use. They're resilient and the difference we made will go on.'

He remains chair of Safe Gorton, a community cafe and young people's project run in conjunction with the Sacred Heart church on Levenshulme Road. The committee was meeting with the priest in the cafe the day we visited, in a bright, warm annexe to the church, with settees and armchairs and eager learning-disabled young people as trainees.

Father Andrew Stringfellow, in charge for the past eight years, notes the changes. Despite Gorton's reputation, rising house prices in central Manchester have sent young middle-class couples out this way, buying Victorian houses overlooking the park. For locals, times have been hard. 'I never used to have people knocking at the presbytery door asking for food. For money sometimes, but not hungry people who can't feed their children, asking for food that doesn't need to be cooked as they haven't money for the gas and electricity for their cooker.'

He points to the shrivelling of institutional support since 2010, the police most of all. 'We've always worked with Damian and his team but I don't know who the police are round here any more.'

———

Once, police cuts would have occasioned alarm and predictions of blood on the streets. Now it's subtler, to do with social cohesion. Inspector O'Reilly's boss is Peter Fahy, chief constable of Greater Manchester. He told us: 'It's not crime as it used to be. It's things that are more complex, domestic violence, rape, child abuse, truanting and issues of chaotic lifestyles. We see the same people, same families, time and again, with problems not best dealt with by the criminal justice system.'

But coalition ministers could not – would not – join policing to social policy, or accept their own welfare and spending policies were part cause of the problem. They left chief constables to get on with it. In the West Midlands, chief constable Chris Sims is spending £25m on consultants Accenture to help redesign policing (after having to cut the force's budget by £100m and with a further £125m to save over the next five years).

The coalition had no strategy for police who are simultaneously doing social work and fighting international crime syndicates. May had gone on the rampage, killing off the National Policing Improvement Agency and the Serious Organised Crime Agency. In came two new quangos, a College of Policing and a National Crime Agency, answering directly to her. Such chopping and changing is bound to affect how well terrorism is policed, both fundamentalist and Irish Republican.

Bang 'Em Up

Hug-a-hoodie barely survived the election; it became bang 'em up. A lot were already locked up. At 85,494 in October 2010 the prison population of England and Wales was at a record high, 2,150 places below the maximum the jails could hold. England and Wales had 148 prisoners per 100,000 people in 2013, the second highest rate in western Europe, after Spain. Labour's record was not inspiring, with the prison population growing by 4 per cent a year to 2008 thanks to a rise in custodial sentences and an increase in the length of sentences.

Lord Woolf, the former lord chief justice who had reported on prison disturbances in 1991, noted how numbers 'have steadily climbed without any benefit to the safety of the public'.[2] That's the point. Crime did not have a coherent relationship with either police numbers or prisoner numbers. But unaccountably the logic that applied to the police was not applied to prisons.

Imprisonment costs £35,000 a year per head, plus criminal justice system costs, and the coalition attempted to make jail cheaper. Prison places were shrinking, with 18 establishments closed or given other functions, losing 6,500 places. More were crammed in, but warder numbers also fell, down by a third during the government's first three years. The Howard League pointed to rising prison suicides as a sign of overstretch, let alone growing prisoner-on-prisoner assaults and attacks on staff, at the highest levels ever recorded.

The government played to the tabloids by restricting inmates' parcels, including books, provoking the ire of the poet laureate among others. Alarm bells were ringing; the Prison Reform Trust reported worsening safety and fewer opportunities for rehabilitation. Prisons are providing less education, work and therapy. The Ministry of Justice itself said 74 out of 119 prisons in England and Wales were overcrowded in mid-2014, with 9,242 more prisoners in jail than the system was designed for and built to hold. The way forward is going to be costly. Super-prisons, a Labour idea, are to be built at Wrexham and possibly as a replacement for the young offender facility at Feltham, keeping children as young as 12 far from home in a gigantic institution. The MoJ has started re-employing staff it had just made redundant.

The government's instincts said outsource. But beyond a certain point even true believers have to yield to the evidence, which said private jails do not perform better, nor – after changes in working practices and regrading in public prisons cut costs – were they any cheaper. The MoJ had tried in 2011 to transfer nine prisons to private companies but, a year later, only one had gone ahead. In its own assessment, two of three establishments of 'serious concern' to the MoJ were run by G4S and Serco. With 18 per cent of inmates in outsourced jails at Easter 2014, the government admitted the proportion was not expected to increase 'over the next few years'.

Rehabilitation Revolution

Bang 'em up seemed to negate a positive policy that the Tories had worked on in opposition: community rehabilitation of offenders, especially repeat offenders. The line was that recidivism at 70 per cent was catastrophic. But cutting reoffending meant spending more in and on prison, also revamping probation and joining together police, councils and charities.

Probation had been run by local quasi-independent trusts that answered directly neither to councils nor Whitehall; it was also shrinking, with staff cut by 12 per cent by 2013. The government rushed ahead with a scheme that was simultaneously to save millions, expand probation to cover short-sentence prisoners, prevent reoffending and secure profits. It was going to be a tall order, even after the MoJ inserted 'poison pill' clauses into contracts, allowing firms to gouge the government for lost profits should Labour win in 2015 and cancel the arrangement.

The plan published in May 2013 stopped short of full privatisation, retaining a rump public service to oversee serious offenders and others with a public reputation in whom the media might be interested: the contractors could not be trusted to respect confidentiality against ever-eager tabloids. In doublespeak, Grayling said the reforms would extend professional freedom, when pursuing profit would diminish the autonomy of probation officers, 99 per cent of whom opposed the plan. Firms are to be paid only if they get results – which builds in an incentive to slough difficult (expensive) clients off to other public bodies or the voluntary sector. Only later did the ministry realise that magistrates are likely in future to use fewer community service sentences and deliberately imprison offenders in order to qualify them for probation. Note, not for the first time, the extraordinary reliance placed by a party steeped in individualism on 'community' action but also how, by sleight of hand, community was elided with profit-making.

This was policymaking that lacked analysis and data and market logic. How would the spoils be divided between the probation firms and the companies running prisons, let alone those trying to profit from DWP benefits assessments? Their interests clashed. Grayling ruled out pilots. The presence in the justice department of a Liberal Democrat minister typically made zero difference. Simon Hughes's ineffectiveness was displayed when he was banned from visiting a women offenders' centre – an alternative to custody introduced under Labour – because it was run by an organisation that might in future bid to take over probation. 'Absolute madness,' said Rachel Halford, director of the Women in Prison campaign.

Courts and Sentencing

Disarray, we keep saying. Here's the home secretary drastically cutting police numbers, with a plausible cover story about crime falling. Here's the justice secretary increasing prisoner numbers with an implausible story about jail and crime. But Cameron's first pick was Kenneth Clarke, who agreed to cut the budget for criminal justice by 24 per cent in real terms over five years, promising efficiency, fewer buildings, layers of management reduced. And, critically, 6,000 fewer prisoners in custody than had been projected for 2015, saving £324m. Defendants could make early pleas of guilty to earn reductions in sentence, saving court and prison costs.

But old vindictiveness was still alive. The Tory press and backbenchers had a seizure at this hint of leniency and No 10 repudiated Clarke. His successor, Chris Grayling, faced having to make the savings implied by lower prison numbers, which helps explain the desperation and recklessness in pursuit of outsourcing to try to cut costs.

The 2011 riots had already added to extra court and prison costs as police in England and Wales recorded over 5,000 riot-related offences in the space of six days. The public mood was vengeful and the courts treated offenders harshly. That mood prevailed for the whole parliament. Here's a paradox. Early intervention in the lives of young people likely to offend could produce a benefit-to-cost saving of 2.5 to 1, but that meant an energetic, resourceful state, which was anathema.

Like its predecessor, the government celebrated coming to power by creating new offences, 634 in its first year – but still not as many as the extraordinary 1,235 created by Labour in the year after May 1997. But 162 courts were to close, so cases were processed more slowly. Cuts in police and probation took their toll: trials not going ahead increased. The digital court-room, announced in June 2013, promised Wi-Fi, evidence screens and new presentation tools, but it might not have lawyers and staff to run it.

The coalition even tried to get rid of expensive justice altogether, with radical plans to privatise the courts service or float it into a non-state body. This proved a contract too far and the government backtracked. The Treasury adjusted allowable costs but by no means enough to modernise IT and buildings; funds are needed to integrate the legal, proba-tion, police and prison services into a seamless conveyor belt dedicated to securing cheaper but more reliable justice. In the meantime, the courts are required to bring in commercial leadership and expertise.

Like its predecessors, the government tidied up and extended the criminal law; for example, toughening punish-ments for stalking and making it more difficult for people to squat. Organised crime and trafficking were also targets. From April 2011 'Sarah's Law' was enacted, allowing anyone to ask for a police check on people who have contact with children.

If they have convictions for sexual offences against children or are deemed to pose a risk of causing harm, the police can tell a parent, carer or guardian. During the initial 12 months the police received over 1,600 enquiries and they made at least 160 disclosures relating to child sex offences. The Legal Aid, Sentencing and Punishment of Offenders Act 2012 introduced 'two strikes' mandatory life sentences for those convicted of a second very serious sexual or violent offence. To deliver a manifesto promise, 16- and 17-year-olds guilty of 'aggravated' knife offences were to get a mandatory minimum four-month prison sentence – again inflating prison numbers.

Justice got meaner and the state took less responsibility for protecting citizens, as the criminal injuries compensation scheme cut awards and restricted eligibility. Yet the Tories, like their predecessors, failed one big test. The commonest type of sentence in England and Wales is a fine, but fines are not collected. The NAO found that only about 35p in every £100 generated by criminal activity is actually confiscated each year; £2bn is outstanding in fines for crimes that are known about.

Legal Aid

Past governments have taken on the law and the law usually won. Labour passed the Human Rights Act and with it expanded judicial discretion, but Tony Blair and David Blunkett took a rough tone with the courts. The Tories, promising but failing to repeal human rights, struck at the lawyers' vitals by cutting the budgets for litigation and attempting to wind back the courts' oversight of government, complaining that judicial review had grown, was often trivial and landed the state with costs. Immigration and asylum cases were rerouted to a new super-tribunal. But the coalition pressed on to restrict judicial review. A first bite would have confined applications to those with a 'direct and tangible interest in the outcome' – ruling out suits by citizens and action groups – which would have wiped out two centuries of precedent, according to former court of appeal judge Stephen Sedley.[3] Instead, the government planned to sift cases more strictly and make litigants carry more of their costs. Meanwhile, duty solicitor contracts for attending police stations and courts in England and Wales were to fall from 1,600 to 525, and criminal court fees fall 17.5 per cent, putting criminal justice at risk, said the London Criminal Courts Solicitors' Association.

Defendants paying for their own defence who were acquitted now had to meet costs, similarly cases where the prosecution offered no evidence. The Legal Services Commission was an unwanted quango and wound up, only to be immediately replaced by the Legal Aid Agency, more directly under the justice secretary's thumb. The cost of legal aid in England and Wales was high by international standards, amounting to some £39 per head of population annually, or 0.17 per cent of GDP, compared with 0.05 per cent in Sweden and 0.02 per cent in France – though no one dared link spend with the quantum of 'justice' in respective systems, and such comparisons usually missed complex differences between systems. Lawyers predicted perverse consequences as, for example, people representing themselves in courts clogged up proceedings, which promptly happened, especially in family cases.

Tests of litigants' means got tighter and assistance for civil suits was restricted. At first the focus was on pushing as many trials as possible to take place in the magistrates court rather than the more expensive crown court. Next, criminal case costs were scrutinised, with competitive tendering for lawyers in most cases. In one of the more unlikely strikes, barristers marched in protest at a proposal to cut fees, for example the £252 full-day rate for a junior dropping to £176. The Bar Council said that a 30 per cent cut coming on top of previous reductions was so severe that QCs were no longer obliged to take complex fraud cases under the convention that they take whatever cases are up. Cameron's own barrister brother was one of the first to walk away from a long fraud case, on the grounds that state fees wouldn't cover his costs. Justice privatised may be justice denied. As the Serious Fraud Office and the Crown Prosecution Service shrank, private prosecutions started to grow, along with the use of private detectives; only the rich can afford either.

Foreign Policy: Keeping Foreigners Out

We began this chapter with *Britannia Unchained* and the fissures in Tory thinking between liberty and order, creativity and constraint, market dynamics and state power. Nowhere was the cleft deeper than over migration. Free marketeers have to believe in the free movement of goods, services, capital … and people. Who's going to pick our fruit and vegetables? wailed the National Farmers Union, complaining that the EU migrants who had previously obliged now wanted jobs in cafes and hotels and not down on the farm. But Tory voters and MPs had deep misgivings, and not just in dusty Fenland towns. Policy was pulled from pillar to post.

Its 2010 election gambit was a promise to cut net migration into the UK to the 'tens of thousands' by 2015 – subsequently spun to imply 'less than 100,000 a year'. The number was implausible, and presented them with an ideological dilemma. It boiled down to low pay. In 1997, of those in low-skill jobs migrants formed 7 per cent; it's now 16 per cent. That contributes to a fair amount of SME profitability. Many migrants are exploited. But the remedy (and a way of cutting immigration) was one the Tories were never going to like – beefing up the enforcement of minimum pay regulation by HMRC (from which a firm can expect a visit once every 250 years and a prosecution once in a million); the Gangmasters Licensing Authority imposes trivial fines.

In 2010 net migration was the highest ever recorded in a single year, at around 252,000 on the ONS count (591,000 in and 339,000 out), though the accuracy of such figures was part of the problem; they were widely disbelieved. In 2014, the ONS reported a net flow of 212,000, with 526,000 in and 314,000 out, up from a net 177,000 in 2012. Of the 2014 arrivals, 201,000 were EU citizens (in the year to March). Not much progress there. Yet Cameron kept flying in the face of the numbers. This was him in May 2014: 'Migration into the UK has been far too high for far too long. It needed a government to come along and change the rules to get it properly under control, and that is what we have done.' It was neither true, nor believed.

Like its predecessor, the government made policy on the back of ropey data. MPs took expert evidence and concluded the main method of estimating migration – the International Passenger Survey – was not fit for purpose. The UK just about counted them in but certainly did not count them out – to get an accurate measure of migration would have meant national identity cards (scouted but rejected by Labour) or huge investment in border checking and control. The goal of full exit checks by the general election in 2015 is not going to be realised. The truth is, migration control involves state intrusion: in labour markets, over national insurance registration, taxation, treatment on the NHS, schools and social services. Cutting migrant numbers would mean uncomfortable increases in regulatory burdens and information requirements: landlords protested when they were instructed to check the immigration status of their tenants.

As far as the analysts could tell, flows into the UK from outside the EU for work reasons had been falling since around 2005, similarly family migration. Student numbers had increased. Public concern, which had risen and fallen since the 1990s on an upward trend, now spilled over into politics as UKIP stoked high levels of expressed concern. Polls also found people greatly overestimating the size of the foreign-born population.

The Cameron response was classic dogma and disarray. In 2011 the number of non-EU work permits was capped at 22,000. A points system allowing in people with skills was tightened at the same time as the red carpet was rolled out for people with money, to come, buy, inflate the property market, leave flats and houses empty. Confusion surrounded students. The NAO estimated that 50,000 bogus students came to work and not study in 2009–10. Here the logic of the government's neoliberal, pro-market position collapsed. Wasn't it good that people moved in pursuit of market opportunities, just as (so Osborne kept saying) it was good that investment capital was footloose and profit-oriented? Or was it the bogusness that was the problem?

The government had reconstructed loan finance and encouraged private universities to attract foreign students and their fees. No more migrants, said the Home Office, as Whitehall departments went to war, the prime minister sidelined. The keep 'em outs insisted on new tests of English and extra inspection of the colleges where they enrolled. Universities would not be recognised as sponsors if more than one in 10 of their applicants were rejected for visas. The former Tory special adviser Nick Hillman, now head of the Higher Education Policy Institute, said it showed the Home Office was 'winning the war of attrition against … the Treasury, BIS and the No 10 policy unit'.[4] Study-related visas fell then rose again, to 219,053 in the year ending March 2014. Further tightening of visa rules came in July 2014.

The government turned on itself, unable to decide between the employers and economists, for whom the beneficial case for more liberal immigration was clear, or the voters, feeling their anxieties were ignored and taking it out on Tory candidates at by-elections. The migration minister James Brokenshire lambasted the 'wealthy metropolitan elite' for relying on cheap overseas workers, providing services to the detriment of the 'ordinary hard-working people of this country'. Who but coalition ministers and Tory MPs, employing foreign nannies (Cameron's from Nepal or Clegg's Belgian), and their supporters in corporate boardrooms, securing cheaper skills and staff, were that elite? Brokenshire could not bring himself to mention his own predecessor, Mark Harper, who resigned when it was discovered he employed an illegal Colombian.

No wonder the government could not specify the exact nature of the problem. Was it health tourism, for which there was some evidence, especially in London? Or was it code for Muslims, most of whom were no longer migrants or even foreign-born, though some were still bringing in foreign spouses?

Heathrow airport was a headache, too. A government that had changed its mind about expansion to accommodate the queues of planes waiting to land now grew agitated about queues in the arrivals hall. Labour had created the Border Force, as part of a new UK Border Agency, which merged bits of the Home Office and customs. May juggled yet again and moved the force from the agency and put the whole lot back inside the Home Office. She protested she had not authorised any loosening of procedure after it emerged that pressured officials facing massive queues had relaxed some checks on incomers. Here was another example, as in NHS, police and social services, where cuts clashed with effectiveness: the official in charge said he had to have flexibility when the UK Border Agency was losing 5,000 staff and UK visa offices around the world were being shut.

The impression of a government lashing out in desperation was heightened when the Home Office launched a fleet of vans for the streets of Brent and other areas of ethnic minority settlement warning (illegal) migrants to 'go home'. Loose wording caused the Advertising Standards Authority to step in. Anti advertising was directed at the inhabitants of Romania and Bulgaria before they acquired their EU rights of free movement to seek work from January 2014, running down the UK, denying it flowed with milk and honey. At first it seemed to succeed. On day one, the expected flood turned out to be a handful, disappointing the media scrum following up their own false tales of packed airlines and convoys of coaches heading our way. Later, the numbers grew: in the year to April 2014, 102,000 Poles applied for NI numbers, along with 47,000 Romanians and 18,000 Bulgarians.

Foreign Policy: Europe the Detested

Migration had for years fuelled resentments about the EU, which was blamed for the increase, not just of EU citizens but others too. Graphic television pictures of Somalis attempting to storm a cross-Channel ferry in Calais port left even EU advocates puzzled: if such migrants were illegal in the UK, why not illegal in France?

Public sentiment had moved against UK membership during the Labour years. Cameron sat, dumbfounded, in the midst of conflicting propositions. He believed in competitive markets, so free movement of capital within the EU had to be paralleled by free movement of labour. No, instead of the EU he wanted a non-intrusive free trade club, but no such organisation was on offer and borders would have to be kept open for bankers and footballers: throwing out the likes of Manchester City's Vincent Kompany – a Belgian – was not going to win votes.

Labour had to live with Blair, like a mad old bat in the attic, preaching hellfire and damnation if the evil tyranny of Islamic fundamentalism were not fought, except in Saudi Arabia and other countries where UK commercial interests were too strong. The Tories proved no more able to come up with a coherent account of national security or the geopolitical fate of a trading society locked by history and commercial logic into detailed and dense engagement with near neighbours, bound into the idiosyncratic edifice of the EU. Every signal from Washington, let alone the Middle East or the Russian periphery, demanded more unity, more sharing of commitments and a stronger European presence on the world stage.

Not for the first time we have to wonder at Cameron's apparent lack of strategic intelligence. Striving to be kind, we could say that with both the EU and Scotland he inherited tensions that had been building for decades. The UK has been detaching from the EU since the creation of the euro. The public mood was moving swiftly in an anti direction, with polls starting to record a majority in favour of exit. Even in Scotland, where Alex Salmond made so much of his Europhilia, the antis were piling up new support. In such circumstances a leader either follows, blaming his passive fate on the tides of history. Or he resists and 'fights, fights and fights again' for the cause. Thatcher bequeathed the Tory party her market convictions but also an unhealed wound.

Alliances had beckoned, with support from the Netherlands, Finland, Sweden and Poland for liberalish positions. The 2014 EU elections showed anti feelings on the march elsewhere, electing broadly anti-EU representatives to fill a third of the parliament, with a looser model for the EU favoured across the parties in the Netherlands and Sweden. A political artist might have tried to reconstruct the Christian Democrat strand in European politics in this direction, which would have involved close engagement with Angela Merkel, the pragmatic German chancellor.

But seeking the leadership of his Eurosceptic party back in 2005, Cameron had made a cavalier gesture and moved to withdraw the Tories from the Christian Democrat caucus in the European parliament. The Tories aligned instead with a ragbag of semi-racists and ultra-nationalists, losing friends and leverage. Alex Stubb, the pro-British Finnish prime minister, was stupefied to see the Tories in bed with his far right enemies, the True Finns. Cameron did no homework on key candidates until far too late.

His attempt to veto the European conservatives' own candidate to head the European Commission, Jean-Claude Juncker, proved how inept he was at the spadework and log-rolling demanded in making this alliance *work*. Cameron fought the fires raging on the Tory backbenches while proving a fitful and disengaged presence at European ministerial meetings during years when financial crisis was testing the eurozone to destruction.

On his domestic flank sit Murdoch and his minions, virulent in their rejection of the EU. The European Union Act 2011 makes future treaty change subject to a referendum. But what an inflammatory word: the only referendum his party wanted was 'Brexit' – shorthand for a British exit from the EU – and if they didn't supply it, they feared the people of England taking their discontent to Nigel Farage and UKIP instead. Cameron's commitment became a promised referendum in 2017 (assuming he was in power and his party in sole control), after untimetabled and unspecified renegotiation. Over the 2011 fiscal compact, the UK tried to stop powerful European countries pursuing their own interests in unity and, for the first time, members of the eurozone realised the departure of the UK might not be a disaster after all. They were increasingly irritated not by British Euroscepticism – most had variants in their own countries – but by the blinkered incoherence of the UK's negotiating stance, which combined bullyboy tactics, hissy fits and the strange stage performance of pointing a gun at your own head and threatening to shoot if 'they' don't give you everything you want, without quite saying what that might be.

Freed of collective responsibility (though that had never much inhibited him) Kenneth Clarke opined that a persistent flaw of Tory prime ministers has been to forget they are not the only people who need to appease domestic audiences and backbenchers.[5] The stakes are high, he said in an interview: it's the UK's standing in the world.

Foreign Policy: the World

This has been a government eager to keep its top table seat, in the G7, the United Nations and Nato, keep the transatlantic relationship 'special', but at the same time it yearned to float free of

Europe and sliced and diced national defence. A former ambassador to Moscow sniffed that 'the British seem to have given up doing foreign policy altogether'. An early sign of incoherence was the decision to cut the BBC World Service, hitting its Arabic output just as the Arab spring was breaking. What the government needs to explain, said the Commons defence committee, is 'what it believes the UK's position in the world could or should be, and the manner in which that is to be delivered'.

In their report in January 2014, the parliamentary committee went further, into uncharted territory, worried about cyber warfare and new threats requiring the government 'to think more strategically about the resilience of the country's critical infrastructure and recovery following a successful attack'. But what if that infrastructure was owned by companies that answered to foreign states from which the threat emanated?

Cameron could not even begin to think what his version of capitalism implied for security. If free trade meant the UK depended on foreign hydrocarbons, did that impair security? What if Chinese engineers had keys to nuclear reactors on the Somerset coast? Cameron's kowtows were self-abasing. UK exports to China had doubled to £15.9bn in the five years to 2013; the UK was fourth as the destination for Chinese overseas investment (against eighth in 2010). But Chinese money was conditional on UK membership of the EU and Chinese commercial relations with France and Germany were more intense. When the prime minister and a large entourage visited China in March 2014 he struggled to avoid giving the impression of a character from *Glengarry Glen Ross*.

Defence: Spending

The UK remained a player, with a defence capability exceptional in Europe, still sixth in world military spending. The UK could still, just about, participate in policing the seas off Somalia, join in the bombing of Libya and possibly even back up the Americans in air operations against Islamic State (Isis) in Syria and Iraq. But foreign policy was becoming a kind of armed voyeurism – looking on while momentous events occurred during the Arab spring in Cairo, and Tunis, then turned sour; looking on while Gaza was bombed by Israel. On Ukraine, the Americans looked principally to Poland and Germany before thinking of talking to the UK. Over Russia, the government's first instinct was Osborne's, or rather those of the City and petrochemical lobby-ists among his intimates – worrying more about their money in London property and banks than incursions in Donetsk or Lugansk. Oligarchs exploited the London courts, while fear of alienating Russia influenced the government's decision to refuse a public inquiry into the death of Alexander Litvinenko, the home secretary admitted; she changed her mind when the government started to respond to Russian aggressiveness.

Defence affordability raised too many difficult questions about the UK's identity and place in the 21st-century world. In Afghanistan, 'continue to fulfil standing commitments' meant complete the pull-out, fingers crossed the benighted country would not descend further into civil war. Civilian casualties had increased during 2013; the counter-narcotics strategy lay in ruins. 'The conflict has been long and arduous. UK armed forces fought with great courage to create and sustain a safer and more stable Afghanistan,' defence committee MPs intoned in their May 2014 report on the conflict. But was it any more stable or safer?

Five years ago Lance Corporal George Anderson, a reservist in the London Regiment, was setting off on a tour of duty in Afghanistan. Sitting in the TA headquarters off King's Avenue in Clapham, the part-time soldier had only a few hours left before departing for Mazar-i-Sharif to train the Afghan National Army. He had already done a tour in Iraq, in 2004, a year after the invasion. 'My first day in Basra I was up in top cover and I could have had my head shot off, but I thought brilliant, this is brilliant. It cuts out the rubbish in your life. There I'd been in my office, listening to someone argue over £5,000 when they were buying a £2m property in Notting Hill, and you think what's the point? This makes you feel alive.'

Since 2010 he has done another stint in Afghanistan, serving for six months at Camp Bastion in Helmand province, where UK forces have taken so many casualties. Bastion then covered an area the size of Reading. 'We ran marathons around the inside of the perimeter.'

Now it is all over, the Iraq and Afghan missions ended, neither accomplished nor glorious. Now 35 years old, Sergeant Anderson (he has added a couple of stripes) looks back over 12 years' service in faraway wars. They are not over for the people of those countries, but there will be no more UK boots on their ground.

'I do believe in the long-term future of Afghanistan,' he told us five years ago. And still? Like Tony Blair, the Americans, the generals and all the troops who slogged through those parched landscapes, Anderson has to cling to a shard of hope that some good was done, a token wish for a better future for their people. But next time, 'everyone will be a bit less gung ho about "Let's go and invade". If there's a next time, there must be more planning, right from the start.'

Training foreign armies is an uphill struggle. Although Anderson learned a bit of Dari — Afghan Persian — communication wasn't easy. 'I could stand up in front of 200 Afghans and make a joke or two,' but mainly they used translators. As for training, 'they don't embrace the concept. They don't see the point. It's all *insha'Allah*, just fate. They don't pick their best men to be trainers, they pick the ones they want away from the front.'

They fired blanks in exercises but the Afghan commander had the men stopping to pick up the brass cartridges to sell, 'so after that they just shouted "Bang!"' They weren't keen on counting how many sit-ups and push-ups the men could do in the British personal fitness test. One night an Afghan was left guarding a fleet of Humvees ready for use next morning: 'Every bit of fuel was drained out of all of them, but of course he hadn't seen a thing.'

The tale could have been told by the veteran of any colonial war at any time during the last 300 years. Perplexed, infuriated, uncomprehending. The week we met Anderson, 45 per cent of Afghans had turned out to vote, inconclusively, for a new president – the Taliban killed 60 voters, 31 election workers and cut off the stained index fingers of 11 elderly men for the sin of participating in an election.

Anderson is shaking the sand off his boots for ever. 'I've done all I can do in the army and it's time to get a real life.' Perhaps back to his old job as a central London estate agent. It's gone mad; he is astounded by what he sees. But until he gets a job, he earns a daily rate recruiting and marketing for the army. To recruit the public schoolboys he goes to Twickenham rugby events. For the working classes, he goes to Millwall Football Club. 'We take from all walks of life … people losing their fitness in their 20s who want to run around in fresh air.' Without war, however, recruiting always drops.

And recruitment to what? The UK is never going to be able again to mount such an operation. The defence budget is shrinking by 7.5 per cent to 2015, implying cuts of 17,000 in service and 25,000 in civilian personnel (later increased to 25,000 and 29,000 respectively). Old connections, through places and families, between civil society and the military are disappearing. Once, the RAF entered general consciousness by providing air-sea rescue capacity. Now the helicopters are being privatised. After faltering and cancellation of a contract amid allegations of 'irregularities' in 2011, the coalition announced that a new (privately owned) civilian-operated search and rescue capability would be established and that military involvement in search and rescue would cease.

Troops

The blueprint for army savings is a 20 per cent cut in regular soldiers – falling from 102,000 to 82,000 by 2018. The coalition wants to boost reserve numbers to compensate for the cuts: trained reserves are supposed to rise from 19,000 to 30,000 over the same period. Despite the efforts of Sgt Anderson in the year to April 2014 they only increased by a meagre 170. A sign of desperation was Cameron's plea to his own permanent secretaries to 'set an example' by giving staff more time off to sign up as reserves.

Media attention focused on the loss of an effective carrier strike capability – a working aircraft carrier equipped with fighter jets – until 2020 at the very earliest. In October 2010, the MoD decided on what the NAO politely terms 'deeply flawed information' to change the type of aircraft to be flown from the carriers under construction at Rosyth. Two years later, it reverted to the original choice of planes. Costs mounted and delays grew. An open question is how to protect the carriers when, with just 19 principal surface combat ships, the navy could not conduct other operations. Operating the carriers will raise the urgency of replacing the Nimrod maritime patrol aircraft scrapped in 2010. Developments in anti-ship technology are already outclassing the navy's ability to defend big ships.

But cuts did not make defence any less attractive to security consultants and arms suppliers. Nor did they plug the looming gap between future costs and likely budgets. Worse, said the NAO, the government's short run cost reductions had the effect of cutting longer-term value for money on projects such as Watchkeeper, the unmanned aircraft, and *Astute*, the nuclear submarine supposed to replace the *Vanguards* now carrying the Trident missile.

Trident

Circumstances (meaning Russian military operations) demanded a rethink of the cost of the Trident submarine-launched missile system, said the Tory chair of the Commons defence committee. The Royal United Services Institute said the UK would not become a nuclear-armed state now if it were not one already. What was missing, over nuclear and conventional capacity, and more obviously in 2015 than five years earlier, is thinking about the UK's 'level of strategic influence and the way the world is changing as well as the identification and prioritisation of the risks to it'. Without it, how could you plan or scope the size of armed forces needed. The government's response confirmed that Britannia is disarming. 'Global influence is not just about the size or even the capability of a country's armed forces. The UK exerts influence in a variety of ways: diplomatic and economic, development assistance, and technological and cultural exchanges, in addition to our capability and willingness to use military force.' This from a government intent on reducing arts budgets, the BBC, clamping down on student visas and evaporating soft power. Where was the strategy? The Commons defence committee said 'we have previously noted that the 2010 "Strategic Defence and Security Review" and the 2010 "National Security Strategy" were governed by the overriding strategic objective of reducing the UK's budget deficit. We have found it difficult to divine any other genuinely strategic vision in either document.'

12

His Obedient Servants

Cameron found it easy to accomplish radical, even revolutionary change. Too easy. What happened to the British constitution's vaunted checks and balances? Shouldn't a party elected by 36 per cent of voters at a time of deep distrust of political leaders have met more resistance to overweening ambitions, restraint when it went manic? Polls continued to show broad approval of the need for savings and (some) cuts, but why was censure of the government's mismanagement and incompetence so mild? Ministers scored more own goals than the blows landed on them by any opposition.

People were grumpy because household income was not keeping up, but – the Tories' fortune – resentment fed not activism but apathy and scepticism. They exploited national (England mostly) masochism, as if we needed to do penance for the fat years. Prodigal Labour was blamed both as previous incumbents and for failing to get over a credible alternative.

Politics usually self-corrects. Because the usual suspects – especially the formal opposition in parliament – failed to push back, others stepped up. Among them were the residents of Scotland, who warmed to the idea of being able to choose whether to sunder ties, then in such large numbers backed the case for escaping this UK: the speed with which independence advanced from possibility to practicality was itself a form of resistance.

Obedient Servants

What needs a note is why the state itself proved so passive despite the coalition's cuts and contumely. Especially the civil service. Leave aside GCHQ, the Security Service and the Secret Intelligence Service; for all MI5's protestations of meritocracy and *Spooks*, Tories and the secret people still seemed kin. Smashing a hard disk containing Snowden material, didn't officials relish the hammer blows that bit more because it was the *Guardian* rather than the *Daily Telegraph*?

In Whitehall, these were dog days and Tory ministers gave the cur a kicking. Despite blows to their pay, pensions and jobs, civil servants were complicit in Cameron's coup. Not once, from 2010 till autumn 2014, did a permanent secretary ask for a 'letter of direction' – a formal statement allowing civil servants to ignore the absence of value for money in such shambolic projects as Universal Credit, abolishing the probation service and setting up academy schools. Not a peep.

In chapter 6 we heard Janet tell how DWP managers forced staff to process fewer claims for benefits. The Wednesday morning meeting of permanent secretaries had never been a gathering of moral heroes, but top officials were now both notably colourless and Trappist.

Special advisers and some civil servants themselves tripped light across the red lines that are supposed to separate party propaganda from neutral government work. Permanent secretaries kept mum because they told themselves the coalition arrangement between the Liberal Democrats and Tories was self-policing. They were wrong. They also wanted, by demonstrating enthusiasm for the new government, to avoid being charged with reluctance, let alone subversion. The Tories' allies on *The Times* stood ready to publicise that one. NHS chief exec Sir David Nicholson admitted how, in health, they fell over themselves to please Andrew Lansley, throwing away all scruples about what he demanded they carry through.

As the man responsible for policing epidemics and guarding the safety of food you might hope Duncan Selbie, the head of Public Health England, would possess intellectual independence. But, asked by MPs about health inequalities, he replied that it would be too controversial directly to address this question. Quango bosses were not going to confront bullies: one was taken aside by the permanent secretary and warned, 'Take Pickles on and you won't get another job.'

In the government's name civil servants put out the Big Lie. Take the BIS growth plan, which in March 2011 talked of 'continuously rising but unaffordable government spending' (under Labour). That 'unaffordable' is value-laden, biased and erroneous as a judgment. In some departments, notably the Treasury, officials probably *believed*, though they still affected world-weary cynicism. Here is the official statement announcing the 2013 spending round: 'Because spending reductions since 2010 have been accompanied by reforms to how services are delivered, crime is at its lowest level in 30 years, school standards have risen and employment is at record levels.' The causality in this sentence is breathtakingly wrong, let alone its 'facts'.

A sign of the times was the drift of rightwing journalists into civil service communications jobs, where they took up cudgels on the coalition's behalf with the bullying enthusiasm characteristic of their newspapers. Noteworthy, in the worst sense, is the press office at the DWP. Its output was not just extravagant and biased but often illiterate. Old barriers to politicisation rotted away. In the Department for Education a new head of news arrived, fresh from a public affairs firm with distinct Tory connections; handpicked appointees were given jobs on the public payroll as 'speechwriters'.

Reforming Whitehall

Civil service was the job of Francis Maude, who pretty much fits our frame: pro-market, a believer that business always does it better. A deep-dyed dynastic Tory (his father had been a Thatcher minister), Maude wanted to shrink the state, and saw in outsourcing and 'mutuals' convenient methods to accomplish that end. But his progress was slow. Members of the cabinet cared about their jobs, perquisites and offices; also, major surgery on Whitehall required the complete and concentrated attention of No 10 and it wasn't interested enough.

Steve Hilton had drafted revolutionary blueprints – cut the number of departments down to four and chop civil service numbers so dramatically that what was left could fit inside Somerset House in the Strand. 'Fundamentally,' said Gove's adviser Dominic Cummings, 'you've got to destroy the concept of the permanent civil service.' It wasn't quite as simple: because of staff cuts Gove found himself swimming desperately in a stew of under-managed school finance and children's services failures that he could not any longer blame on councils.

Instead, Maude presided over a less radical deprivileging operation. Reform was much needed. NAO reports shone a glaring light on persistent amateurism, unwillingness at the very highest levels to acquire the skill, say, to let a contract to Serco and not be fleeced. This posed Maude problems as contractor-out-in-chief: outsourcing only works if there are smart, highly paid state servants. His record is inconsistent. At first he had had an easy win. In its last year Labour was spending £789m on consultants and a further £215m on bought-in interims. They were banished, for a while. They were soon back, the MoD admitting it paid Deloitte £14.8m in consultancy fees in 2012–13, a week after the PAC said it failed to control project costs. Consultants say they are technocrats, offering capacity to stretched departments (which were busy cutting posts). This was specious. They carried ideology like a virus; its DNA was pro-market, anti-public sector; they were preferred because their world-view chimed with the government's. Consultants never say 'no minister' – though civil servants now rarely did, either.

What we consistently find, said the NAO, are the same fundamental weaknesses around strategy, lack of good management information and accountability of individual officials, departments ignoring the needs of government and lack of modern management skills. The success of one new agency, the Major Projects Authority, exposed the wider problem. To remedy that, Maude imported corporate executives, as Tory governments had before, only to find they went native or never quite understood the complexities of politics and public management. The efficiency of government – which to Maude's surprise was not related to its size – failed to pick up. Perhaps because of their views about the state, Tory ministers could not be modernisers of the thing they wanted to maim. And ministers themselves had always been part of the problem. In the coalition they weren't ascetic; they, too, liked the chauffeurs and the perks; the civil service was never going to be rationalised when ministers were the acme of amateurism, prizing media and in-fighting skills over all others. Cameron consulted no management textbook (nor anyone else for that matter) when he split the jobs of cabinet secretary and head of the civil service because it suited him to have a head courtier (Sir Jeremy Heywood) close at hand. The botched experiment lasted barely three years and left the civil service head, Sir Bob Kerslake, a forlorn and discredited figure.

The Tory chair of the Commons public administration committee, Bernard Jenkin, was another dynastic Tory. But now he offered a bipartisan way forward – MPs and peers to consult on the future shape of the civil service. Maude, however, was 'loath to believe that fundamental change is needed' (as he said in a 2013 lecture at Policy Exchange). He proposed to go on slicing and dicing, and the civil service continues to decline in prestige and effectiveness.

Politics as Usual?

Maude and colleagues were as tempted to leak, brief and diss each other as the denizens of Westminster ever are. Coalition introduced no new puritanism, no forswearing the juicy pleasures of politicking. Prizes for obsequiousness in this parliament went to Liberal Democrats, in front of whom the greasy pole shimmered. But backbenches must also include the disappointed, the ambitious and the principled, who will all veer off message. An optimist might even say the innate pluralism of politics checks ideological commitments.

Governments control parliament; if they didn't they wouldn't get bills through. But MPs and occasionally peers do scrutinise, oppose and sometimes halt. In their condemnation of the British centre, the Scots were too hard on Westminster. Inside parliament, this has been a golden age for bolshie backbenchers.

A Labour reform now allowed backbenchers to vote on select committee chairs, and parliament's foot soldiers also won more control of Commons business. Despite the party whips, certain select committees took off. The PAC relished its powers of scrutiny, deploying the NAO to crawl over contracting and tax collection. The public administration committee affirmed the vital independence of the UK Statistics Authority; if ministers and advisers knew the watchdog was alert, they had to be more honest with the figures. Perhaps. The Treasury committee provided spiky commentary not just on the conduct of economic and monetary policy by ministers, but also on the performance of the Bank of England and the OBR.

But parliament was inconsistent and unreliable in its role as checkweighman for executive decision. Spending approval was still disjointedly organised through 'estimates' that no one understood. MPs paid little attention to movements on the state's balance sheet, despite the creation of Whole of Government Accounts. Select committees did not collaborate and were still persuaded to water down reports at the behest of the party whips.

The Commons' decision in August 2013 to reject the potential deployment of military force to Syria was greeted as momentous. Now it feels like a one-off exhalation, caused by poor political management. It led to no thoroughgoing scrutiny let alone revision of the doctrine of royal prerogative, the power of ministers and civil servants to make it up as they go along, without parliamentary approval before or after the fact. At the same time as MPs were patting themselves on the back for their opposition to the use of prerogative powers over Syria they ignored the use of power by the secret state, especially GCHQ, despite the Snowden revelations. The Commons home affairs committee complained that scrutiny should not be the exclusive preserve of the vetted members of the intelligence and security committee. Oversight remained ineffective, diminishing accountability and public faith in parliament's effectiveness.

Fair Voting Scuppered

Parliament's legitimacy and, who knows, public trust could have been immeasurably improved, but for massive political failure by the junior partners. For many Liberal Democrats the one reason for coalition, worth the humiliation of becoming the Tories' legislative fags, was the glittering prize of fairer votes. And there, at last, the coalition agreement temptingly laid out a referendum on reform. Never mind it was only an alternative vote, which Clegg had once called a miserable compromise short of full proportionality, matching votes cast with seats won.

He miscalculated. He failed to secure the prime minister's commitment to bring Tory MPs on board. In the referendum they were well organised and financed in fighting for a no vote. The UK population was no dumber than those in the many other countries voting proportionally for their parliaments; indeed various voting schemes were already in use here. Joining the coalition had diminished Clegg and his party and now they were to be punished. All the no campaign had to do was put his face on leaflets. Cleggmania became Cleggphobia.

In parliament's other chamber the adhesion of the Liberal Democrats to the Tories produced a usually unbudgeable majority; although among crossbench peers were individuals of distinction, too few of them turned up to oppose even bills as broken-backed and unloved as what became the disastrous Health and Social Care Act 2012. Still, the Liberals had been pledging reform since 1911 and their successors pressed the issue. They failed, but delivered a sucker punch. Lords reform got Tory backbenchers on their feet. Market forces could destroy entire communities and bedroom tax force people from their dwellings, but they would die in the last ditch to protect the green benches of the unelected House of Lords. But Tory intransigence had a price when Clegg withdrew support from the reciprocal vote on reviewing constituency boundaries, which would have cut Commons constituencies from 650 to 600, and levelling their populations. If the review had gone ahead, Labour would lose and the Tories gain up to 20 seats.

The same conservatives who fought to preserve their lordships in aspic were prepared to see ancient constituency boundaries grubbed up. Surveyors took a pair of compasses to the map without regard to history or nature to create, for example, a Mersey Banks seat that included places in Cheshire, the Wirral and outer Liverpool on either side of the river, unconnected by any nearby bridge or tunnel. Liberal Democrat MPs did their psephological sums. The turkeys did not vote for Christmas.

More and Less Democracy

Reform had a habit of going ahead where it was likely to be electorally beneficial. That is why, despite austerity, the government is spending £200m on shifting voter registration to individuals away from households. Ostensibly it's to combat electoral fraud and improve the accuracy of the register in the light of allega-tions about voting irregularities in London and the big cities (which were often coded attacks on ethnic minority support for Labour). But what if, in switching, millions seize the opportu-nity to decouple from registers; studies suggested 16 million potential voters could be lost, especially young adults, students, movers, ethnic minorities, many of them poorer citizens with an interest (it could be argued) in progressive taxation, amelio-rative social policy and decent schemes for work and welfare. Whether they are potential Labour voters is debatable; they might not be voters at all. It felt a partial, isolated measure. Other radical changes were watered down, such as petitions to recall MPs deemed guilty of serious wrongdoing.

Constitutional Rules

In opposition, Cameron talked grandly of restoring trust in the political system, code for blaming Labour. In office, trust eroded further. Coalition reforms 'have done little to restore trust, build bonds or address cynicism and anger. The govern-ment's promise of and subsequent failure to secure reform may have damaged public faith even further,' said the Electoral Reform Society.[1]

Tory innovations included directly elected mayors in cities, a distinctive commitment given how antipathetic the Tories had once been to Ken Livingstone in London. Elections were now seen as a way of mobilising the people against incumbent Labour politicians – Labour traditionally being stronger in urban politics. This was democracy of a kind few turned out to want. Following a Labour lead, e-petitions were instituted, to require parliamentary discussion of designated subjects. The public or, as it transpired, determined lobbies, could sign up online; when they did, objects included stopping the badger cull and, this one presumably organised by the Kop, to confer a knighthood on Kenny Dalglish.

Governments never have a clean sheet; there are always leads and lags and commitments that can't be shaken off. The coalition inherited from Labour's Equality Act a duty to review the effect of their policies and, although it took until May 2012, the Equality and Human Rights Commission did eventually squeeze out a report. This quango had survived, shrunken and cowed; its report did not get much official publicity. Had the Treasury analysed the impact of the benefits cap, or the effects of cutting the education maintenance allowance? Using the most convoluted phrasing, the EHRC could only conclude: no.

Changes in the law operate on a glacial timescale and the coalition found itself carrying forward legislation plotted years previously to ban age discrimination. Labour had outlawed workplace age discrimination in 2006 and we are now on the way to abandoning retirement as a specific or actuarial event.

Cameron was metrosexual enough to desire the approval of luvvies, which was not readily forthcoming. But they loved him for enacting gay marriage. A pretty banal step from civil partnerships, some said, which under Labour's Equality Act could now be celebrated in religious buildings, though not against the wishes of the mullahs or priests who owned them. Queen Victoria might not have known what lesbians were, but her great-great-granddaughter signed the Marriage (Same Sex Couples) bill, and the first same sex weddings in England and Wales took place on Saturday 29 March 2014. Cue pictures of the happy pairs.

Tory MPs muttered about human rights and mutter still. The Tories did try, setting up an inquiry on replacing convention rights with a British bill of rights, but it spluttered into inconsequentiality. Accommodation between libertarians and reactionaries was uneasy and legislation veered in opposite directions. To please the petrol heads, the government inserted into law a public right to challenge the use of CCTV and automatic number plate recognition. A promise made in opposition was redeemed when the Home Office scrapped what remained of Labour's identity and registration plans. The government is committed to scaling back the power of the state and restoring civil liberties, the minister for policing, Damian Green, intoned. By 2014, amid the Isis jihadi scare, the Tory frontbench was back on Labour's track.

Special Advice

This litany could sound like: they promised, got elected, changed their minds and ended up not dissimilar from predecessors. It's what incites 'they are all the same'. For example, the coalition agreement pledged to limit special advisers and did indeed move smartly to impose a limit of two per cabinet minister. A cry of we want more soon went up: coalitions mean more internal negotiations. Quietly, officials disappeared from the No 10 policy unit to be replaced by political appointees reporting solely to the Tory portion of the coalition. Ministers joined suit. Spad numbers went up from 85 to 98 in defiance of the pledge. The cost of special advisers rose by £1m in a year, to a 2013 total of £7.2m, compared with £6.8m in Brown's last year.

Here, apparently, was a part of the state they did believe in. Adam Smith, special adviser at the Department for Culture, Media and Sport, had fewer moral sentiments than his illustrious namesake and lobbied hard over News Corp's bid to take over BSkyB; he loyally took the fall for his minister, Jeremy Hunt. When Cameron ostentatiously appointed as his political strategist a professional lobbyist fresh from working on behalf of tobacco and fracking companies, advisers got the message: do what's necessary on behalf of minister and interest groups, just don't get caught. Even better, construct a high-toned argument saying lobbying is good for you. Giles Wilkes, former adviser to the business secretary, did just this. 'Politicians have to govern on matters far beyond their experience. Lobbyists are well placed to understand the disquieting levels of ignorance that surround political decision-making writing.'[2] And remedy the ignorance by corrupting public decision-making?

Labour had taken money from Bernie Ecclestone, who was not averse to splashing cash to gain advantage. But since 2010 money has seemed more unashamed, unabashed. Will Hutton said 'the fiction of our times is that all business is entrepreneurial, all business aims to behave well, all business accepts that it should pay the social costs of its activities and that any effort to shape business activity is counterproductive'.[3] In fact, successive industries demonstrated their 'unnerving and effective capacity to block efforts at making them work more in the social and public interest'. The UK drinks industry had had 130 meetings with ministers in the runup to the abandonment in July 2013 of the promise to set a minimum price for a unit of alcohol. Food processors, housebuilders and developers were all at it.

The Top Table

Being a Tory means being at ease with wealth so it's unreasonable to be surprised that ministers should so unashamedly break bread with rich donors, media barons and the very people who caused the crash – investment bankers. On the list of attendees at a Tory fundraising dinner at the Hurlingham Club in summer 2014, you would have found a property magnate on one table, a Goldman Sachs banker on another. In plutocracy, rich people make key decisions, so it's logical to appoint a party donor to the Bank of England's financial policy committee. Wealth secures *proximity*. Michael Hintze, a billionaire hedge fund owner, had donated £1.5m to the Tory party. Knighted in 2013, he was another ex-Goldman Sachs banker – few tales of politics and business in recent times escape the tentacles of that octopus – and adept at minimising UK tax payments, which some might say is an odd qualification for a major state honour. He set up a charitable foundation, which funded Adam Werritty, the special adviser to defence secretary Liam Fox, before it was struck off the register for 'lacking charitable purpose'. He also contributed to the Global Warming

Policy Foundation, the vehicle for climate change deniers. Fox had resigned in 2011 for failing to acknowledge his connexion with Werritty.

Why not just make corporate chieftains *the government*? The list of new Tory members of the House of Lords announced in August 2014 illustrated the Tories' close ties to such companies as Marks and Spencer and TalkTalk. Or put business panjandrums in charge of the state? Lord Browne, former chair of BP, chairman of Cuadrilla, a mining company keen to frack the night away, became 'lead non executive director' in Whitehall, sitting at the topmost table.

You could call this web of connections the establishment. Or compare them to a tribe of permanent winners, who intermarry and ensure their offspring bond with the right people. Matthew Freud, who had attended Clegg's public school, was married to Murdoch's daughter, Elisabeth, who is part of the Cotswolds set. Freud's advertising and public affairs agency had grown fat on Labour's anti-obesity campaign Change4Life. Under the coalition, PR spending had at first been cut, but then business picked up and Freuds won the contract to handle all the Department of Health's public health campaigns, on a contract worth £85,000 a month. A smaller state could still be lucrative. And permit some patronage, allowing Cameron to give his hairdresser a gong and try to put his personal photographer on the public payroll.

In such a closely connected world, lobbying seems almost otiose. But it flourished. Not long after ceasing to be housing minister, Mark Prisk becomes adviser to a property developer. Lord Hill, appointed a European commissioner, was a lobbyist by profession, who had known Cameron since the 1980s; former clients included the Saudis, Bahrain, HSBC and Gazprom. Hill had founded the public affairs company Quiller; he sold it to a company, Huntsworth, chaired by Lord Chadlington, Tory donor and brother of former Tory minister John Gummer (with Matthew Freud a £4m stakeholder in the company) – and immediate neighbour in a village near Witney. Quiller's former chief executive (who, like Cameron, was a graduate of the Conservative party research department) is now an adviser to the head of Santander UK.

Louche Metropolitans

At the same Hurlingham dinner Cameron committed to play a tennis game with Lubov Chernukhin, wife of the former Russian deputy finance minister and pal of Vladimir Putin, who shelled out £160,000 as a donation to the Tory party for the privilege. Love–15 to Moscow. When Gove was removed from education, a prominent *Daily Mail* columnist tweeted her anger. But this was no objective commentator – she was Sarah Vine, Gove's wife. Peter Oborne of the *Daily Telegraph* said 'the phone hacking scandal exposed a louche, selfish, privileged metropolitan elite at the heart of British public life', deploring a 'coterie of chancers'; he might have observed that his own newspaper often seemed like an annexe to Tory party HQ.[4]

Murdoch's Media

Tory instincts were standard – palliate the press, kowtow to Murdoch and browbeat the BBC. The coalition announced straightaway that it was letting the NAO loose on the BBC accounts and, along with a new licence fee, settled in October 2010, came in a new chairman, a Tory politician, albeit of a liberal, patrician kind. Unfortunately for his reputation, Lord Patten, the last governor of Hong Kong, was on watch when history came back to bite the BBC in the ghoulish shape of Jimmy Savile. Patten had already shown a disappointing lack of political awareness in not seizing the post-crash moment to shame the BBC's executive cadre into more proportionate pay arrangements. A public service ethos burnt fitfully among BBC programme-makers and news executives but was hard to discern among presenters and executives, as they exploited the pretence there was a market for their services outside. Ominously, among senior recruits to the BBC was James Harding as director of news and current affairs, who had served Murdoch so loyally at *The Times*. The BBC bent to the prevailing wind. When *Newsnight*'s Jeremy Paxman conducted his farewell, he turned the occasion into a gigantic puff for a serving Tory politician, Boris Johnson.

As for the wider broadcasting landscape, Murdoch had implanted friends and advisers at the heart of power. Their influence shows in what the Department for Culture, Media and Sport had to say about 'media plurality'. By some over-sight the discussion document fails to mention Murdoch's vast holdings across print and broadcasting. This was his stock in trade: by manipulating regulators he could approach monopoly, using his newspapers to tighten the screw on the politicians who controlled the regulators.

Conventional wisdom calls Cameron's selection of Andy Coulson as his press chief a spectacular lack of judgment. On the contrary, this was meant to cement the alliance; it was the equivalent of Tony Blair in 1996 travelling all the way to Australia to bend his knee at the court of King Rupert. Little did the monarch imagine, however, that he, his queen and the servile prime minister would later be embroiled in sleazy tabloid allegations.

With Coulson ensconced, no wonder other ministers cosied up, and their special advisers put Murdoch's men on speed dial. And a woman. The rise and fall of Rebekah Brooks was emblematic even if, again, Blair had been there before, as it were. But she, a well-schooled Murdoch apparatchik, knew how swiftly and ruthlessly to transfer allegiance.

Murdoch's News Corporation wanted to acquire all the shares in BSkyB, to bind the broadcaster even more tightly into its global networks of production and distribution. Vince Cable, with utmost stupidity, allowed himself to tell undercover

Daily Telegraph journalists he had 'declared war' on Murdoch. If only. Adjudication of the Murdoch bid passed to Jeremy Hunt, as culture secretary.

Hunt's special adviser might have been called Adam Smith but Murdoch's was the invisible hand. The plot nearly succeeded. But then, at the last gasp, a revelation appeared that ironically turned out to be a symbol of a wider truth about the journalistic culture Murdoch and the other tabloid owners had fostered. The *News of the World* had hacked murdered teenager Milly Dowler's mobile after her death. The law gave Ofcom a duty to consider Murdoch's fitness. Public revulsion was immediate and irresistible. Cameron was capable of massive misjudgments of the public mood – for example over the NHS – but on this he caught the breeze. Murdoch's bid became unacceptable.

Leveson Thwarted

No 10 appointed a high court judge to conduct a thorough review of press practice and (absence of) self-regulation. That this judge or any independent mind would conclude in favour of statutory regulation was so obvious; it's extraordinary in hindsight how little attention was paid to the methods by which the newspapers would seek to thwart it.

Their power is anachronistic. The London press, as newspapers elsewhere, are bleeding readers and revenue. The success of some online ventures does not redraw the bigger picture. Despite that, Murdoch, the Rothermere clan and their malevolent *Daily Mail*, combined with a sad collection of do-gooders mindlessly incanting freedom of the press, thwarted a once-in-a-generation opportunity to break the political spell exercised by the London front pages.

Lord Justice Leveson played to the gallery, literally, as his hearings were broadcast, providing many hours of entertainment to the media and political classes and, as with previous inquiries into the press, mounds of incontrovertible evidence of corruption, moral and financial, and massive dysfunction in the newspapers' influence on parliament and politics and their debilitating effect on public service, in the police, armed forces, anywhere a backhander could be proffered to purchase titillating or politically damaging information. When those methods failed, outright criminality followed, as phones were hacked and privacy torn to shreds.

But people wearily said, we sort of knew they did it – rarely adding that in a just and civilised society such suspicion would have led to regulatory action and expulsion of the culprits and their employers from any decent public place, including No 10 Downing Street and the House of Commons.

Leveson's 'Inquiry into the Culture, Practices and Ethics of the Press' was published in November 2012, and in October 2013 a final draft royal charter on the independent self-regulation of the press was published, following cross-party agreement. Cameron had declared that unless Leveson's recommendations were 'bonkers', he would accept them. They were rejected. It follows, a wit wrote, that Cameron thought Leveson, his own appointment, was mad.

Leveson's suggestions were far from crazy, but they are complex. To avoid the charge of political interference with the press (as if Murdoch and the *Daily Mail* were not doing politics day in, day out), the press would continue to write its own code of conduct, but a regulator (at double arm's length from government) would adjudicate breaches. By now the criminal trial of Murdoch's lieutenants, including Brooks and Coulson, was in full swing, washing their linen among other sordid items. But political leadership on reform had gone awol. No cabinet ministers stood up to rebut the misinformation put out by the *Daily Telegraph* and others – presumably because it was 'their' paper and they feared its revelations and wrath. ('Their' paper was owned by a couple of businessmen, the Barclay Brothers, whose commitment to the UK was demonstrated by their residence in an offshore tax haven.) 'With very few exceptions,' said the University of Westminster's Steven Barnett, 'led by the powerful triumvirate of News International, Associated Newspapers and the Telegraph Group, our newspapers have indulged in a litany of obfuscation, distortion, personal vendettas and exaggerated concerns about the potential impact of these proposals.'[5]

Quislings

But society and politics are full of naysayers, people willing to stand up and be counted, to buck the prevailing trend – aren't they? The coalition made a show of being a broad church, parading the likes of Dame Clare Tickell, chief executive of Action for Children, and John Dunford, general secretary of the Association of School and College Leaders, to carry out reviews. Former Labour ministers were also recruited, including Frank Field. Alan Milburn's social mobility commission spoke truth to power, saying 'fiscal consolidation has been regressive, with the bottom 20 per cent making a bigger contribution than all but the top 20 per cent'. Telling the government that instead of abolishing child poverty by 2020, as it had pledged, some two million children would then be in poverty wasn't likely to win invitations to soirees at No 10, but Milburn sweetened the bad tidings with praise for 'considerable effort and a raft of initiatives'.

Professor Julian Le Grand, a former Blair adviser, headed a government panel propagating 'mutuals', viewed by Tories as merely a precursor to privatisation. Another Labour health professor, Paul Corrigan, joined hardliners at the Reform thinktank arguing for maximal competition in the NHS, long after the disaster of the Lansley reforms had been enacted and displayed. We must end 'false loyalty' to equity, he said.

Many who might have spoken out were struck dumb. The children's commissioners were hardly audible. The third sector, a hotbed of political naïfs, wanted to think the best of ministers, whatever they said. Perhaps they were merely self-interested, despite the patina of saintliness charities liked to paint themselves in. Some simply wanted to keep in with the powers that be. Sir Stephen Bubb, head of the Association of Chief Executives of Voluntary Organisations, enlisted to sell the Lansley health reforms. Later, he lost his favoured status when Tory MPs rounded on him for defending charities' right to pay chief executives (such as Sir Stephen?) handsome salaries. Sir Martin Narey, the former head of Barnardo's, became Michael Gove's adviser on children's social services, where he took it upon himself to defend the private sector's role in child protection. Perhaps that is Narey's sincere belief, but his intervention was conveniently timed from the government's point of view.

Earlier we heard Sir Stuart Etherington of the National Council for Voluntary Organisations finding his voice. Some did speak out. Frances Crook, director of the Howard League, said the government's view of charity was Victorian: 'It believes that charities should provide the safety net that the state is increasingly withdrawing from.'[6] She challenged the Ministry of Justice to release correspondence referring to her charity. Presumably it wasn't flattering and ministers refused. Academics wrote a report for the charity Elizabeth Finn Care on benefits stigma, a good report, but what cowardice to mention only once the name of that enthusiastic instigator of stigma, Iain Duncan Smith.[7]

Evidence and Data

The DWP secretary became a byword for abuse of numbers. Once the Tory gadfly Alan Clark could joke about being economical with the *vérité* but now, the coalition not having dared abolish the independent statistics regulator created under Labour, a custodian of truth was at hand. Sir Andrew Dilnot, chair of the UK Statistics Authority since 2012, occasionally but tellingly delivered swingeing ex cathedra judgments.

Environment secretary Owen Paterson, deeply unimpressive as the waters covered his green wellies, claimed the government was spending record amounts on flood defences. The UKSA pointed out his figure only made sense by including money spent by *private firms*. The House of Commons library, another unimpeachable source, calculated that in fact public spending from 2011 to 2015 was £247m less than in the previous four years.

Cameron himself was a serial offender. In the Commons he blandly asserted that the 'average waiting time' in A&E had been 77 minutes under Labour, while under the coalition it was 30. The House of Commons library said typical waits in A&E before assessment and before treatment had remained static. The statistics watchdog ticked the health secretary off for repeating the assertion, noting there was barely a minute's variation in waits for assessment over the previous five years.

Ministers did have a way with figures. The LSE's Tony Travers showed how, in the spending review for 2015–16, Osborne shifted funds from health into social care but then double-counted the sum, so it appeared in both columns.[8] Gove had obviously not done much maths at school. Asked how it was possible for all schools to exceed the national average, as he had demanded, he replied 'by getting better all the time'.

Still, data had become sexy and so, oddly enough, had evidence. Dogma and data, ideology and evidence made uncomfortable bedfellows. In the first flush of power, 'openness' was espoused: the government would push public bodies, including Whitehall departments, to shower the public in data. According to the Department for Communities and Local Government, the public would become 'armchair auditors', quizzing and querying extravagant expenses claims by officials, unearthing evidence that government was fat and profligate and deserved the starvation diet prescribed by the coalition. Unfortunately, the amateurs did not do the digging and Transparency International later concluded that local government had been opened to a greatly increased risk of corruption. The Centre for Counter Fraud Studies at Portsmouth University found a 'marked decline in the counter-fraud culture in local government' from 2010 onwards.

Osborne patted himself on the back for publishing data from the Treasury's Combined Online Information System (Coins). But spending data is complex and ambiguous. Look, Pickles sneered, here's a figure for a delivery of flowers to the town hall, incontrovertible evidence of municipal extravagance. In fact, it was a fully costed purchase on behalf of a couple getting married at the register office. The Coins data (how they chortled at the acronym) proved indecipherable. There was data and data. The coalition destroyed the Labour scheme to pool and share information about children. The redisorganisation of health corrupted data about how many people lived in clinical commissioning group areas. Later, it came a cropper when it tried to force GPs to pass on patient data to a central collection point, where privatisation opportunities involving pharmaceuticals and possibly insurance companies beckoned.

The Tories scored an own goal when party HQ tried to erase old, pre-election speeches and press releases from its public-facing website, and tried to remove speeches from internet search engines. So much for open data. They even played fast and loose with the data they needed to show whether the government's own policies were working. Its proposed sale of the Land Registry and cuts to the Valuation Office Agency would jeopardise land price statistics, complained experts such as Kate Barker. (The Land Registry made a surplus, which is perhaps why ministers were so keen on giving the private sector a share of the action; in summer 2014 Vince Cable let it be known he had successfully opposed the £1.2bn sell-off.) Ordnance Survey and the Meteorological Office were simultaneously told to make more data available and be more commercial, meaning sell more data to business users. The government created a Data Strategy Board (a new quango) to buy data from these agencies, and advise on how to 'unlock growth opportunities for business' – devising apps to repackage data, say, around transport, weather or house prices.

The government, said Cabinet Office minister Francis Maude modestly, was a 'world leader in open data'. That did not stop records of Sure Start children's centres being deleted from the official website, perhaps because they detailed the 600 closures over the three years from 2010. After claiming the 'cull' of quangos had saved billions, the NAO checked the data and found it ropey. The government paraded data.gov.uk, a portal offering 14,000 open datasets, but they don't include one of the most valuable, the Postcode Address File, containing all known delivery points and postcodes in the UK. It was sold along with Royal Mail.

Evidence and Ideology

With a climate change denier at environment, it's no surprise that health secretary Jeremy Hunt should believe in homeopathy, which the chief medical officer, Dame Sally Davies, declared on the basis of the evidence and her clinical experience to be 'rubbish'. Hunt's predecessor had attacked the NHS without evidence. 'Just as new medicines are subjected to clinical trials before they are used more widely,' the IFS's Paul Johnson said, 'the health reform proposals could have been piloted, their effectiveness measured and the final policy tailored accordingly. The same is true of swaths of government policy.'

At education, Michael Gove did appoint the blogger and activist Ben Goldacre to look at 'how to improve the use of evidence in schools'. Goldacre co-authored what he claimed (without evidence) to be an 'influential' Cabinet Office paper on bringing randomised trials into government. Perhaps Goldacre was what the Soviets once called a useful idiot, since education policy was neither evidence informed or open: the department was placed under 'special monitoring' for its refusal to comply with the Freedom of Information Act. What need did a conviction politician have for analysis or empirical findings before dismantling councils and establishing academies and free schools? Gove had been to Sweden and saw all he needed. This was policymaking by faith and assertion.

However, interesting small-scale work was done by a behavioural insights team in the Cabinet Office before they were privatised. With the support of the Economic and Social Research Council, the government did establish several 'what works' centres to pull together evaluations and knowledge about ageing, local economic development, policing. It's time for us to gather the evidence on what Cameron's coup accomplished.

Conclusion

Cameron has governed Britain for his own kind. From Notting Hill to the Cotswolds, he sees his own people, timelessly at ease, unruffled. If the state receded, they would pay less tax. He has ruled with a mental half-map of the country, the rest of it places to be visited in a hard hat for a photo opportunity. As for Scotland, Wales and Northern Ireland ... here be dragons.

Witney, by contrast, is the comfort zone, 98.4 per cent white and mostly affluent. This England he understands. Cameron, with 59 per cent of the Witney vote, is no fantasist. His England exists, sustained by that blue sea of permanently Tory seats south of the line from Wash to Severn, plus well-heeled outcrops in Macclesfield, Bury, Tatton and the rural hinterland of the Midlands and northern shires. At best that's a bit more than a third of UK votes. His England can taste of paradise. Stroll around Witney beside the Windrush in the summer and you can't help but be charmed by its market square, corn exchange, the Blanket Hall and the town's curious old council chamber jutting out above the street. Don't think about the contrast between the civic spirit of the olden days that built these things, and the shrunken aspirations of today's Tories. In a somewhat forlorn bit of a park, the concrete paddling pool has been closed. Nowadays, local government isn't for doing things, beyond keeping the place neat and the verges mowed.

The public realm is being hollowed out; police station and post office closed; care for the elderly harder to get; day centre fees up; bus fares soaring and hospital transport cut. There's a Witney food bank, hidden in a garage attached to a suburban house on the edge of town. It's not small because the need is small but because there is no room, not even in Witney's churches, few of which seem recently to have read as the lesson Matthew 26:11 ('the poor you will always have with you...'). The council refuses to find a room in any of its buildings, perhaps embarrassed. Instead the needy troop to a windowless slot of a shed piled high to the ceiling with tins, packets, jars, emergency rations and toilet paper. 'It's two miles from the jobcentre,' says Julie, one of the two women who keep it going with collections and appeals. 'Lots of people are sent here with a voucher when they've been sanctioned.' The other day when a man came in with four huge bags, she almost wept with gratitude: he'd unexpectedly won his DWP appeal for sick pay and he spent it on food to repay them for saving him in the weeks when he had nothing.

People here work in Oxford, but the A40 road from Witney is gridlocked daily. An average house costs over 12 times average pay but 'Hands off Hanborough' is resisting the building of 430 new homes. There's plenty more. A woman tells me that when she was offered an NHS pain clinic appointment – a year ahead – they informed her she could be seen right away if she paid privately. In Chipping Norton, part of the Witney constituency, a specialised home for severely disabled children has closed, its therapy pool no longer available. Half the tenants of a Witney housing association have gone into rent arrears because of the bedroom tax.

'But, you know,' says one of our guides to the darker heart of Cameron country, 'I have to say, this is also a fabulous place to live. In Chipping Norton we have a wonderful theatre, a lovely independent bookshop and really nice people. Just make sure you never need anything, never need a home or a social service.'

Here enough people own their own homes, didn't lose their job in the recession and get by even when salaries have stagnated for a decade. The Treasury's partisan calculation has been that people will tolerate the rich getting fabulously richer as long as homeowners (still in a clear majority of tenures) can enjoy their own property values booming too. As for the rest – rebrand bad luck as bad character, this is the preaching of the prosperity gospel. Wealth and property are self-evident proof of merit. Poverty and disability signal lack of 'aspiration', so turn the tax-paying majority against the tax-spending residue and celebrate the comfortable and the copers. In that frame of mind, you can walk a long way on the sunny side of the street in Britain and never see the shadows, unless you look. Time was when Tory fear of rebellion, trade unions or rising crime was a check on neglecting the downtrodden. Now the calculation is, how far can you tread them down with no ill effect on anyone else? Osborne promises to cut another £12bn from welfare benefits after 2015, so a second term would test to destruction what remains of the post-1945 settlement. Where's the limit?

After five years of coalition the country feels harder and meaner. Cameron has not healed or soothed. After Duncan Smith sent out press releases with anecdotes of fraudulent claimants, disabled people reported an alarming rise in public abuse and contempt, and even people in wheelchairs are accused of malingering. Such attitudes had been brewing before 2010, but then intensified and spread. Not just in Scotland, Cameron has been the great divider. There's a scratchy discontent in the land, where people are quick to bear grudges, whether in frenzies of online trolling or sudden random upsurges of wrath – NHS managers, defence lawyers, football managers, even television amateur cake-bakers were not safe – though these are often orchestrated by tabloid journalists. Enthusiasm and idealism are in short supply.

Tomorrow

For optimism, don't we look to the young? But young adults are now more individualist, doubtful about the value of state support and suspicious of redistribution through welfare. Perhaps this is what inter-generational strife feels like: the dull ache of resentment rather than demonstrations. Good news for the right: the young are less collectivist by instinct. But research shows they are strongly tilted anti Tory. They are not inactive over what they think are important, but drawn to single-issue politics.

Social Immobility

Social mobility depends not just on origins but on destinations. It is hard to spot any effort to open up the closed spaces of elite Britain, whether it be in the boardrooms or round the cabinet table. Even the CBI admits who you know and your social background were having an even larger impact on the job you are likely to get. The government's own commission reports that 71 per cent of today's judges, 65 per cent of army officers, 55 per cent of permanent secretaries, swathes of the media and half the House of Lords, not to mention orchestral horn players (and other instruments they don't teach in state schools), come from the small pool of the privately educated.

Structural reform was never going to happen. Instead, the coalition preferred 'aspiration', so every individual who fails to get their foot on the ladder can be blamed for not trying hard enough. The top are there on merit, of course, so let's offer bursaries for the very brightest of the indigent to attend the best schools and universities. The alternative is to even up the ever more unequal distribution of wages, profits and wealth. But that would require progressive policies, state programmes and public spending.

Yesterday's People Today

Comparing the over-65s to the 25 to 35 age group, the British social attitudes survey found them twice as likely to be interested in politics and twice as likely to vote. The bloc is formidable and rich. But Cameron has never got his head round how to placate his favourite voters and yet cope with their galloping extra need for health and care. Fiscal adjustments could cope with demography – but only if those in power took the long view, were strategic and prepared to think openly and without prejudice about levying extra tax on the wealth accumulating on property owned by the old, with collective saving and investment.

Ageing isn't tomorrow's problem, it's today's. Age UK reports 800,000 frail old people receive no care at all from their councils, yet would have been cared for before 2010. They warn of the soaring gap between council revenues and care needs. But then (this is the leader of Norfolk county council, George Nobbs) 'the sort of support from central government that local government has been used to throughout our lifetimes is now a thing of the past'. Along with 'doing more for less', that 'thing of the past' is a catchphrase of the era, showing how deeply fatalism has entered the political blood stream. Nobbs isn't even a Tory. He became leader after Labour did well in the 2013 elections. But his resigned voicing of the conventional wisdom is a measure of Cameron's success. Local authorities are passing the point of no return on staffing and capacity, so a future government may find rebuilding impossible.

Austerity and spending cuts have been successfully sold; belief in what councils or government departments can do has been undermined. The trick of Tory leadership over many years has been to normalise unfairness. A status quo that favours those who possess property and wealth is *all that there can be*. TINA, said Margaret Thatcher, and George Osborne wept at her funeral.

Less Bread, More Circuses

Thatcher's obsequies made a spectacle even if it was greeted with more indifference than passion. The state, much derided by her and her mourners, could still do pomp and circumstance, ditto great sporting events – the Olympics, despite failing contractors – and the royal jubilee, despite the rain. A more imaginative government might have used the Olympics to inspire fitness, anti-obesity initiatives and emulation. But no real connection was made between PE in English schools (not one of Gove's favoured subjects), council maintenance of playing fields (falling) and the post-Olympics announcement by the Department for Culture, Media and Sport of £125m of lottery and government money only for elite sport, not for the grassroots.

Sport England did claim progress: in 2013, 1.4 million more people took part in sport at least once a week than when the UK was awarded the Olympics in 2005. But Labour's free swimming for children and pensioners disappeared in most areas. Tim Lamb, chief executive of the Sport and Recreation Alliance, said 'initiatives have been quietly dropped and millions in government funding promised for school sport have been withdrawn'.[1] So what, fans might say, as long as their team was winning. Yet the poor state of school sport and municipal pitches does have to do with tax and policy – and the way television rights are regulated. England's failure at the Brazil World Cup prompted *Guardian* sportswriter Barney Ronay to say it's not the hapless England footballers who need to apologise, but it's us: 'Sorry for the disappearance of our vital inner city and suburban green spaces. Sorry for standing by while the shared national treasure that is state-school sport atrophies into underfunded inactivity. Sorry for sitting on my sofa enjoying the brilliantly dressed product that is another six-hour soaraway *Super Sunday*, created by a system that while extremely successful in its staging, is clearly incompatible with also expecting English football to produce players capable of bestriding the globe at a World Cup.'[2]

Health, Whose Responsibility?

Sport, like health, exhibits both the limits of markets and the impact of policy decisions on everyday life over time. Tory MPs tried the line that obesity stems from 'lifestyle choice', ignoring the reams of evidence linking it and ill health to income; right-wing thinktanks took up the usual refrain with a clamour for charging for GP visits. But even residents of gated communities breathe the same polluted air, need herd immunity from mass vaccination and rely on food quality inspection. Antibiotics are losing their effectiveness: most don't now work against ubiquitous gram-negative bacteria such as *E. coli*. But only governments' collective action can control prices, invest in life sciences and manage how and what NHS GPs prescribe. If you nod through mega deals by pharmaceutical giants geared to short-run profit, labs won't work on long-run problems. The government chief scientific adviser, Sir Mark Walport, wrung his hands.

The incidence of type 2 diabetes is soaring; diabetics now number 3.8 million, up from 1.4 million two decades ago. In August 2014 Coca-Cola announced with a flourish that it was to remove advertising, not Coca-Cola, from the 4,000 vending machines it has installed in schools, as if that were a public health triumph. The coalition refused to bring in the minimum alcohol pricing it once proposed. The fast-food industry was invited to sign up to a 'responsibility deal' in lieu of banning pre-watershed television advertising of sweets and drinks. The chief medical officer wrung her hands.

Things Deliberately Left Undone

Bishops take sins of omission as seriously as sins of commission and we should too. The coalition inherited from Labour a pile of things languishing in the 'too difficult' tray. The Lords had not been reformed, party funding and political lobbying was corrupt. Scotland, we now know, was rethinking the UK while the UK slept. Banks and the City were still mis-selling, traders at Barclays were fiddling foreign exchange rates and Libor, the economy still unbalanced in its overdependence on finance and property: all were happening when the coalition came to power and most still are.

Media – An Opportunity Missed

History landed Cameron with the opportunity and duty to snap the incestuous bonds between politics and the press. He failed to rise to a unique opportunity. A small man in so many ways, what came first was his immediate party interest and his set: the editors and the media barons' glamorous children were his chums. Leveson disclosed a nexus of politics, power, public officials and police infected by the media as blackmailer, intimidator, briber and seducer. And the cesspit extended to Edinburgh, where the Scottish nationalists were bowing down to Murdoch, too. Of course, Blair and Brown had abased themselves before the contemptuous and contemptible press barons. But Cameron too was lickspittle and threw away a chance to give democracy the upper hand. He deserves no credit for setting up Leveson: the *Guardian* journalist Nick Davies disclosed the hacking scandal only days before Murdoch was gifted broadcasting media dominance. Once the prime minister, a PR man by background, had called lobbying 'the next big scandal', but he was not the man to clean it up.

Public Squalor

The government could and still can borrow for almost nothing, yet instead of seizing the chance to invest, rebuild and improve tomorrow's productive capacity, Osborne allowed the great backlog of capital spending projects to grow. British companies, guided only by immediate share value, don't invest long-term and the government neither offered carrots nor arm-twisted them to change. While the eye-catching HS2 project grabbed headlines – its costs safely postponed to tomorrow's balance sheet – the mundane roads people drove and cycled along daily were springing potholes, complaints rising. In 1997 Labour inherited a threadbare legacy of schools with leaking roofs and outdoor toilets, and they left the public estate in a much better shape – though it had also bequeathed its ill-written PFI contracts. Now the cycle of underinvestment leading to public squalor began again, for another government to repair.

The Necessity of State Action

Some might say we are crediting Cameron with too much, in both devising a grand plan and his capacity to carry it out. If you want to do less, tax less, and say 'there's nothing to be done, the state is powerless', it does make for a peculiar statecraft and a paradoxical style of government. A social democratic optimist might argue that any project to deconstruct the state can only be a passing phenomenon, because only government can do the heavy lifting in the years ahead. Look at threats from Russia and terrorism, ageing, energy, carbon emissions, research, skills training – all demand a smart, enabling and providing state of a certain size. If you live in one of the 5.4m properties in England at risk from sea, rivers or flash flooding you may worry that between now and 2021 that state is shrinking; £1.4bn less will be spent on flood management than the Environment Agency says is needed. At today's pace it will take 54 years before the engineers get round to you. The government has been reluctant to arrange fairer risk-sharing for dwellings, as that would mean encroaching on 'the market', so insurance premiums for those properties are rising. In a free-market England of Conservative imagining, flooding would be someone else's problem – but that captures the issue: people will always expect the state to *do something,* hence Cameron's Wellington-booted splash in the

Somerset Levels in 2014. His environment secretary might not believe in manmade climate change, but scepticism won't stop winters getting wetter.

Cameron's War of Belief

Climate change was not the only instance where prejudice confronted evidence and fixed belief won. 'What works' research had to contended with the evidence-free conviction that government doesn't work. Ministers, not just Duncan Smith, were loath to let the truth get in the way, and their media scapegoating of the poor as scroungers was contemptible. The Tories resumed their vocation as the nasty party, spreading a stain across the country, censuring generosity, pity or sympathy for life's losers, even attacking anti-poverty charities for trying to do good.

If Thatcher attacked the postwar consensus on what the state should own, Cameron went further by attacking what the state should provide. The party's journalist courtiers applauded his political victory in selling austerity: the public swallowed the cuts without much demur, persuaded they were necessary. But the road is rocky. Public resentment at bankers' bonuses and boardroom greed did not abate, knowing that top pay was unrelated to top performance. If the historic task of Tory governments is to normalise inequality and privilege, this one had mixed success, as people kept telling pollsters they wanted more boardroom responsibility and regulation. Abashed, even company remuneration committees occasionally tried to snip a few noughts off the annual increment of their chief executives.

Yet the government of the UK has become more plutocratic, more beholden not just to moneymen, but to foreigners such as Murdoch to the west and shadowy oligarchs and Chinese state combines to the east. Hedge fund managers with overseas accounts and property magnates seeking planning permissions made political donations, and the very least of the return was a gong or peerage. Growing numbers of large state contracts went to companies that put their profits through tax havens, happy to take taxpayers' money but not to pay tax themselves. Taking Murdoch's man Andy Coulson into the very heart of the state as his intimate colleague and press spokesman infected government with a toxin.

'The ruling values of Thatcherism always had the potential to corrupt,' wrote the Oxford historian Ross McKibbin, and Cameron showed the results. 'The dismissal of what we might call public spirit, of the idea that someone might do something disinterestedly, of the notion of collective endeavour, has left Britain open to a corrosive and shameless individualism of which the attitude of the bankers to their bonuses is the archetype. The increasingly ambitious programme of privatisation and the sale of under-priced public assets, often for political reasons, confirmed that everything could be bought and sold: power companies as well as opinions or stories in newspapers.'[3]

It went wider than that. The Tory project was to kick the welfare state about, confusing and confounding the wider public sector. Locally, the project was to denigrate and incapacitate councils by stripping them of power and money. In education, teachers, inspectors, civil servants and councils were lumped together as the 'Blob'. Attacking health managers, putting hospitals and trusts into the crudest of league tables, the project was to blame practitioners and distract attention from the basic social facts that determine mortality and morbidity.

Show Us the Money

A cynic or self-styled realist might say to all that: does it really matter, provided the government delivered? If the country's GDP is improving now, that's his accomplishment. Votes will always follow the money. But there is no answer to the question: whose recovery was this? Some are better off, of course. It is the Tories' historic destiny to boost the interests of property, share prices and profits. This they did. Share prices rose in anticipation of recovery. Corporate profitability is high. But earnings did not rise, nor did household income. Most people have less in real terms than they did five years ago, and rising interest rates could yet sink many more.

Osborne's mission was to do as much as he could to restore pre-crash economic conditions essentially unchanged – except for the state, which would be smaller. Reluctant to reshape banking in any fundamental way, Osborne fired the gun that reignited house price mania, simultaneously the reason for the crash and the feelgood that preceded it. 'This time it's different,' swore the Treasury. It always is, until it isn't.

In the British model, pre-crash as now, short-term profit is preferred to long-term returns. The UK, says John Kay – his government-commissioned report on short-termism in the City already gathering dust on the shelf – remains a happy hunting ground for predators. This tendency may even have strengthened, as the business secretary admitted. Yes, Cable told a House of Lords committee, all the evidence shows most mergers and acquisitions end up costing everyone, except the fixers and some of the short-term shareholders in the target company. 'But we must let this market operate.'

The UK model also ensures an increasingly smaller proportion of the proceeds of growth ends up in pay, especially not in the wages of the bottom half of the population. They work on zero-hours contracts for companies that avoid innovation by using low-paid, low-skilled workers. More corporate effort and innovation goes into tax dodges than growth-creating investment plans. Companies complained they lacked job-ready staff and yet had an exceptionally poor record in staff training.

Come the recovery, six out of 10 engineering firms were saying they feared a shortage of qualified people. International studies showed English 15-year-olds did have good creative problem-solving skills. But too many – one in six – failed to get to the skills baseline and the UK has a higher proportion of low-skilled jobs than any other OECD country except Spain. One in five jobs need nothing more than a primary education, compared with one in 20 in Germany. At the same time, a third of workers are overqualified for the work they do.

The coalition created more apprenticeships, but employers used them to retrain their own adult staff rather than take on the young. Productivity worsened. Output per worker in the UK was 21 per cent lower than the average for the G7. Lack of productivity explained why earnings growth was negligible.

That points to a judgment that says: not only did incomes not rise during the course of the parliament but future UK growth capacity may have been jeopardised. A foundation of growth is schooling and here the coalition's approach was divisive and dogmatic. The quasi-privatisation of schools through academies and free schools has not improved aggregate national outcomes. For lack of good vocational choices, the talents of large numbers of young people continued to be wasted. School-to-work transition is still neglected. Schools were graded on academic successes and vocational subjects were downgraded or abolished. Standards might continue to rise, as they had done under Labour, but a high-quality, high-status technical training route looks as distant as ever.

A Government of the South

Recovery spread across the territory but at nowhere near the rate or intensity needed to diminish disparity in income and opportunity, let alone health and wealth, between the regions of England, or Wales and Northern Ireland. Referendum rhetoric painted Scotland as an oasis of prosperity, but within that country, too, great fissures separated well-off towns and cities from the west central conurbation and the rust belt. Anomalous London is ever more resented for its wealth and jobs, despite disparities that could no longer be easily packaged as inner and outer; some of the suburbs, Enfield and Croydon, now had dense concentrations of poverty and deprivation in the midst of plenty.

We said earlier that Cameron presents the diagnosticians with a puzzling case of geographical aphasia. Once, Tories with his provenance at least affected a noblesse oblige interest in the 'provinces'. Now their tin ears completely failed to hear the Scots' plaint, but were deaf too to the English badlands, which now included Cornwall and the Kent and Essex coast as well as the former industrial Midlands and north. His government made token gestures to appease anger at London's centripetal force. Glasgow got the Commonwealth Games, the north got vague promises of an extension of HS2 and a link between the northern cities. But London loomed ever higher and mightier over the land, the Shard a sky-piercing symbol of the global city. Open to high rollers and tax dodgers, London was embodied in its louche mayor, Boris Johnson, infatuated with money and glitz.

No sooner a parliamentary candidate in 2014 than Johnson tacked away from his previous espousal of migration. Here was the issue, wicked and persistent, that split Tory sensibility: strong borders versus market freedom. Its electoral politics are tricky, too. The ethnic vote remains a strong marker for Labour: Cameron was warned how many marginals would be lost because of ethnic refusal to vote Tory. Pollsters found immigration stayed top of the resentment list: nothing could assuage unease at changes in the look of streets, estates and local shops or a common-sense reckoning that more new people must be adding to the worsening housing crisis.

UKIP is a confection of contradictory views: anti-gay marriage, anti-speed cameras and against a ban on teachers smacking children, but polls find supporters against selling off utilities and public services and in favour of renationalising the railways. Odd bedfellows for the free marketeers, they blame Brussels, but the real enemy is the globalisation that had taken their livelihoods to China and India and brought foreign competition for jobs to their own neighbourhood. By encouraging that sense of state impotence, the Tories made a rod for their own back. When markets ripped right into people's lives, and they were unconvinced about Labour, UKIP beckoned.

What Next?

The landscape ahead is arid. Though national output got back to its pre-recession levels, wages hardly keep pace with prices. Recovery, already slowing in 2015, may be further jeopardised by the ending of quantitative easing, what Gavyn Davies calls the delicate procedure of weaning an economy off this experimental treatment.[4] The Resolution Foundation warns that 2.3 million low-income, over-borrowed homeowners would find a rise in interest rates unaffordable. Struggling households were acquiring yet more debt, with the revival of hire purchase agreements.

The self-employed are predicted to outnumber public sector employees by 2018, mainly signifying a shift from decent jobs to insecure low pay. The IFS thinks, all things being equal, 1.13m public jobs will be gone by 2019, and public sector pay will be 8 per cent below equivalent work in the private sector, the deepest differential for 20 years. All work will become more insecure, more 'flexible' than ever, for the benefit of employers.

To abolish the deficit altogether, austerity phase two requires epic additional cuts. Only half the consolidation plotted in 2010 has been accomplished, so far by including some tax increases and almost eliminating capital investment, as well as cuts in public spending. Osborne plans to eliminate the rest of the deficit by using spending cuts alone. The next years of austerity mean fiscal tightening (cuts, in plain talk) reaching £190bn by 2018–19. The picture gets even darker now the Tories are trying to tempt electors with tax cuts. To pay for the income tax cuts being dangled, let alone the hinted-at inheritance tax cuts, yet more would have to be cut from welfare and public services.

Then add in more ideology. Home secretary Theresa May, making a leadership pitch, talks about 'the need to reduce the huge demand for public services in the first place'. Stopping people becoming criminals, she said; preventing old people getting to the point where they need care, she implied. But how, short of some massive programme of state intervention and early years schemes, which she certainly did not mean. Nor is she likely to want what NHS England's chief executive demands – powers for councils to veto fast-food outlets and ban the sale of tobacco in order to minimise future calls on the NHS.

What May's view does portend is more markets and more privatisation. If the Tories win in 2015, fiercely Thatcherite MPs will predominate, according to surveys of candidates. They have been selected by a dwindling band of the Conservative party's mostly very old, very Europhobic local members. The 2010 intake of Tory MPs, the young thrusters who wrote *Britannia Unchained*, will be joined by a yet more Eurosceptic and anti-state set, predominantly male. Cameron is already promising to repeal the Human Rights Act. A Tory win would see benefits for families hit again, the benefits cap tightened and housing benefit further restricted.

In education, for-profit companies would run chains of schools to make money. Never mind the evidence from Sweden that private free schools have both pushed the country down in the international rankings and become more socially segregated. Whitehall would be reduced to five departments, the declared plan for civil service to cut it to a third of its 2010 size. Remaining public servants would find their pay frozen, national pay scales abandoned, people paid less in already poor areas. With house prices diverging, isn't it common sense to pay lower wages in cheaper places?

But, at this point, the narrative muddies. There's also Tory talk about instilling a 'greater sense of national identity'. Which nation would that be? English nationalism in an English parliament sounds like a Tory winner, but what about 'national' unity? Already a Tory guru is predicting that London will pull 'further away from a country that it communicates with via cheque, winning the right to issue its own work visas'.[5] The effect would be a yet deeper rift between south and north, London floating further away on its cloud of global gold, much of it tax-avoiding or money-laundering.

Little England nationalism, spurred on by UKIP pressure, would bring in all the restrictive practices and the potential barriers to capital that the Conservative party's current business backers would fear. How do global companies thrive in a little half island adrift from the EU? Nor does English nationalism come ready-made. To invent it, you need the schools to teach a single curriculum and teachers to sing their pupils patriotic songs. Yet Osborne says they must take on 'leftwing socialist ideology in the teaching unions' – and you could not let schools run free. English national identity is most strongly felt in those great bastions of togetherness – the NHS and the BBC. But both these emblems of unity are viscerally detested by many Tories. The Murdoch media and other commercial predators would seize the opportunity presented by the BBC's charter renewal in 2017 to end the affront of a successful non-profit, quasi-state broadcaster flourishing on their turf, admired across the globe.

Against such a background expect the next Scottish referendum soon, bringing the final dismemberment of the UK. Having come frighteningly close last time, is the Tory party really prepared to throw away what remains of the great in Great Britain? Perhaps for the new Tories, it's good riddance. The international standing of the UK is already problematic. Cameron's chosen gift to Chinese Premier Li Keqiang when he visited in 2014 was a copy of the shooting script for the first episode of *Downton Abbey* – as ersatz an imitation of faux Britishness as you could find. The official Chinese newspaper *Global Times* advised its readers: 'A rising country should understand the embarrassment of an old declining empire and

at times the eccentric acts it takes to hide such embarrassment.'
That cut to the quick.

Decline long predates the coalition, and continues. Even
if money were found for Trident, it could only come at the
expense of severe cuts to the armed forces that would forbid
not just grand adventures in desert sands but small coastal
interventions. Could Tory identity really withstand the end of
the flag and global heft?

A Europe referendum would make the next period tumultuous. Cameron or any substitute Tory prime minister would
return from a bogus renegotiation with no more than token
changes. Ahead lies confusion: the UK out of the EU, Scotland
gone, that prized seat on the UN Security Council unsustainable. But doesn't that mean delusions of grandeur finally
extinguished, and not before time?, you might say. But what if
rightwing sentiment then turned in upon itself, in authoritarian
forms? If Cameron were ousted by his insatiables, he would be
replaced by one of them.

Those are versions of what could happen after the 2015
elections. The British once had a penchant for muddling
through, avoiding confrontations and sharp edges. But who
are 'the British' now? An election result leaving the Tories at
the helm would destroy much and conserve little. As we write
this we have to hope for some better prospect of expressing
who we are, what we value in our state and our public services,
and where we belong in the world.

ENDNOTES

CHAPTER 1: UNJUST BRITAIN

1. Jesse Norman *Compassionate Economics – The Social Foundations of Economic Prosperity*, Policy Exchange, 2008
2. Professor Glen Newey – http://www.independent.co.uk/arts-entertainment/books/reviews/conservatism-by-kieron-ohara-2313602.html

CHAPTER 2: BRITAIN 2015 – A SNAPSHOT

1. Janan Ganesh *FT Magazine*, 28/29 June 2014, p.27
2. UK Commission for Employment and Skills 'The Labour Market Story – An Overview', July 2014

CHAPTER 3: OUR DISUNITED KINGDOM

1. Charlotte Leslie – http://blogs.spectator.co.uk/coffeehouse/2014/03/labour-run-wales-is-a-nightmare-vision-of-what-ed-miliband-would-do-for-britain/
2. Peter Bingle – http://www.prweek.com/news/bulletin/UKDaily/article/1051960/?DCMP=EMC-CONUKDaily

CHAPTER 4: CAMERON'S COUP

1. Janan Ganesh *Financial Times*, 25 March 2014
2. Quoted in Peter Snowdon *Back from the Brink – The Inside Story of the Tory Resurrection*, Harper Press 2010
3. Will Hutton *Observer*, 21 July 2013
4. Professor Simon Wren-Lewis – http://mainlymacro.blogspot.co.uk/2013/06/how-greek-drama-became-global-tragedy.html
5. http://blogs.telegraph.co.uk/finance/jeremywarner/100025496/oh-god-i-cannot-take-any-more-of-the-austerity-debate/
6. Professor Tim Bale *Fabian Review*, Vol 126, No 10–11

CHAPTER 5: THE CUTS

1. http://www.ft.com/cms/s/0/7dff69d6-850f-11e3-8968-00144fe-ab7de.html#axzz2rbOfLvPW
2. John Kay *Financial Times*, 11 September 2013
3. Brian Henry '*The Coalition's Economic Strategy – Has It Made a Bad Thing Worse?*' quoted by *William Keegan Observer*, 29 December 2013 – http://www.theguardian.com/business/2013/dec/29/big-society-cutting-welfare-coalition-big-lie
4. Chris Giles *Financial Times*, 26/27 July 2014, p.3
5. John Hills *Good Times, Bad Times – The Welfare Myth of Them and Us*, Policy Press 2014, p.223
6. http://www.localgov.co.uk/1000-jobs-set-to-be-axed-at-Coventry/36853
7. http://www.derbytelegraph.co.uk/Lives-lost-Derbyshire-County-Council-plans-make/story-21339910-detail/story.html#a5wxY1Z BqScAQJfs.99

CHAPTER 6: WAGING WAR ON WELFARE

1. http://www.oecd-ilibrary.org/social-issues-migration-health/society-at-a-glance-2014_soc_glance-2014-en
2. Jonathan Portes – http://bit.ly/1r8sSGJ
3. http://www.jrf.org.uk/publications/universal-credit-mis
4. DWP 'Evaluation of Removal of the Spare Room Subsidy', July 2014

CHAPTER 7: RECOVERY – PALLID AND PARTIAL

1. *Financial Times*, 26 August 2014, p.19
2. Guardian – http://www.theguardian.com/politics/economics-blog/2014/jun/08/george-osborne-economic-policy
3. Chartered Management Institute press release – http://www.managers.org.uk/about-us/media-centre/cmi-press-releases/major-report-outlines-plan-to-defuse-ticking-time-bomb-of-myopic-management
4. Evidence at Commons public administration committee, 5 December 2012
5. John Plender *Financial Times*, 12 May 2014 – http://www.ft.com/cms/s/0/37793a70-d9b8-11e3-920f-00144feabdc0.html#axzz3EcxDlxCD
6. *Financial Times*, 1 July 2014, p.17
7. http://www.archbishopofcanterbury.org/articles.php/5353/archbishops-lecture-on-the-future-of-banking-standards
8. Quoted in *Financial Times*, 20 July 2014 – http://www.ft.com/cms/s/0/413b5012-0e73-11e4-a1ae-00144feabdc0.html#axzz3EcxDlxCD

9. *Observer*, 20 July 2014 – http://www.theguardian.com/business/2014/jul/20/jurgen-maier-siemens-british-productivity-catching-germany-manufacturing

CHAPTER 8: INFRASTRUCTURE UNDERMINED

1. OECD Economic Survey of the United Kingdom. February 2013, p.29
2. Quoted in *Guardian*, 19 July 2014, p.7
3. http://www.theguardian.com/environment/2013/nov/21/david-cameron-green-crap-comments-storm
4. *Guardian*, 12 May 2014 –http://www.theguardian.com/environment/2014/may/12/ukraine-crisis-shows-europe-must-not-turn-its-back-on-renewable-energy
5. http://www.northdevonjournal.co.uk/Lord-Krebs-calls-pilot-badger-culls-8216-complete/story-20306535-detail/story.html#ixzz2njxNPeiP
6. Martin Wolf *Financial Times*, 10 October 2014 – http://www.ft.com/cms/s/0/aa1c9dfa-30ea-11e3-b478-00144feab7de.html#axzz3EcxDlxCD
7. http://www.bbc.co.uk/news/blogs-the-papers-28537650

CHAPTER 9: SCHOOLING THE NATION

1. Andreas Schleicher 'PISA's Hard Lessons', *OECD Observer*, 2013, Issue 4
2. Peter Wilby – http://www.theguardian.com/commentisfree/2014/feb/03/state-schools-independents-michael-gove
3. Royal Society of Arts 'Unleashing Greatness'. The Report of the Academies Commission, January 2013
4. Dominic Cummings quoted in *Guardian*, 11 October 2013 –http://www.theguardian.com/politics/2013/oct/11/genetics-teaching-gove-adviser
5. *Oxford Review of Education*, 2014, Vol 40, Issue 3
6. JRF report 'Does Money Affect Children's Outcomes?' – http://sticerd.lse.ac.uk/dps/case/cr/casereport80.pdf
7. Alasdair Smith *Public Finance*, June 2014

CHAPTER 10: HEALTH RE-DISORGANISED

1. *Health Service Journal*, 16 September 2013
2. http://www.dailymail.co.uk/news/article-2608139/NHS-watchdog-chief-goes-private-hip-operation-avoiding-three-month-wait-patients-face-hospitals-hes-meant-improving.html#ixzz2zbqejhQs

3. Noel Plumridge *Public Finance*, September 2014
4. http://www.independent.co.uk/life-style/health-and-families/
health-news/elderly-spend-weeks-too-long-in-hospitals-due-to-lack-of-
housing-age-uk-warns-9707325.html

CHAPTER 11: BRITANNIA UNCHAINED

1. http://www.theguardian.com/politics/2013/nov/27/boris-
johnson-thatcher-greed-good
2. British Academy 'A Presumption Against Imprisonment: Social Order
and Social Values', July 2014, p.33
3. Sir Stephen Sedley *London Review of Books*, 6 March 2014
4. Nick Hillman *Times Higher Education*, 31 July 2014, p.6
5. *Observer*, 20 July 2014 – http://www.theguardian.com/politics/
2014/jul/19/kenneth-clarke-views-no-10

CHAPTER 12: HIS OBEDIENT SERVANTS

1. Electoral Reform Society 'Reviving the Health of our Democracy',
2013
2. Giles Wilkes *Financial Times*, 7/8 June 2014
3. Will Hutton *Observer*, 12 January 2014
4. http://www.telegraph.co.uk/news/uknews/phone-hacking/
10925485/Prime-Minister-and-his-gang-havent-learnt-their-lesson.
html
5. *The Political Quarterly*, July–September 2013, Vol 84, Issue 3
6. http://www.howardleague.org/francescrookblog/politics-
charities-and-civil-society/
7. Elizabeth Finn Care 'Benefits Stigma in Britain', November 2012
8. Tony Travers *Public Finance*, March 2013

CONCLUSION

1. Tim Lamb quoted in *Walk* magazine, Summer 2012, p.1
2. *Guardian*, 23 June 2014
3. *London Review of Books*, 2 August 2012 – http://www.lrb.co.uk/
v34/n15/ross-mckibbin/money-and-the-love-of-money?utm_source=
newsletter&utm_medium=email&utm_campaign=3415&hq_
e=el&hq_m=1870344&hq_l=7&hq_v=b847b3c49b.
4. *Financial Times*, 21/22 June 2014, p.13
5. Janan Ganesh *Financial Times* – http://www.ft.com/cms/s/0/
fa4aad86-de7d-11e2-b990-00144feab7de.html#axzz2c2iDNGp2

INDEX

AbbVie 139
Abramovich, Roman 7
Adonis, Lord 166
Age UK 225, 230, 287
Alexander, Danny 75–6, 126
Anderson, Sgt George 254–6
apprenticeships 35, 135, 137,
    295
AstraZenica 138
Aycliffe, Peter 132

badgers 176–7
Baker, Julie-Ann 230–1
Baker, Maureen 231
Bale, Prof. Tim 73
banks 72, 87, 90, 96, 97, 143–5
Barclay Brothers 275
Barker, Dame Kate 228, 279
Barlow, Gary 96
Barnes, Ann 236
Barnett, Steven 276
BBC 43, 253, 272, 299
bedroom tax 26, 33, 45, 76, 108,
    113, 125–6, 185
    see also infrastructure: housing
Beecroft, Adrian 137
Beischer, Neville 187–9, 209
benefits:
    cap on 113, 268, 298
    children and mothers hit by cuts
        in 36; see also child poverty
    cuts to, versus tax rises 72
    deepest cuts in 17
    and DWP bullying 115–16

and entrenched family poverty
    109–10
and inflation measure 112–13
poor targeted in cuts to 101,
    110–11
thresholds for 114–15
unclaimed 111
    see also housing benefit
Bennett, David 217
big society 56–9
Big Society Capital 60
Bingle, Peter 56
Black, Prof. Dame Carol 120
Black, Guy 64
Blair, Tony:
    claimed virility of 31
    and Islam 250
    and Murdoch 273
    and NHS 214, 218
Blanchard, Oliver 88
Blanchflower, Danny 15
Blunkett, David 71, 244
Boles, Nick 68–9
Boyle, Danny 215
Brain, Tim 235
Britannia Unchained (Kwarteng et
    al.) 233, 298
Britnell, Mark 217
broadband 151–2
Brokenshire, James 248–9
Brooke, Andy 162, 163–4
Brooks, Rebekah 5, 10, 273, 275
Brown, Gordon:
    and Britishness 45